the Creation Explanation

a scientific alternative to evolution

Robert E. Kofahl
Kelly L. Segraves

Harold Shaw Publishers
Wheaton, Illinois

Creation-Science Research Center
San Diego, California

This book is dedicated to two mothers, Nell Segraves and Beatrice Kofahl, whose labors, faith, and support have had much to do with the successful completion of *The Creation Explanation*.

table of
contents

List of Figures   *x*
List of Tables   *x*
Preface   *xi*
Acknowledgments   *xv*

1 Living Evidence of Design   *1*

Design in Living Creatures   *2*
The Beetle That Carries a Gun   *2*
A Lizard on the Ceiling   *3*
Do Drinking Giraffes Have Headaches?   *5*
Bats and Whales That "See" with Their Ears   *6*
Each Creature a Designed, Integrated System   *6*
Animal Instinct   *8*
Bird Navigators   *8*
Spider Aquanauts   *8*
Symbiosis   *9*
The Dirty Fish That Blushes   *9*
Ants in the Plants   *9*
Predation and Defense   *10*
Slugs with Stolen Stingers   *10*
Cyanide Is Good for the Millipede   *10*
The Cowboy Fungus   *11*
Design in Communities of Living Things   *12*
Design in Atoms, Molecules, and Water   *14*
Design in the Earth-Sun System   *16*
Man's Place in the World   *18*

2 The Changing World 21

Processes of Change 22
Cyclic Change 24
Work, Energy, and Energy Transformations 24
Units of Matter Interact and Rearrange 28
The Energy Conservation Law and a Finished Creation 31
The Natural Law of Degeneration 32
Life and the Energy Laws 35
Matter, Energy, and Intelligence 37

3 The Primeval World 39

Two Approaches to the Evidence 39
Do Fossils Speak for Evolution or Creation? 41
Geology—Gradualism or Global Catastrophe? 45
Rock Structures and Earth History 46
Fossils and Earth History 50
Do All Fossils Appear in Evolutionary Order? 52
Fossils and Strata—A Creationist Interpretation 55
Pre-Cambrian Strata 56
Cambrian Rocks 57
Carboniferous Strata 57
Mesozoic Strata 58
Cenozoic Strata 59
Evolution and Extinction—Why? 59
Conclusion 61

4 Life—Miracle, Not Accident 63

What Is Life? 63
Cellular Life 65
The Structure and Composition of Cells 65
Living Things Are Classified 68
Living Things Work Together 70
The Pyramid of Producers and Consumers 71
Environment and Heredity 73
Mendel's Laws 74
Genetics 77
The Building of a Gene 78
Replication of DNA—the Foundation of Genetic Inheritance 78
Transcription of RNA upon DNA Templates 85
RNA in the Synthesis of Proteins 86
Building a Protein Molecule 88
A Library in a Molecule 89
The Materialist's Dilemma 90
Mutations 90

Enzymes by Mutation?   92
Recent Enzyme Research   93
Summary of Mutation Effects   94
Where Does Life Come From?   95
Spontaneous Generation in a Primeval World?   96
Proteins by Chance—Faith in the Impossible   98
Life in a Test Tube?   102
Mechanism in Biology: A Materialist or Theistic Concept?   102
Conclusion   104

5   Man in His World   105

Man Is Different   105
Science and the Study of Man   106
The Scientific Method   107
A Modern Myth   110
Creation and the Study of Man   111
Can a Scientist Be Mistaken?   113
Science Is Self-Correcting   114
Is This Really Science?   114
The Origin of Civilization   115
Language and "Primitive" Cultures   115
The Model for the Evolution of Civilization   116
Cultural Evolution—The Facts   117
Fossil Men and Physical Anthropology   119
The Fossil Evidence: Five Kinds Used to Classify Fossils   119
Classification by Fossil Form   119
Analysis of Fossil Finds   124
Interpreting Fossil Forms   124
Classification by Strata and the Associated Flora and Fauna   125
Classification by Radiometric Dating of Fossils   128
Classification by Associated Cultural Remains   128
Classification by Geographical Location   129
Biblical Interpretations of Fossil Man Data   129
Conclusion   131

6   Design in the Universe   133

The Design of the Atom   133
The Nucleus of the Atom   137
The Solar System—Designed or Evolved?   140
The Age of the Solar System   144
Stars—Evolved or Created?   146
The Galaxies   149
Did Galaxies Evolve?   151
Is the Universe Expanding?   152
The Origin of the Universe   155

7 Beliefs and Interpretations of Evidence   *159*

Philosophies of Beginnings   *159*
Comparative Anatomy and Taxonomy   *162*
Comparative Protein Structure   *165*
The Development of the Embryo   *169*
Vestigial, Rudimentary, and Atavistic Structures   *171*
Animal and Plant Distribution   *172*
Mutations   *173*
The Fossil Horses   *175*
Physiology, Philosophy, and Tacit Assumption   *177*
Conclusion   *179*

8 The Age of the Earth   *181*

Biblical Chronologies   *181*
Time and Evolution   *182*
Time Defined and Measured   *182*
The Age of the Oceans   *184*
The Atmospheric Helium Clock   *185*
The Erosion and Sedimentation Clock   *186*
The Meteoritic Dust Clock   *190*
The Population Growth Clock   *191*
The Age of the Mississippi River Delta   *191*
The Gas and Oil Seepage Clock   *192*
Geostatic Pressure   *192*
The Earth's Magnetic Moment   *193*
The Cooling of the Earth   *194*
Radiometric Clocks   *195*
Radioactive Decay Curve and Half-Life   *196*
Common Radiometric Methods   *199*
Anomalous Ages   *200*
Discordant Ages   *201*
Radioactive Disequilibrium   *201*
A Last Look at the Moon   *202*
Radioactive Halos and Instantaneous Creation   *203*
Some Conclusions   *204*
Carbon-14 Dating   *205*
Is the Carbon-14 Reservoir in Balance?   *207*
Reinterpreting Carbon-14 Data   *208*
A New Chemical Method for Dating Bones   *210*
Conclusions   *211*
Jesus Christ, Lord of Time and the World   *212*

9 The Ultimate Design   *215*

Ultimate Evidence of the Designer   *215*

He Has Spoken to Man   *217*
He Has Spoken in the Bible   *217*

Appendix A   A Creation Model   *221*
Appendix B   Biblical Chronology   *231*
What the Scriptures Seem to Say   *231*
The Meaning of the Word "Day"   *231*
A "Gap" Between Genesis 1:1 and 1:2?   *232*
Interpretation of the Biblical Genealogies   *233*
Appendix C   Theistic Evolution   *235*
Conflicts with the Teachings of the Bible   *235*
Conflicts with Scientific Evidences   *236*
Conflicts with Evolutionary Theory   *236*
Appendix D   Basic Probability Theory   *239*

Footnotes   *241*
Bibliography   *247*
Index   *251*

list of figures

figure 1-1   The Bombardier Beetle   3
figure 1-2   The gecko's foot pads   4
figure 1-3   The honeybee   7
figure 1-4   The nematode worm   11
figure 1-5   Charges in the water molecule   14
figure 1-6   Solar radiation   17
figure 2-1   Potential and kinetic energy   26
figure 2-2   Energy and probability law   33
figure 3-1   The *Archaeopteryx* bird fossil   43
figure 3-2   Empire Mountains overthrust   48
figure 3-3   Fossil pollen grains in Grand Canyon   53
figure 3-4   Trilobite fossils in sandal print   54
figure 4-1   Photomicrograph of lily leaf   66
figure 4-2   Biomass pyramid in grasslands   72
figure 4-3   Photomicrograph of onion root tip cells   74
figure 4-4   Mendel's law illustrated   76
figure 4-5   Hydrogen bonds in nucleotides   80
figure 4-6   Deoxyribose and phosphoric acid in nucleotides   81
figure 4-7   DNA strands   82
figure 4-8   Shape of DNA double helix   83
figure 4-9   DNA helix prior to cell division   84
figure 4-10 DNA-RNA flow chart   87
figure 5-1   Important fossil skulls   122-123
figure 6-1   Atomic orbit of electron   134
figure 6-2   Decreasing energy of electron   135
figure 6-3   Prism spectroscope   135
figure 6-4   Balmer series   136
figure 6-5   Electron cloud patterns   136
figure 7-1   Photomicograph of bird's flight feather   162
figure 7-2   Photomicrograph of chick embryo   170
figure 7-3   Core body temperature control   179
figure 8-1   Helium in earth's crust   187
figure 8-2   Grand Canyon fossils   188
figure 8-3   Decay curve of radioactive atoms   197
figure 8-4   Bismuth-210 decomposition   198

list of tables

table 1   Uniformitarian Geological Time Scale   42
table 2   Important Humanoid Fossils   120-121
table 3   Basic Atomic Particles   134
table 4   Periodic Table of the Elements (Partial)   138
table 5   Four Forces (Interactions) in a Nucleus   140
table 6   Cytochrome *c* Amino Acid Sequences   167
table 7   Differences in Vertebrate Cytochrome *c*   168
table 8   Parent/Daughter Isotope Pairs   199
table 9   Samples of Carbon-14 Dating   207
table 10 Comparison of Carbon-14 Dating   208

Preface

Creation and evolution are now being debated in public, even in the mass media, and in the schools and universities.* Those who are materialists (and therefore believe in evolution) have long dominated the scientific, educational, and literary realms. But a reaction is setting in, and those who believe in creation are increasingly being heard. Yet in the minds of the general public and of those who believe the Bible, there is still much confusion and little solid understanding of the relationship of science to creation and evolution. Often the public debate is not well informed and misconceptions are spread and believed by many.

The Creation Explanation is written to correct some of these widely held misconceptions and to bring together facts from science which support the biblical record of creation and the Flood of Noah. It also brings critical analysis to bear on some of the evolutionary theories and the evidence which is used in their support. But rather than a frontal attack on evolution, the principal purpose of the authors is more to bring together

*Creation: All things were designed and created by an intelligent, purposeful, omnipotent Creator. Evolution: All things are the result of purely materialistic causes, all design has arisen out of the properties of matter, and all living things including man arose from inanimate matter by unplanned, purposeless, random chemical and physical processes.

a positive structure of supporting evidence for intelligent, purposeful design, that is, for creation. Nevertheless, some critical response to the claims of evolutionary theorists is necessary. Their data, we believe, do not necessarily support their thesis, but can be accommodated within a creation model of the world, often in a more satisfactory manner.

The most powerful evidence for creation and against evolution is, in our opinion, to be found in specific evidences of intelligent, purposeful design. This evidence is all around us and is something the layman as well as the scientist can appreciate. Therefore, we open and close *The Creation Explanation* with this kind of information. In general, the aim of the book is to bring the pertinent facts and concepts down to the level of high school students and people who are not trained in science. Because many readers lack a scientific background, part of the second chapter is devoted to a rudimentary explanation of some basic science. In later chapters a few rather complicated topics are discussed which may seem rather technical to some readers. Yet the consistent attempt has been made to explain everything in basic terms. Such subjects are included because they are either important to recent evolutionary arguments and therefore need critical analysis, or because they provide important support for creation. We hope all of our readers will find most of the book easy as well as interesting reading, and that they will be able to work their way through the few more difficult sections for a better understanding of the principles involved.

The most pervasive of the misconceptions about the evolution-creation controversy which are propagated by the mass media and by many educational institutions is the allegation that evolution is science whereas creation is religion. The error of this claim can be seen as soon as the so-called "scientific method" is clearly defined. The scientific method, discussed in some detail in Chapter 7, is simply that process whereby every observation, opinion, and theory about the world is continually subjected to attempts to prove it false by means of observation and experiment. A theory which cannot be subjected to potentially falsifying tests is not scientific. It belongs in the realm of metaphysics (philosophy and religion).

But can any theory about origins be falsified by experiment? The answer is *"No!"* It is not possible to devise experiments which have the possibility of conclusively falsifying either the evolutionary or the creation model of the world. Neither one, therefore, is science. They are equally religious; the one is part of the religion of materialism, the other of theism. The view called *theistic evolution* is discussed in Appendix C.

Materialism traces all reality and being to the properties and processes of eternal matter. Theism traces all reality and being to infinite-personal

Spirit. Neither view can be established by science. They are both belief systems. Nevertheless, circumstantial evidence may be adduced from the present world in support of the two contrasting world views. All of the data of science may be interpreted from the viewpoint of either theory of origins. Which view do the data of science better fit, evolution or creation? The authors believe that the scientific facts pointing to intelligent, purposeful design and therefore to creation are very persuasive. Our readers must come to their own conclusions.

As a corollary to the definition of the scientific method given above, it follows that there is no absolute knowledge in science, for every scientific theory must be open to potentially falsifying tests. It may be overthrown tomorrow by new evidence.

Is there, then, any source of *absolute* knowledge? There can be only one, God Himself, disclosed in divine revelation. And this is what the Bible claims to be, divine revelation. The authors of *The Creation Explanation* accept the claim of the Bible to be the Word of God. They accept the opening chapters of Genesis, therefore, to be true to scientific fact. This is their fundamental postulate and they make no apology for it. They do not claim to "prove" creation by means of science, although the Bible says that the evidence to be found in nature for the real existence of a personal God is conclusive, rendering all men everywhere accountable to God (Romans 1:19, 20). But the Bible also says that the Bible and creation are to be received as true by faith (Hebrews 11:3). Nevertheless we are commanded to persuade men (2 Corinthians 5:11), using every reasonable means, including the "foolishness of preaching" (1 Corinthians 1:21).

In Peter's first epistle we are admonished, " . . . be ready always to give an answer to every man that asketh you a reason of the hope that is in you with meekness and fear" (1 Peter 3:15). So we present this book with no confidence in the flesh, not depending upon any knowledge or persuasive power of our own. We make no claim to have specific answers to all of the questions which confront creation-science today. In fact, a few of the as yet unsolved problems are indicated in the book so that the reader may not be taken by surprise if such problems are used in an attack upon his faith. Evolutionists in a century of effort have accumulated persuasive arguments and massive evidence to support their case. However, we believe that taken as a whole and entirely on the basis of logic and supporting evidence, the case for creation is by far the better one. This case is open to all men everywhere. Indeed, the Scriptures assert this as fact in Psalm 19:1-7. Nevertheless, in this life we walk by faith, regardless of how great or how limited our knowledge may be. The essential foundation for security, stability, and effectiveness in the Christian life is "faith which worketh by love," a faith which is expressed in unwavering confidence in and humble obedience to God's Word, the Bible.

It is our earnest desire that *The Creation Explanation* may prove to be enlightening, encouraging, and persuasive to the end that every reader may have joyful, satisfying faith in Jesus Christ and in His Word. We also hope that this book may help every reader to see true science in its proper perspective, as a searching out of the handiwork of the Creator for the glory of the triune God—Father, Son, and Holy Spirit.

Acknowledgments

We are indebted to many who have written before us and to many colleagues who have contributed their knowledge and suggestions along the pathway of authorship. Most of those whose works have proven invaluable to the present authors are recognized in the footnotes and bibliographical lists. Others who have served on the staff of the Creation-Science Research Center and made definite contributions to this book include Miss Carole Barklow who searched the stars; Dr. James DeSaegher and Mr. John Atkinson, who perused early stages of English composition; Mrs. James DeSaegher, who typed much of the manuscript with a sharp eye for errors; and Dr. Robert F. Koontz, our resident entomologist, who inspired our respect for the complex little creeping creatures which inhabit the jars and boxes in his office-laboratory. Also incorporated in the book are important technical contributions due to three members of the Board of Trustees of the Creation-Science Research Center—Mr. Everett Purcell, Mr. John Read, and Mr. James Honeyman. Dr. John N. Moore offered constructive criticisms of the original manuscript. We are also much indebted to Dr. Victor L. Oliver for his very helpful contribution as final reviewer of the material relating to "Man."

Finally, as staff members of the Creation-Science Research Center, the authors wish to express their gratitude for the exceedingly valuable and growing body of research and study in creation-science which has been carried out and published by the Creation Research Society and its members over the past decade and more. We will feel satisfied if to their work we have added just a very few original insights and perhaps some fresh approaches to several specific problems.

Robert E. Kofahl & Kelly L. Segraves
San Diego, California
January 1975

1
Living Evidence of Design

Man is a rational and responsible being, created in the image of God. This is what the Bible teaches. Man was uniquely framed to worship and obey the God of creation. Even if he had never seen or heard of the Bible, the evidences of intelligent, purposeful design obvious in the world all around him speak to man's intellect concerning the power and deity of the Creator. The unbeliever then, in the words of Romans 1:20, is "without excuse," having ignored or rejected the forceful testimony of the evidence.

What are some of the evidences of intelligent and purposeful design? To answer this question, we will present a selection of remarkable instances of design in living things and in the structure of physical things ranging from atoms to the solar system. The facts presented will require an explanation. What was their origin? The biblical record of creation attributes the design and origin of all things to the intelligent will of an omnipotent Creator. In contrast, the evolutionary explanation proposes that a blind, unplanned, and purposeless materialistic process brought all things into being and originated all species of living creatures.

The mechanism advanced for the evolutionary development of all life from primeval "simple" cells is that of random mutations (accidental changes) which have been selected by the pressure of environmental conditions. Mutation upon mutation upon mutation—minute changes by the million occurring over millions of years, each selected mutation being one which conferred an advantage to the creature—is the process which supposedly produced all of the structures and relationships of living things, past and present. Can such a scheme offer a rational explanation for the origin of all kinds of living things? The reader is asked to consider the evidence, exercise his powers of reason, and be the judge. He should not feel that the conclusions of "authorities" or "experts" are always trustworthy. Listen to your conscience in the light of the evidence. The decision and the responsibility are yours.

Design in Living Creatures

The beetle that carries a gun   The Bombardier beetle, *Brachinus,* protects itself from its enemies by firing a hot charge of chemicals from two little swivel tubes in its tail. In 1961 Professor Schildknecht in Germany published the results of a careful investigation.[1] *Brachinus* possesses in its body twin sets of apparatus consisting of two glands producing a liquid mixture, two connected storage chambers, two "combustion chambers" (this term is Professor Schildknecht's), and the two external tubes which can be aimed like flexible guns in the tail of a bomber.

Upon analysis, the stored liquid was found to contain ten percent hydroquinones and twenty-three percent hydrogen peroxide (used in rockets). Such a mixture, Schildknecht reported, will explode spontaneously in a test tube. Why not in the beetle? Apparently the mixture contains an inhibitor which blocks the reaction until some of the liquid is squirted into the combustion chambers, where an enzyme is added to catalyze the reaction. Immediate violent reaction, an explosion, takes place; the resulting products are vaporized and fired boiling hot at the enemy (at a temperature of 212° F.) Spiders, ants, and even predators as large as toads are effectively repelled by *Brachinus*' chemical warfare.[2]

Note that a rational evolutionary explanation for the development of this creature must assign some kind of adaptive advantage to each of the millions of hypothetical intermediate stages in the construction process. But would the stages of one-fourth, one-half, or two-thirds completion, for example, have conferred any advantage? After all, a rifle is useless without all of its parts functioning. One small part missing or malfunctioning renders the rifle useless except, perhaps, as a club.

Is the Bombardier's artillery any different in this respect? Before this defensive mechanism could afford any protection to the beetle, all of its

figure 1-1. The Bombardier Beetle, *Brachinus tschernikhi*. This is a specimen found near San Diego, California, and preserved in the collection of the San Diego Museum of Natural History.

parts, together with the proper explosive mixture of chemicals, plus the instinctive behavior required for its use, would have to be assembled in the insect. The partially developed set of organs would be useless. Therefore, according to the principles of evolutionary theory itself, there would be no selective pressure to cause the system to evolve from a partially completed stage toward the final completed system. This singular defense mechanism, so perfectly designed, raises a major problem for evolutionary theorists who imply that their theory explains everything.

To recapitulate, the problem is simply this: If a particular type of organism, organ, or behavior did, in fact, originate by natural selection of random mutations, it should be possible to devise a rational succession of hypothetical mutations covering the entire hypothetical history of the supposed evolutionary process. Furthermore, it should be possible to demonstrate logically that each proposed intermediate stage or mutation would confer a selective advantage upon the organism. According to the theory, there would be no reason for selection of intermediate stages unless they were advantageous. This is why we say that evolutionary theory fails to explain *Brachinus* and the other organisms which are described below. If a theory fails to explain the data in any science, that theory should be either revised or replaced with a theory that is in agreement with the data. Now examine the following evidence and draw your own conclusions.

A lizard on the ceiling The gecko lizard can walk across your ceiling upside-down without falling off. How? Until a few years ago scientists did not know, though they proposed several conflicting theories. Examination of the toe pads of the gecko with optical microscopes at up to 2000 diameters magnification revealed thousands of little fibers arranged like the tufts of bristles in a toothbrush. Yet the question remained unanswered. An answer was finally provided by the powerful scanning electron microscope, which was able to take a series of remarkable photographs magnified to 35,000 diameters or more.[3] What was revealed?

The gecko has on its toe pads many millions of fine fibers tipped with little suction cups, each about eight millionths of an inch in diameter. In conjunction with this, the lizard's feet are designed so that the toe joints bend or curl upward (try it sometime) so that he can peel the suction cups off gradually at each step and not get himself too firmly stuck to the surface. It is estimated that the gecko has at least 500 million suction cups on his toes. The extraordinary microscopic structure of the gecko lizard's toe pads clearly indicates intelligent, purposeful design. No remotely plausible scheme for the origin of the gecko's suction cups by random mutations and natural selection has yet been proposed by evolutionary theorists. And should some scientist with a clever imagination succeed in devising such a scheme, he would still be without a scrap of fossil evidence to demonstrate that the hypothetical process of evolution actually took place in the past.

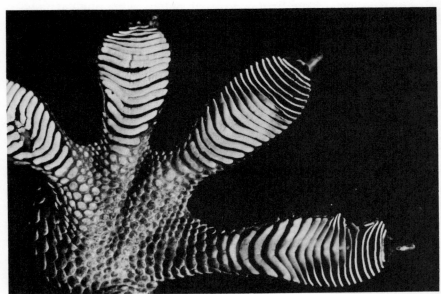

figure 1-2. Each chevron-shaped ridge of the gecko's foot pads is composed of millions of fibers tipped with microscopic suction cups.

Do drinking giraffes have headaches?   Darwin wrote in his *Origin of Species* that he had no difficulty in imagining that a long period of drought could have caused some hypothetical short-necked ancestors of the giraffe continually to stretch their necks higher and higher to reach the diminishing supply of leaves. He had no fossil evidence, of course, for such an evolutionary history. He also apparently was not aware of certain problems peculiar to giraffes which make his easy assumption of giraffe evolution even more difficult to accept.

The giraffe heart is probably the most powerful in the animal kingdom, because about double normal pressure is required to pump blood up that long neck to the brain. But the brain is a very delicate structure which cannot stand high blood pressure. What happens when the giraffe bends down to take a drink? Does he "blow his mind?" Fortunately, three design features have been included in the giraffe to control this and related problems. In the first place, the giraffe must spread his front legs apart in order to drink comfortably. This lowers the level of the heart somewhat and thus reduces the difference in height from the heart to the head of the drinking animal, with the result that excess pressure in the brain is less than would be the case if the legs were kept straight.

Second, the giraffe has in his jugular veins a series of one-way check valves which immediately close as the head is lowered, thus preventing blood from flowing back down into the brain. But what of the blood flow through the carotid artery from the heart to the brain? A third design feature is the "wonder net," a spongy tissue filled with numerous small blood vessels and located near the base of the brain. The arterial blood first flows through this net of vessels before it reaches the brain. It is believed that when the animal stoops to drink, the wonder net in some way controls the blood flow so that the full pressure is not exerted on the brain. It is also believed by scientists that probably the cerebrospinal fluid which bathes the brain and spinal column produces a counter-pressure which prevents rupture or leakage from the brain capillaries. The effect is similar to that of a *g* suit worn by fighter pilots and astronauts. Leakage from the capillaries in the legs due to high blood pressure is also probably prevented by a similar pressure of the tissue fluid outside the cells. In addition, the walls of the giraffe's arteries are thicker than in any other mammal.

Some careful investigations and measurements of blood pressure have recently been made in live giraffes in action. However, the exact manner in which these various factors operate to enable the strange creature to live has still not been clearly demonstrated. Nevertheless, the giraffe is a great success. When he has finished his drink he stands up, the check valves open, the effects of the wonder net and the various counter-pressure mechanisms relax, and all is well. Not even a headache.[4]

Bats and whales that "see" with their ears   Bat echo-location capabilities are well-known but bear another look.[5] The small insect-eating bats are master sound technicians. When hunting in the dark, they emit rapid sequences of hypersonic chirps, for the most part inaudible to human ears. Each chirp lasts about two milliseconds and is frequency-modulated; that is, it begins at a very high frequency, around 100,000 cycles per second, and sweeps down to about half of the initial frequency. It is believed that this enables the bat to determine the size and other characteristics of objects which reflect echoes to the bat's ears. The shorter wavelengths reflect better from the smaller objects. The bat cannot be fooled by a pebble but will only capture insects.

We will only briefly allude to the underwater sonar capabilities of dolphins, porpoises, and whales, which enable these creatures to perceive their obscure watery surroundings with amazing accuracy. The United States Navy has failed to duplicate their sonar technology.

Each creature a designed, integrated system   Every living creature is an integrated system which lives and functions as a whole. An excellent example of this is provided by the worker honeybee. Consider certain parts of the worker bee's body and their vital functions:[6]

1. Compound eyes can analyze polarized light for navigation by sun in cloudy weather and for flower recognition.

2. Three single eyes on the head probably have some navigational function.

3. Antennae supply sense of smell and touch.

4. Grooves on front legs clean antennae.

5. Hairs on head, thorax, and legs collect pollen.

6. Pollen baskets on rear legs carry collected pollen.

7. The tube-like proboscis sucks nectar, honey, and water, curls back under the head.

8. Mandibles crush and form wax for comb-building.

9. A honey sac provides temporary storage of honey.

10. Enzymes in honey sac begin transformation of nectar to honey.

11. Glands in abdomen produce beeswax, which is secreted as scales on rear segments of body.

12. Long spines on middle legs remove wax scales from glands.

13. Pronged claws on each foot cling to flowers.

14. Glands in head of adult worker make royal jelly for the develop-

figure 1-3. The honeybee was created according to a highly integrated design. The numbers refer to the numbered design features listed on pages 6 and 7.

ment of a new queen bee.

15. Marginal hooks fasten front and rear wings together for flight, disengage at rest for compact storage of wings.

16. Barbed poison sting serves for defense.

17. Complex instincts cause entire hive to function as a single organism.

Without all of these design features and many more the worker bees could not function in the hive; as a result the hive would perish. Actually, the entire hive of bees functions as a single living organism. The queen controls the life and development of the hive by means of chemical substances called pheromones which circulate through the hive population in the food supply. The social organization in the hive is truly marvelous. One of the most remarkable features of this organization is the dance language used by a returning worker to inform other bees of the location and preferred course to a new source of nectar. The honeybee is surely the result of intelligent design.

The same may be said of the orb weaving spider. The selection of several distinct protein formulations which she incorporates in up to seven different kinds of silk and the complex spinnarets having hundreds of microscopic holes through which the precisely formed threads are spun have not been explained on the basis of accidental, purposeless evolution.[7] The beautiful design of the orb web is a miniature engineering wonder, but the spider learns her web building technique from no one. The spider was, so to speak, hatched with a degree in web engineering. It may also be pointed out that no fossil evidence exists for the evolutionary origin of spiders, but the mute little spider bears eloquent witness to the reality of design in nature.

Animal Instinct

Bird navigators   The navigational abilities of birds remain largely a mystery to science. A species of warbler summers in Germany, where the young are raised. At the close of the season the parent birds depart for the headwaters of the Nile in Africa, leaving the young birds behind, for they are not yet ready for the long flight. A few weeks later the young birds take off and fly to Africa, traveling thousands of miles without a guide over a path they have never seen to join their parents. How do they accomplish this? German scientists proved that they navigate by the stars.[8] These birds are hatched from the egg with this ability and with the pre-programmed navigation and flight instructions already in their little bird brains.

More recent research reveals that a pigeon has two independent mechanisms for determining direction. In sunny weather the pigeon tells direction by means of the sun, but in cloudy weather it tells direction by means of some kind of magnetic compass located somewhere in its head.[9] The common pigeon guards an even more mysterious secret of navigation. It has knowledge of a map which it reads as it travels to its destination. This map is entirely independent of surface features on the earth, yet is strangely influenced by the geographical location in which the bird finds itself. Scientists at Cornell University and other research centers are striving to learn the pigeon's secret.

Evolutionary science has absolutely no explanation as to how bird and animal navigation capabilities could have evolved. The reasonable explanation is that these creatures were designed this way by the Creator.

Spider aquanauts   Most spiders do not like water. They are dry land creatures. But *Argyroneta* lives *under* the water![10] These clever creatures live in little silken diving bells a foot or so under the surface of ponds and streams in Europe. At the surface they capture bubbles of air, which cling to the hairs of their abdomens, and they fill their diving bells with bubbles brought down from the top. The female *Argyroneta* lays her eggs in her diving bell, and the little spiderlets begin their life there beneath the surface. When they are ready to begin an independent life, they dart out into the water sheathed in a silvery bubble of air borrowed from their mother's diving-bell home. We challenge evolutionary science to come up with a rational explanation for the origin of *Argyroneta.*

Symbiosis

The dirty fish that blushes   The blushing fish of tropical seas provide a striking example of symbiosis (living together). Symbiosis is the term for a relationship between two creatures which is beneficial to one, the other, or both of them.

A certain species of tropical fish, the yellow-tailed goat fish, mostly white in color, swims in small schools. In common with most of the scaled fish, this species is bothered by infestations of parasites in their scales and gills, and from time to time the fish need a cleaning job. When one of the fish needs such a cleaning, the small school swims over to a coral reef where small black and yellow French angel fish have set up a neighborhood fish wash station. When the dirty fish blushes a bright rust-red color, the little cleaner fish knows that the blushing fish wants a wash, not a fish dinner. He darts out, gives the blushing goat fish a good cleaning, and then darts back into the safety of the coral. The blushing fish stops blushing and the school swims off.[11]

Several dozen such cleaner relationships have been observed in tropical waters, involving a number of different species of small cleaner fish as well as various species of tiny, beautifully decorated cleaner shrimp. The cleaners are often eaten by the larger fish, so it is only after the proper signal is given that they will leave their protective lairs to venture out on cleaning missions. These signals, in addition to color change, include the adoption of an attitude of rest with gills and fins flared, or a vertical position in the water with head up and fins flapping.

One researcher removed the cleaner shrimp from two coral heads and found that within two weeks there were fewer fish at these coral heads than at others in the area. The fish present often showed frayed fins and ulcerated sores. This strongly suggests that the cleaner relationships are essential for the larger fish and constitute an integral feature of the community life of the coral reef. The idea that such symbiotic arrangements could be evolved and not designed stretches the evolutionary imagination to the breaking point. Does not the evidence lead one to believe that these creatures were designed and created to help one another?

Ants in the plants   Another marvelous example of symbiosis is afforded by the myrmecophytes, plants which are inhabited by ants. The South American Bull's horn acacia serves as the home of a species of fierce ants which are nourished by certain parts of the tree. In exchange, the ants protect the tree from all intruders, be they insects, birds, or foraging animals. But even more amazing, these ants nip off and prune back any encroaching vines, bushes, or other plants, thus maintaining ample growth space for their home tree. If the ants are removed from the tree, within two to fifteen months the tree is defoliated, overrun by neighboring plants, and it perishes.[12] Who taught these ants to be gardeners?

Predation and Defense

Slugs with stolen stingers   Predation is combined with defense in a most amazing way by *Eolidoidea* spurred nudibranchs, a type of sea slug which feeds primarily on sea anemones. But anemones are armed with tiny stinging cells which explode at the slightest touch and plunge a poisoned dart into any intruder. The sea slug, however, can tear an anemone apart violently, chew it up, swallow and digest it without either exploding or digesting the stinging cells. And the most fantastic part of this story is yet to come.

Leading from the sea slug's stomach to small pouches in the fluffy spurs on its sides are very narrow channels lined with moving hairs or cilia. The cilia sweep the stinging cells out of the stomach and up the channels to the pouches, where they are arranged and stored for the sea slug's defense. If an unwary fish should nip at a sea slug, it would be stung in the mouth by stinging cells which the hapless sea anemone had prepared for its own hunting and defense.[13]

Cyanide is good for the millipede   The millipede, species *Apheloria corrugata,* is a very clever chemist. On both sides of each segment of its body where a pair of legs attach, subsurface glands produce a liquid containing a chemical compound, mandelonitrile. When the millipede is attacked by ants or other enemies, it mixes the mandelonitrile with a catalyst, causing it to decompose to form benzaldehyde, a mild irritant, and hydrogen cyanide gas. Hydrogen cyanide is the deadly poison used in the gas chamber to execute criminals. For chemistry enthusiasts the equation for the reaction is as follows:

$$\overset{\displaystyle OH}{\underset{\displaystyle H}{C_6H_5 - C - CN}} \rightarrow C_6H_5CHO + HCN$$

mandelonitrile $\rightarrow$ benzaldehyde + hydrogen cyanide

There the millipede sits, happily basking in a cloud of lethal fumes, while his attackers flee in all directions. When the coast is clear, he crawls off, for some unknown reason totally unaffected by his own deadly poison.[14]

The cowboy fungus   Our closing example of intelligent and purposeful design in living creatures is that of the predatory molds. There are many species of soil mold which capture and feed upon the tiny, exceedingly numerous nematode worms which inhabit the soil. Some of these molds grow sticky knobs with which they entrap the worms. But the star predatory molds species is *Arthrobotrys dactyloides,* which lassos its prey like a cowboy lassos steers. Only when nematodes are present in the soil does this mold grow tiny loops, each one formed of three cells. When a worm sticks its neck into one of the loops, within one-tenth of a second the loop cells swell and the loop clamps shut on the worm, strangling it. The worm is then digested at leisure.[15]

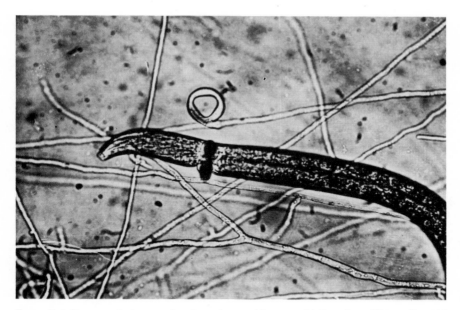

figure 1-4. The nematode worm has been trapped in a constricting ring of the earth mold, *Arthrobotrys dactyloides,* magnified 363 times in this photomicrograph supplied by Dr. David Pramer, Director of Biological Sciences, Rutgers State University, New Brunswick, New Jersey.

We have offered thirteen examples of design in living things, design for which there is no evolutionary explanation. These things point unmistakably to an infinitely wise and powerful Designer and Creator. The list of such wonders is endless. However, we need not look only to the unusual and bizarre for evidence of intelligent and purposeful design, for such evidence can be found in every creature, beginning with the intricacies of the simplest single cell and including the basic structures of plants and animals and the human body and brain.

The Psalmist expressed his wonder concerning such things in Psalm 139:14, "I will praise thee; for I am fearfully and wonderfully made: marvelous are thy works; and that my soul knoweth right well." In Psalm 111:2 he said, "The works of the Lord are great, sought out of all them that have pleasure therein." We can take great pleasure in studying the marvels of God's creative handiwork and in giving Him the glory and praise.

Design in Communities of Living Things[16]

All living creatures form an interdependent system linked with the purely physical earth environment. Providing significant evidence of design by a Master Designer, ecological studies of particular localized communities of living things reveal in such communities an intricate, integrated web of interdependencies among the various living things. Ecological communities are characterized by self-adjusting balancing mechanisms and also by conservative cycles by which the materials used by plants and animals are continually circulated and reused.

The most obvious balanced interdependence is that between plants and animals. By the process of photosynthesis plants are able to capture the energy of sunlight and use it to transform water and carbon dioxide from the atmosphere into carbohydrates and other energy-rich organic compounds plus oxygen gas, which is released into the atmosphere. Animals eat plant materials and use oxygen from the atmosphere to oxidize the energy-rich plant products, producing energy which powers animal life processes, releasing carbon dioxide into the atmosphere. Thus a double cycle of carbon and oxygen powered by the energy of the sun is basic to all life upon the earth.

In every ecological community there are food cycles which intermesh with various material cycles involving chemical elements essential to life. The greater part of photosynthesis takes place in the oceans, carried out by the microscopic plants of the plankton suspended in the upper layer of seawater within a couple of hundred feet of the surface. Carbon dioxide absorbed into the water from the atmosphere is used by the plankton, and oxygen is released into the water, some going back into the air, the remainder serving as the oxygen supply for the animal life of the oceans. Many of the smaller sea creatures eat the microscopic plant life;

small fish eat them, larger fish eat the smaller fish, and on up the food chain to the largest denizens of the sea, which thus are ultimately dependent upon the photosynthesis performed by the microscopic plankton in the upper water layers.

On the land a characteristic food chain or cycle would consist of photosynthesizing plants, plant-eating grasshoppers, hopper-eating toads, toad-eating snakes, and snake-eating birds of prey, the highest members of the food chain. The bird dies, falls to the ground and is decomposed by bacteria or eaten; the essential chemical elements are finally returned to the soil to be used once again by plants. And again the energy source is sunlight harnessed by plants.

Mutually dependent and beneficial relationships between plants and insects provide extensive evidence of intelligent and purposeful design in the natural order. The most familiar of these is that between many pollen-bearing plants and the honeybee, for bees need nectar and pollen, and the flowers need a mechanism by which pollen can be transported from blossom to blossom. The fig tree and the fig gall wasp are similarly interdependent, and in a manner that is so wonderfully unique that one may only conclude that one was specifically designed for the other. The yucca plant and the pronuba moth are related in a very similar manner. Nature is replete with these marvelous fingerprints of infinite intelligence, purpose, and creative ability.

The preservation of all species of plants and animals inhabiting an ecological community requires the automatic maintenance of balance between the different kinds of living things. For instance, too many deer will strip the food supply from a forest area until increasing deer population and decreasing food supply bring about catastrophic waves of sickness, starvation and resulting depopulation of the deer herd. Reestablishment of a healthy herd of deer in that area may require decades. The Designer of the forest community included among its fauna predators, such as coyotes, wolves, and mountain lions, which limit the size of the deer population. Thus the balance is maintained between predator, plant, foraging deer, and the plant food supply. Then man comes upon the scene with his domesticated sheep and cattle, and some of these fall prey to the predators native to the region. When an all-out campaign is mounted to exterminate the predators, the natural balance is destroyed and the forest and the deer herd suffer disastrous damage.

Man is learning, often too late, that natural balance must be preserved for man's own welfare. Would not greater awareness of divine design in nature and a more profound sense of man's responsibility before the Creator have helped to prevent many unfortunate episodes throughout the history of man's interaction with the balance of nature?

Design in Atoms, Molecules, and Water[17]

Modern scientific research depends upon the principle that nature is orderly, subject to laws which man can discover by repeatable observations and measurements. Indeed, at every level, from the nucleus of the atom to the distant galaxies, structured order and design have been discovered. Consider the design of the water molecule, which consists of one oxygen atom and two hydrogen atoms (H_2O).

Hydrogen and oxygen gases react to form water molecules because of the design of the nuclei of hydrogen and oxygen atoms and the associated arrangement of the electrons which form a structured cloud around these two kinds of atoms. The water molecule has a "V" shape with the oxygen atom at the apex of the "V." The oxygen atom is classified as more "electronegative" than the hydrogen atoms, for it attracts electrons toward itself away from the hydrogen atoms in the molecule. Therefore, the oxygen end of the water molecule has more negative charge, the hydrogen atoms more positive charge.

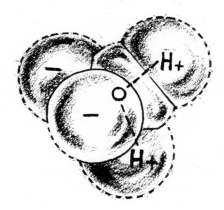

figure 1-5. The hydrogen atoms on the right side of this water molecule carry an excess positive charge, whereas the electron clouds on the left side carry negative charge.

Thus we say that water is a "polar" molecule, for it has negative and positive ends or poles. This is important to the properties of water, for the polar molecules tend to attract each other and clump together in the liquid form. In addition, the hydrogen atoms of water can form a special kind of bond between the oxygen atoms of adjacent molecules. This bond mediated by a hydrogen atom is called a hydrogen bond. Hydrogen bonds are described in more detail in Chapter 4. Because of polar attraction and hydrogen bonding between molecules, it requires considerable energy to break the molecules in the liquid state loose from each other to produce water vapor or gas in which the molecules are not in contact with each other. We say that water has a high "heat of vaporization."

When water is frozen, the "V" shape of the water molecule, its polar character, and its ability to form hydrogen bonds cause water to produce a beautiful geometric structure which takes up more space than the liquid water. Thus ice is less dense than liquid water. Moreover, the polar character of the molecules causes them to cling together in the ice crystal so that a large amount of energy is required to melt water. We say that water has a high "heat of fusion" (melting).

This singular combination of properties found in the water molecule results from the unique design of the two constituent atoms. Now consider the place of water in the world around us. The polar character of water, combined with its stability and also its very slight tendency to break up (ionize) into two charged ions, H^+ and OH^-, makes water the ideal solvent for living systems. Water can dissolve a greater variety of substances than any other solvent, but it draws the line at oily (non-polar) substances, which are not soluble in water. On the other hand, the polar character of water makes it possible for so-called "surface active" molecules which are polar on one end and non-polar on the other to carry oily substances into colloidal suspension in a water system. These capabilities of water are vital to life processes.

Now let us consider the function of water in the oceans and atmosphere. As indicated earlier, water expands slightly upon freezing so that ice floats. Only one other pure substance, the metal bismuth, has this characteristic. What if ice were heavier than water? When winter approached, the circulation in oceans and lakes would slowly cause the entire body of water to cool to the freezing point. If the first ice formed at the surface, it would immediately sink to the bottom. Any ice formed at the bottom would stay there, and the entire body of water would become solid ice from top to bottom. When spring and summer came, is it likely that large lakes or oceans would be able to melt before the next winter arrived? No.

Soon most of the water in the earth would be locked up in great glaciers and ice sheets near the polar regions, never to be released, and the rest of the earth would primarily contain either very hot or cold deserts with little available water. And, of course, life in most bodies of water would be very scarce, for total freezing would kill everything under the surface.

But ice floats because the Creator designed it that way, and when the snow and ice come, we can enjoy them (sometimes) because we know they will melt in the springtime.

Just as the energy of the sun provides the life energy for all living creatures on the earth, it also powers the circulation of the atmosphere, which is responsible for weather and climate. Air is the principle energy-carrying medium for this engine, but also partially responsible is water vapor, particularly effective because of its high heat of condensation which, as was explained earlier, results from the design of the water molecule.

In addition, a body of water can store a great deal of heat energy, which is subsequently released in winter time and moderates the cold weather. Conversely, in the summer such a body of water cooled during the winter can soak up much heat energy and thus moderate hot summer weather nearby. In another important function, water vapor in the atmosphere teams up with carbon dioxide gas to absorb heat radiation from the earth's surface and keep it within the atmosphere. This is a major mechanism for moderating temperature extremes on the surface of the globe. All of these capabilities depend upon the design of the water molecule.

We have given just an introduction to the important properties of water, deriving from the design of the water molecule, which are essential to the existence of life on the earth. When we realize that the universe's only known concentration of water in the liquid form essential to life is located on the earth, and that the temperatures and pressures required for the existence of water in the liquid form depend upon a finely balanced set of conditions peculiar to the earth, the rational mind must recognize that there is, indeed, weighty evidence for intelligent, purposeful design of the earth and the solar system.

Design in the Earth-Sun System[18]

The balanced design features of the earth-sun system include the following:

1. The average distance of the earth from the sun provides the average temperatures required for life.

2. The sun's temperature is correct to provide the right kind of radiation to sustain life.

3. The nearly circular orbit of the earth limits temperature variations.

4. The water vapor and carbon dioxide in the atmosphere produce a

"greenhouse effect" which moderates the temperature extremes.

5. A high altitude ozone layer effectively absorbs the lethal fraction of solar ultraviolet rays which in minutes would destroy life on the earth's surface.

6. The 23½ degree inclination of the earth's axis of rotation from the

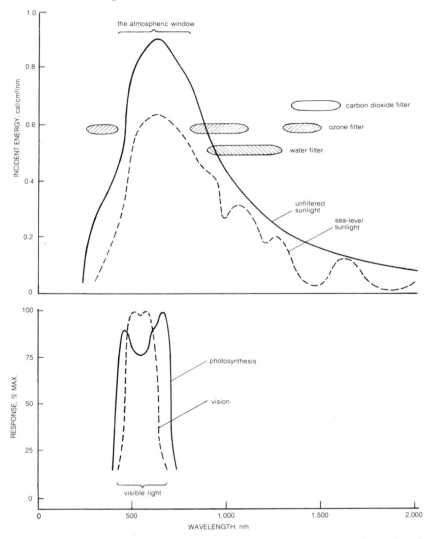

figure 1-6. The peak in solar radiation in the center of the visible range of wavelengths, coupled with the peculiar absorption characteristics of the earth's atmosphere, provides an ideal radiation environment for living things. Needed wavelengths are admitted and deadly ultraviolet light of wavelengths shorter than 400nm are largely excluded from the earth's surface. (From Helena Curtis, *Invitation to Biology,* Worth Publishers, New York, 1972, p. 91)

plane of its orbit provides for the seasons and probably prevents the locking of excessive amounts of water in polar glaciers. Average equatorial temperatures are probably lower and desert areas less extensive than would be the case were the axis not inclined.

7. The earth's magnetic field, extending tens of thousands of miles into space, shields the earth's surface from the lower energy cosmic rays and high energy solar wind particles which would be deleterious to life.

8. The lunar gravitation provides important tidal circulation effects in the oceans, which make conditions much more suitable for sea life in the shallow zones along shores and in estuaries.

9. The mass and size of the earth are adjusted to provide gravitational force and atmospheric pressure suitable for life.

10. The two major constituents of the atmosphere, oxygen (twenty-one percent) and nitrogen (seventy-eight percent), are balanced to make up the ideal medium for the support of life.

11. The elements essential to life, such as nitrogen, carbon, oxygen, and phosphorus, are contained in the earth's crust, hydrosphere, and atmosphere considerably or even greatly enriched over the average content of these elements observed in other parts of the cosmos.

The obvious question at this point is, "Where does the weight of the evidence lie—the evidence from living things, ecological communities, the structure and properties of the water molecule, the balanced conditions upon the earth's surface and in the solar system, and the chemical composition of the earth?" Does the weight of evidence lie with the thesis of origin of all things by random, purposeless, unplanned, materialistic processes, or does it lie with the thesis of origin by intelligent, purposeful design and creation by an omnipotent and omniscient Creator? You must answer this question for yourself.

Man's place in the world The Bible tells us in Genesis 1:26, 27 that God created man in His own image with dominion over the creatures. That this image in man is not a physical but a spiritual, intellectual, and moral image is made clear by all the scriptural teaching concerning God, and specifically the teaching of Christ in John 4 that God is a spirit and in Luke 24 that a spirit does not have flesh and bones. The image of God in man, therefore, is the complex of essential attributes that make man *man*, not animal—his intellect, affections, will, and moral capacity. Alone of all creatures on earth, man uses symbolic language and logic, reasons inductively and deductively and is capable of abstract thought, plans for the future and preserves the intellectual accomplishments of the present for use in the future, and makes use in the present of the accomplishments of men in the past. Man alone possesses and exercises a sense of moral responsibility; he alone shows compassion and concern for others arising from moral and spiritual capacities. He alone evidences awareness of a supernatural world or feels any responsibility to know, worship, and obey the God of Creation.

The dominion over all other creatures which God gave to man in his original created state of perfect holiness and wholeness to a large extent was lost when man, through sin, forfeited rational dominion over his own soul. The responsibility, nevertheless, remains, and even apart from God men often demonstrate a sense of this responsibility for preserving the natural order for the benefit of all. Only man has the intellectual capacity for comprehending the complex ecological systems which make up the world of living things, including the human race. Man alone has the ability to apply knowledge and reason to the solution of the difficult problems of imbalance, destruction, and pollution caused primarily by man's activities. It is now almost universally recognized that such problems are of extreme importance to all peoples, because of the need not only to keep the earth a livable place, but also to preserve its order and beauty which only man has the aesthetic sense to appreciate.

The person who honestly accepts the testimony of the scientific evidence which points to intelligent, purposeful design in nature should be more responsible and concerned for its preservation. Especially is this so if he goes on to perceive the biblical teaching that God created man with dominion over the created world and all its creatures, giving him responsibility to dress and guard it. The knowledge of science and creation such as that offered in the present and succeeding chapters of this book, should lead every sincere seeker after truth to praise and glorify the God of Creation to Whom the beauty, order, and design of nature so powerfully testify. This is the God who created all things by and for His Son, Jesus Christ.

2

The Changing World

Of old hast thou laid the foundation of the earth: and the heavens are the work of thy hands. They shall perish, but thou shalt endure: yea, all of them shall wax old like a garment; as a vesture shalt thou change them, and they shall be changed. But thou art the same, and thy years shall have no end. Psalm 102:25-27

The Psalmist saw that the world around him was continually changing, never static, never the same today as it was yesterday. Even the most stable, rocky mountains were slowly wearing down. Perhaps David could not detect change in the starry heavens, but the Spirit of God taught him that the heavens, too, were changing. God alone changes not, the Creator God of the Bible, whom David worshipped, trusted, and served.

The processes of change in the physical world are among the most important subjects of scientific research. The physical laws which govern such change have profound significance for the Christian as he reads the Genesis record of divine creation and compares it with the theories which unbelieving scientists have devised to explain the origin of all things—the universe, earth, life, and man. An understanding of these physical laws discovered by scientists can serve to undergird the Bible-believer as he contends with science falsely so-called.

A satisfying understanding, however, of these laws of energy and change requires some rudimentary knowledge of such things as force, motion, and energy, which are fundamental concepts in physics. The objective of this chapter is to impart a basic comprehension of those concepts and principles which are necessary for the appreciation of those very fundamental physical laws which afford powerful support for the biblical record of creation. These ideas are really quite simple, and they will be explained in as simple and direct a manner as possible. To grasp them is to comprehend a great deal about what we see going on in the world around us, as well as to understand how physical science supports the Bible. So let us observe the changes occurring around us all the time and try to understand just what is happening.

Processes of Change

Change and the processes which bring about change give significance to existence in the physical universe. We have all observed many different kinds of change, some obvious and some more subtle, but all important to our lives. The most obvious type of change merely involves the relative motion of objects, as in the case of the apparent motions of the sun, moon, and stars, an airplane or meteorite hurtling through the sky, a stone rolling down the hillside, a walking man or flying bird. Viewed superficially, most of these changes do not seem to necessarily produce permanent effects, for the objects can be returned to their former positions.

Another kind of change involves the alteration of the shapes of material things, as in the flow of water or wind, the breaking of glass, or the bending of a pipe. In the case of breaking or bending, the changes are more permanent in character than are the changes involving mere relative motion of objects, but flowing water and wind also seem to obey rules which make them flow only in one direction, that is, from high pressure to low pressure.

Flow of heat through the bottom of a metal frying pan, the transmission of light and other radiations through space, and the transmission of radio waves are more subtle processes of change which seem to be less permanent in their effects. Even with these processes, however, there appear to be governing laws which cause change to take place in only one direction. For example, heat is always observed to flow or radiate from warm objects toward colder objects.

Chemical reactions, producing changes continually in our environment, are basic to life. Living creatures absorb food and oxygen from their surroundings and combine them chemically to build tissues and to provide energy for life processes, releasing carbon dioxide gas and water vapor into the air. By the process of photosynthesis, plants absorb energy from the sun with which to transform water and carbon dioxide gas from the air into sugar, cellulose, and other substances necessary for plant and animal life.

We observe, however, that whereas non-living substances containing carbon and hydrogen do combine with atmospheric oxygen to produce carbon dioxide and water and release heat and perhaps light to the surroundings, they never accomplish the reverse process. For example, the burning of a candle transforms the wax into carbon dioxide and water, releasing heat and light, but the reverse process never occurs spontaneously in nature. A candle never "unburns," that is, the water, carbon dioxide, and energy released to the air are never observed spontaneously to collect and reform once again into a candle, even if heat and light are introduced in ample amounts. On the other hand, green plants *can* absorb carbon dioxide and water and, using the energy of sunlight, synthesize wax which could be used to produce a candle.

Though modern scientific research has uncovered many of the mysteries of photosynthesis, much remains to be learned. And the more scientists learn, the more the scientific facts suggest that the photosynthetic process, the complex structures required, and the complicated enzyme systems and cycles involved are the result of intelligent design.

All living things are characterized by metabolism (consumption of food for energy and building materials), growth, response to environment, and reproduction—processes of change which distinguish living from non-living substance. But concurrent with the growth process, aging inevitably occurs, so that continually some of the initial organizational excellence of the creature is being degraded. Ultimately the creature dies, and processes of decay soon destroy all vestiges of the ordered structures and systems which made up the living thing.

The universal tendency of all things toward degeneration and decay is common to our experience. The works of man seem particularly vulnerable to this law of degeneration, regardless of how precisely and strongly they are constructed or how carefully they are maintained and protected. Metals corrode, paint cracks and chips, wood decays. Clothing and machinery wear out, automobiles and toys end up in the junkyard; indeed, anything that money can buy progresses finally to dust and ashes. No doubt this is one of the reasons that the Lord Jesus Christ admonishes us in Matthew 6:19, "Lay not up for yourselves treasures upon earth, where moth and rust doth corrupt, and where thieves break through and steal."

Cyclic Change

Many kinds of change are coordinated with reverse processes so that a continually repeating cycle of change results. The water cycle illustrates cyclic change in nature. Radiation from the sun causes liquid water in the oceans to vaporize and disperse into the atmosphere. Wind currents carry the moisture laden air to high altitudes, where the reduced pressure permits the air to expand and thereby become cooled below the dew point so that the moisture condenses as snow or rain. Falling on the land, this condensation ultimately finds its way back to the sea whence it came, and so the water cycle is closed. At first glance this cycle might appear to cause no permanent change, but such is actually not the case. For example, energy has left the sun never to return, and the rain waters have produced permanent erosional changes on the earth's surface. The flow of solar energy keeps the weather cycle going, but the sun and the earth are permanently changed.

The biblical author, Solomon, writing in a supposedly pre-scientific age, accurately described the global cycles of water and wind, in Ecclesiastes 1:6, 7.

The wind goeth toward the south, and turneth about unto the north; it whirleth about continually, and the wind returneth again according to his circuits. All the rivers run into the sea; yet the sea is not full; unto the place from whence the rivers come, thither they return again.

Other examples of cyclic change in nature include the annual revolution of the earth in its orbit and its daily rotation, the carbon and oxygen cycles which intersect in the photosynthetic activity of plants and in the respiration of animals referred to above, the nitrogen cycle, and a number of other material cycles which are vital to the continued existence of life on earth. On first view one might conclude that no permanent changes are brought about by these cycles, but more careful examination reveals in each case that permanent loss of useful energy occurs and that consequently the cyclic process cannot be eternal.

Work, Energy, and Energy Transformations

Work and force are familiar terms to most people, and the average person has some intuitive notion of what they mean, even though he may not know their technical definitions. Force applied to an object produces change only if motion results, and some motion, however slight, always results from applied force unless it is counteracted by an equal and opposite force.

Thus, when a force is applied to a coil spring, there is motion, for the spring is compressed; or, when a lifting force is applied to a lead weight, there is motion and the weight moves upward. In each case there is a resisting force: the spring resists being compressed, and the force of gravity resists the lifting force.

This leads us to the definition of work: *Work is the transference of energy which occurs when a force is applied to a moving object in the direction of motion. Quantitatively, work is defined as the product of force times distance:* $W = F \times D$ (where F is the component of the force which is in the direction of the motion).

Once the spring has been compressed and the compressing force is released, the spring can expand and do work in the process by exerting force on a moving object. The raised weight can be allowed to return to its initial lower level while doing work in a similar fashion. Thus we say that a compressed spring and a raised weight have the capacity to do work.

This leads to another important definition: *Energy is the capacity to do work.* Thus the compressed spring and the raised lead weight in the previous illustrations possess energy. There are a number of different kinds of energy, and these are classified as either potential or kinetic. *Potential energy is possessed by a system of objects by virtue of their relative positions.* Thus the compressed spring possesses potential energy of deformation because its parts have been moved with respect to one another. Likewise the lead weight possesses gravitational potential energy because of its position relative to the earth.

Kinetic energy, on the other hand, *is energy which an object possesses by virtue of its motion.* If the compressed spring is used to propel an object through the air, the spring loses its potential energy, but the moving object has gained kinetic energy. If the raised weight is released, it immediately starts to lose potential energy as it falls, but gains kinetic energy as its speed increases. These are two examples of energy transformation which will be discussed in more detail below.

Note that when the raised weight is left free to fall, the only force acting upon it is the force of gravity downward. The weight immediately receives an acceleration in the direction of the gravitational force acting upon it. The compressed spring in a toy gun applies force to a projectile and accelerates it. Magnetic force acting on a piece of iron can accelerate the iron, and gas pressure in a rifle barrel produces a force on the end of a bullet which accelerates it to high velocity in the barrel.

From these examples of the effect of force, we may derive a definition for force: *A force is any influence which is capable of accelerating an object.* From this definition we may draw the conclusion that if an object is either

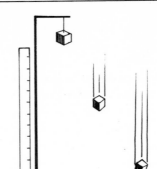

figure 2-1. The stationary weight at the top possesses potential energy. As it falls, its potential energy is transformed into kinetic energy.

stationary or moving at constant velocity, the sum of all forces acting on it is zero, because it is not being accelerated. On the other hand, if the velocity of an object is changing—either increasing, decreasing, or changing direction—a net force is acting on that object, because it is being accelerated.

Observe that force is an interaction between two objects which, when there is relative motion, transmits energy from one object to the other. Thus as a force compresses the spring or lifts the weight, these objects gain potential energy. And as expanding gases in a rifle barrel exert force on a bullet, they perform work on the bullet, which is accelerated and gains kinetic energy.

We have explained force and its relation to energy only qualitatively, but just this rudimentary understanding can give much insight into common processes happening all around us in the world. Now let us return to the subject of energy.

The common kinds of energy include mechanical (potential and kinetic energy of objects large enough to be seen and handled), heat, radiant, chemical, gravitational, electromagnetic, and nuclear energy.

In view of the definitions of work and energy, it should be clear that work involves the transformation of one kind of energy into another or its transmission from one object to another. Thus, when an object falls under the influence of the force of gravity, potential energy is converted into kinetic energy as the object is accelerated.

When a gun is fired, the chemical energy of the explosive is converted into the heat energy of hot, compressed gases in the barrel, which is then converted into the kinetic energy of the bullet. In a hydroelectric power generating system, the gravitational potential energy of the water at the top of the dam is converted into electrical energy by the turbine-generator system at the bottom of the dam. When a moving auto is stopped, the vehicle's kinetic energy is converted by friction into heat energy in the hot brake drums. And as a final example, when a man does manual labor, chemical energy stored in his body which came from the food he consumed is converted into heat and mechanical energy. As we shall see in a later section, whenever energy is transformed, none is lost; it is merely changed to a new form.

In theory, motion need not necessarily involve work. If a moving object does not exert any force upon another object in the direction of its motion, no work is being performed. The energy of the moving object remains constant. Let us consider two examples. First, imagine a skater gliding across a perfectly horizontal and absolutely frictionless ice surface. Neglecting air resistance, the skater would continue in a straight line indefinitely with the same velocity and the same amount of kinetic energy, performing no work. His acceleration would be zero because the total forces acting are zero. But if there is some friction between the skate and the ice or the skater and the air, the skater does some work on the ice and the air, and the frictional force slows him down (negative acceleration); he thus loses some kinetic energy.

For the second example, consider a timely one, that of a satellite in circular orbit around the earth far outside the atmosphere. The earth's gravitational attraction is exerted at right angles to the direction of the satellite in its orbit. Therefore, the satellite does no work, because there is no component of force along the direction of motion. Thus it continues at a constant speed in the same orbit with constant kinetic energy and constant gravitational potential energy (because it remains at a constant distance from the earth's center). Acceleration caused by the gravitational force is a continual change in direction, toward the center, not a change in the speed. If, however, as is the case, there is a slight amount of very thin atmosphere through which the satellite moves, friction between the satellite and the gas molecules will result in a drag force which will slow down the satellite. The satellite in turn will do work and lose kinetic energy.

What happens to the kinetic energy lost by the skater and the satellite? Friction transforms it into heat energy in the ice and in the atmosphere. The production of heat by friction will be considered in more detail in the next section.

Note that, except for nuclear energy, geothermal energy, and the energy of tides, all of the energy sources available to man lead finally to the sun as the ultimate energy source on earth. Present living things obtain their energy from the sun through photosynthesis as did living things in the past. But most of the fossil fuels—coal, oil, and gas—are believed also originally to have received their energy stores from the sun. Finally, hydroelectric power stems from the solar energy which powers the water cycle to lift water from the oceans to the tops of mountains.

For the Christian, these sources and stores of energy which are so important to modern civilization are a mark of the gracious providence of God. With the Psalmist we can say, "O LORD, how manifold are thy works! in wisdom hast thou made them all: the earth is full of thy riches" (Psalm 104:24).

Units of Matter Interact and Rearrange

Now that the basic definitions of force, work, and energy have been considered, we may begin to examine how force and energy are involved in the structures and processes which the Creator in His wisdom ordained for the natural world. We will find that the physical laws which govern the actions of forces and the transformations of energy are in accord with the biblical record of creation. We will see that these universal physical laws discovered and enunciated by scientists support the biblical report that living things were designed and created by an intelligent Creator, that they could not have arisen by any spontaneous process of chemical reactions or evolution. To reach this conclusion we must first delve more deeply into the forces which help to organize atoms which form the physical objects in the universe.

All of the changes and the examples of work cited above in this chapter are characterized by interactions (forces) exerted between units of matter and by the movement of units of matter relative to each other. There are four classes of interactions or forces between particles of matter: gravitational, electromagnetic, the nuclear strong interaction, and the nuclear weak interaction. Gravitational force is exerted mutually between every object or particle in the universe and every other object or particle. Electromagnetic force is exerted mutually between charged particles. Nuclear forces are exerted between the fundamental particles inside the nuclei of atoms.

It is by means of these four kinds of interactions or forces that units or particles of matter become organized into various forms and structures. Gravitational force is long-range in action and is mainly responsible for the organization of matter into larger units such as planets, stars, the solar system, and galaxies. Electromagnetic force in general acts at shorter or intermediate ranges and is responsible for the organization of the outer electronic structure of atoms and for the organization of atoms in molecules, crystals, liquids, all solids, gases, and plasmas (ionized gases).

Finally, the nuclear forces operate at exceedingly short distances in conjunction with electromagnetic force to organize the neutrons and protons inside the nuclei of atoms.

Because all of the changes which are observed taking place in the physical universe result in the reorganization of units of matter, and because mutual forces of interaction act between material particles, work must be accomplished when the changes occur, and energy must be transferred or transformed from one form to another.

Thus, when a weight falls toward the earth, work is performed on the weight by the force of gravity, and potential energy is transformed into kinetic energy of the moving weight. When the rock strikes the earth and stops, the directed kinetic energy of the moving rock is transformed mostly into heat energy (random kinetic energy of the atoms and molecules) in the rock and the soil. When ice is melted in a pan by means of a gas flame, first the molecules of natural gas and the free oxygen molecules of the air are reorganized into combustion products, i.e., molecules of carbon dioxide gas and water vapor, and the chemical (actually electromagnetic) potential energy of natural gas and oxygen molecules is transformed into the heat and radiant energy of the hot combustion products. The heat and radiant energy is transferred to the atoms of the metal pan which in turn transmit it to the ice. This energy serves to break the bonds holding the water molecules together in the solid ice crystals, and the water molecules are reorganized into liquid water.

How is heat transmitted from molecule to molecule when the heat is conducted through a solid substance? Since heat is essentially the random kinetic energy of trillions of molecules or atoms which make up the solid, heat is conducted by the collisions of adjacent molecules. By this means kinetic energy moves from molecule to molecule, the faster-moving molecule performing work on the slower-moving molecule.

In the preceding section the production of heat by friction was alluded to in connection with the illustration of the skater and that of the satellite. How does friction produce heat? As was just mentioned, heat is essentially the kinetic energy which atoms and molecules possess by virtue of their random, rapid motions and jostlings back and forth in solids, liquids, or gases. When the skate moves over the surface of ice, the atoms on the surface of the skate runner come into contact with and collide with those on the surface of the ice, and the atoms in the ice are given more kinetic energy because they have been caused to move faster. We say that their temperature has increased.

Likewise, when the satellite or the skater collides with the molecules of air in the atmosphere, kinetic energy is imparted to the air molecules.

The temperature of the air increases. Friction always results in the production of heat. We conclude, then, that friction transforms organized kinetic and other forms of energy into random kinetic energy of atoms and molecules, which is called heat.

Can electromagnetic radiation such as visible light do work on atoms or molecules? When an atom or molecule absorbs a quantum of radiation, the quantum transfers its very small amount of momentum. The atom or molecule moves slightly, but the work accomplished is quite small. However, the energy of the quantum of radiation can increase the internal energy sufficiently to break a bond and split the molecule, to raise an electron to a higher energy level, or eject an electron from the molecule. In this way electromagnetic radiation such as visible or ultraviolet light can bring about chemical change. Outstanding examples of this are photosynthesis in plants and the production of a photographic image in the film of a camera. In photosynthesis, the chlorophyll molecule of the plant absorbs the sun's radiant energy. The plant is then able to use this energy to separate the carbon from the oxygen in carbon dioxide and combine it with water to produce sugar and starch.

In the photographic process, light energy is believed to dislodge electrons in the microscopic crystals of silver bromide or silver iodide in the film emulsion. As a result, some free silver atoms are produced which then serve as a latent or invisible image, made visible by the development process. Thus photography is based upon changes which light is able to produce in chemicals in the film emulsion to bring about the reorganization of atoms in the silver bromide crystals.

For our final illustration of energy transformations and reorganization of matter, let us consider the use of food and oxygen by our bodies (known as metabolism). Remember that we are dependent ultimately upon plants for our food supply. Using the sun's radiant energy, plants reorganize carbon dioxide, water, and compounds of nitrogen and phosphorus, plus many other elements in trace amounts, to produce sugars, fats, proteins, vitamins, and other compounds necessary for our bodies. These substances are absorbed from the plant materials eaten by animals and by man.

Particularly the sugars, fats, and proteins contain large amounts of chemical energy which comes originally from the sun as radiant or light energy. These important organic compounds also have another characteristic which is vitally significant for life. They are much more highly organized, possessing much more intricate chemical structures than do the simple substances, such as carbon dioxide and water which the plants started with. Furthermore, man and animals are capable of using the highly organized compounds they gain from the plant kingdom to fashion other substances which are even more highly organized. And these substances contain very high energy content, actually called "free energy", because it is energy which is available to do work when the complicated molecules are broken down into simpler molecules.

Thus living things—plants and animals—are capable of using the sun's energy to organize simple, low-energy substances into exceedingly complex organic molecules which contain much energy. Moreover, plants and animals can then use these complex "bio-molecules" to construct almost unfathomably complex living cells, subsequently organizing these cells into all the vast panorama of living things with their almost endless variety of structures, functions, abilities, and interrelationships.

The fundamental food supply for any community of living things is provided by the photosynthetic plants which use the radiant energy of the sun to transform low-energy carbon dioxide gas from the air plus water and other simple substances from the soil into carbohydrates (sugars, starches, and cellulose), proteins, fats, and other energy-rich organic compounds. Animals consume the energy-rich plant products and use them to maintain their bodies in a high-energy state. When a plant stops absorbing the sun's energy, or when an animal stops consuming high-energy plant or animal products, the creature dies and its body soon decomposes into low-energy substances.

A tiny seed sprouts, begins to photosynthesize, and slowly from the elements in the air and soil builds a great, complex structure, a Sequoia tree. A microscopically small fertilized egg, just a single cell, begins to divide, absorbing energy-rich substances from its mother, and the end result is a powerful lion or a man possessed of intellect and personality.

This coupling of energy for the transformation of disorder into structured, energy-rich complexity is peculiar to living organisms. That non-living systems cannot accomplish this feat is the consistent conclusion which must be drawn from all the scientific evidence yet observed. Non-living systems appear to be characterized by processes of change which uniformly transform highly organized, energy-rich chemical structures into disordered or less organized substances of lower free energy content. This matter will be discussed in detail below where we will see that the most fundamental physical laws discovered by scientists afford powerful support for biblical creation.

The Energy Conservation Law and a Finished Creation

Scientists carefully observe and measure the things which they are investigating, accurately recording all of their observations. Then they repeat their experiments and observations, and other scientists will probably do the same, to verify that the data are reproducible. From the time several centuries ago that scientists first became interested in carefully defining and accurately measuring force, work, and energy, their experimental data have proved to be consistent with the theory that energy is always conserved. This means that in every physical process that scientists have been able to investigate quantitatively, the destruction of energy has never been observed. Energy may be transmitted from one point to another, or it may be transformed into other kinds of energy, but it is never destroyed. This principle has become established as the *First Law of Thermodynamics* or the *Law of Conservation of Energy: In any physical system the sum of all forms of energy remains constant unless energy flows into or out of the system.*

The discoveries of modern physics require a single modification of this law, since it has been established that matter can be converted quantitatively into energy and vice versa. Therefore, the conservation of energy and the conservation of matter have been combined into the Law of Conservation of Matter-Energy, which simply requires that the total of matter and energy be conserved. However, except in the case of nuclear reactions or high-energy physics, the original simple energy conservation law uniformly applies.

What significance does this fundamental law of science have relative to the problem of the origin of all things? Simply this: Science has never observed any process capable of bringing matter-energy into existence. Therefore, science can tell us nothing about the origin of the universe except that a power outside of and greater than the universe must be responsible, and further, that creation is no longer occurring. Thus this fundamental law of physics supports the biblical teaching of special creation recorded in the opening chapters of Genesis and summarized in Exodus 20:11: "For in six days the LORD made heaven and earth, the sea, and all that in them is, and rested the seventh day."

The Natural Law of Degeneration

The second great fundamental law governing energy was formulated as a result of efforts by engineers and scientists to improve the efficiency of steam engines. They discovered that a certain portion of the heat energy produced by combustion of the fuel consistently could not be transformed by the engine into work, but was lost as unusuable heat. Subsequently it was realized that all spontaneous processes increase the disorder or randomness in the energy and structure of matter. A quantity called *entropy* is used to measure the increase in unavailable energy and disorder of a system. These observations were generalized in the *Second Law of Thermodynamics: In all spontaneous processes the entropy of the system and its surroundings increases.*

For a simple explanation of these ideas, imagine ten Ping-Pong balls arranged in a neat pyramid-shaped pile on the fourth step up from the bottom of a staircase, as shown in Figure 2-2. Let these be very special Ping-Pong balls which are perfectly resilient so that they bounce without losing any of their energy. Two of the balls colliding can pass some energy from one to the other so that one then has more energy and the other less, but the total energy of the ten balls remains equal to the original energy total.

This original energy total is simply the gravitational potential energy the balls possess in the elevated position on the fourth step. They also

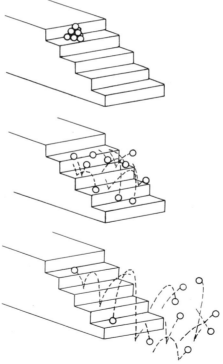

figure 2-2. It is highly probable that the carefully arranged pyramid of Ping-Pong balls will collapse and that the balls will bounce down the steps. Even if the balls were perfectly resilient so that they would bounce forever without losing their total initial energy, the probability that they might bounce back and reform the pyramid on the top step is essentially zero, even though the exact amount of energy remains to accomplish the restoration to the initial condition.

possess order in the neat pile. If they are slightly jarred, the pile will collapse and the balls will roll over the edge of the step and bounce down the stairs to the bottom. They will now be continually bouncing, continually transforming potential into kinetic energy and vice versa. Their original order is lost, both the order of arrangement in the pile and the ordered storage of all their energy in the form of potential energy. Now the pile is no more, and the energy is partly potential and partly kinetic.

Most of the balls will be bouncing down on the lower landing, but occasionally a ball may be knocked by a collision so that it bounces back up to the original step where the pile was located. But it will soon bounce back down. And even though the balls have the right total amount of energy, it is exceedingly unlikely that all ten of the balls will spontaneously bounce back up to the fourth step and rearrange themselves in the form of the original pyramid, even after a billion years of random bouncing. The occurrence of such an event would be interpreted as almost positive proof of intervention by an intelligent, purposeful agent.

The equilibrium arrangement is for most of the balls to be bouncing down on the lower landing, with an occasional ball bouncing up onto an upper step. This more disordered final situation corresponds to a state of high probability, that is, of high entropy. Compared to this state of the system, the stack of balls on the fourth step is most improbable, corresponding to a state of low entropy. To cause the balls to return to the pile would require intelligently directed work. In fact, it seems very probable that some human being stacked up the pile of balls in the first place.

When the balls were still on the upper step, their potential energy could pretty easily have been coupled and used to do work as they came down the staircase. But after they have started bouncing wildly and unpredictably, it is more difficult to put their energy to work. Thus, available energy has been transformed into a form less available to do work.

Now to make the analogy explicit, the balls correspond to atoms and the pyramid to a highly structured, energy-rich molecule. The initial gravitational potential energy of the pyramid of balls on the upper step corresponds to the free energy of an energy-rich molecule. The natural tendency is for the molecule to break down, just as for the pyramid to collapse and the balls to roll down the stairs. The free energy of the molecule can be coupled to do work, but once it has been transformed into random kinetic energy of disorganized atoms, it is exceedingly unlikely that the atoms will ever spontaneously put themselves back together into a molecule with the energy again stored as free energy in the molecule.

This example, though not a perfect analogy, illustrates the requirement of the Second Law of Thermodynamics that spontaneous processes always lead to a loss of free energy and an increase in entropy. Also illustrated is the corollary of the Second Law, the principle of equilibrium, which relates to the direction of spontaneous processes and to the final state reached by the process. Thus, all spontaneous processes, since they result continually in increased entropy, must be moving toward some state of maximum entropy under the limitations which are placed on the system. This state is called the equilibrium state, and when it is attained the process of change stops.

The Second Law is of great significance for the problem of origins, as is the First Law, which requires that observed natural processes cannot be responsible for original creation. The Second Law requires that the universe cannot be infinitely old, for if it were, the increase of entropy resulting from natural processes would long ago have brought the universe to a state of maximum entropy, i.e., the state of maximum disorder and unavailable energy. This hypothetical final equilibrium state has been termed the "heat death" of the universe, a state in which all concentrations of energy and all differences in temperature will have been dissipated.

The scientists who worry about such supposed problems for the most part believe that the universe evolved into its present state by natural processes. Yet the Second Law of Thermodynamics seems to preclude the possibility of the natural evolution uphill to a highly ordered low-entropy state of the universe. So concerned are some cosmologists with this impasse that they are actually trying to discover a way to reformulate the science of thermodynamics without including the concept of entropy.[1] All reproducible observations of science, however, point to the universal validity of the entropy concept—that spontaneous processes always produce increased entropy, i.e., increased randomness and decreased free energy.

Life and the Energy Laws

This Second Law of Thermodynamics is of great import also for any theory of spontaneous origin of life. Such a theory proposes that chance arrangements of physical conditions and mixtures of simple inorganic chemicals—maintained for billions of years—made possible, probable, even inevitable the formation of some complicated, energy-rich proteins and other bio-molecules from which the original living cells then were formed by random combinations.

However, this chemical evolution would require the spontaneous production of organic compounds extremely rich in free energy and low in entropy, and the spontaneous assembling of fantastically complex structures of living organisms. It is most difficult to imagine how this could occur spontaneously without violating the Second Law, to say nothing of actually demonstrating such a process experimentally. It is, of course, pure imagination. Since the Second law has not yet been faulted or invalidated, theories of spontaneous chemical origin of life call for extreme skepticism on the part of honest scientists.

Just what is going on in a plant or animal which is so different from inorganic chemical processes? A living creature is a self-contained metabolic engine maintaining itself in a high-energy steady state which is not in equilibrium with its surroundings. The creature obtains energy with which to preserve this energy state in one of two ways, depending upon whether it is a plant or an animal.

If a photosynthetic plant, it is able to couple the energy of the sun's radiation. If an animal, it makes use of energy-rich substances produced by plants or other animals which feed on plants. In the processes of metabolism, energy and building materials from the surroundings flow through the living system continually, and it is thus enabled to maintain its high-energy steady state and also carry on the other functions characteristic of life, i.e., growth, response, and reproduction. Plants couple the solar energy and produce an excess of energy-rich chemicals. Animals feed on this excess from the plant world and excrete into the environment simpler substances containing less free energy. Other animals may use these and extract more energy, but plants ultimately recycle the building materials.

When the living creature's source of energy or food is cut off, or when the ability of the creature to metabolize ceases, death occurs. The creature no longer maintains its high-energy steady state; its chemical structure starts to move toward the state of equilibrium with the environment, the design disappears, and there remain only relatively simple chemicals which are unable to carry out the reactions unique to the living creature.

How do living creatures accomplish what chemical reactions in non-living systems cannot do? First, the process of photosynthesis and all metabolic processes of plants and animals require exceedingly complex metabolic systems or motors. These metabolic systems are obviously the product of intelligent, purposeful design. Moreover, the metabolic motors require instructions to direct them to carry out the correct reactions necessary for life. This information is carried by the mechanism of genetic inheritance which will be discussed in Chapter 4.

An immense amount of coded information is required to describe the structure and functions of any organism. Each living cell contains all of the information necessary for the description of the organism. This information must be copied when cells divide to form new cells, and it must be transmitted to places in the cells where proteins are being constructed.

Finally, the information must be translated to guide the construction and control activities of the cells. The mathematical laws of information theory predict that in any transmission or translation of information, the amount of noise or non-information will spontaneously increase.[2] The mathematical equation describing this increase of noise is identical in form with the equation for entropy increase. The theory that the genetic code and genetic information originated spontaneously and that the information has spontaneously and continuously increased for billions of years is called the theory of organic evolution. This theory violates the laws of information theory which are just as soundly based as the laws of thermodynamics, and are, in fact, identical with them.

Non-living chemical systems have neither the cell structures, the coded instructions, nor the translation machinery to enable them to accomplish what living systems can do. In a limited way coded instructions originating in the brains of chemists, and complex equipment in the chemists' laboratories, have produced outside of living systems a few of the reactions and products characteristic of life. However, chemical reactions planned and controlled by intelligent chemists are in no way comparable with hypothetical random reaction of simple chemicals in some hypothetical primeval ocean.

Some scientists have pointed out that non-living chemical systems are raised to higher, non-equilibrium energy states when high-energy radiation is flowing through them, and rather complicated chemical compounds can be produced under such circumstances.[3] But the similarity to living systems is limited to the maintenance of a somewhat elevated energy level, a more complex mix of chemicals, and the existence of rudimentary chemical cycles in the mixture. Such systems have never been observed to exhibit the combination of properties and functions defining life: a stable, complex structure, metabolism, growth, homeostasis, response to environment, reproduction, and coded information. These properties of living systems are defined and discussed in Chapter 4.

Matter, Energy, and Intelligence

In this chapter we have found that the myriad changes we can observe all around us in both living and non-living systems involve interaction of units of matter, reorganization of matter, and the transmission or transformation of energy. These processes of change were shown to be subject to two fundamental principles called the First and Second Laws of Thermodynamics, so that energy is conserved and entropy increases.

The conclusion which we draw from these laws of physics is that the reorganization of matter and the energy transformations which would be required to bring life into being cannot be accomplished without the influence of directing intelligence. Order does not arise from disorder without the application of intelligent planning and intelligently controlled energy. The laws of physics operating apart from intelligence must result in the transformation of order into random disorder and of free energy into random heat energy. This is the only consistent interpretation of the data of science. Theories of spontaneous origin, of order from disorder, of life from non-life, and of intellect from impersonal atoms guided only by physical law are not science but philosophical or religious speculation.

The observations and physical laws of science can better be fitted into the biblical record of the origin of the universe and of life than into any theory of materialistic evolution. In the opening chapter of Genesis we are told, "And God said. . . ." By the intelligent word of the infinite, eternal, omnipotent, and omniscient Creator were the universe and all living creatures brought into being. "By the word of the LORD were the heavens made; and all the host of them by the breath of his mouth" (Psalm 33:6). The living Word of God, the Lord Jesus Christ, is the One by Whom all things were created and by Whom all things are preserved (John 1:1-3, 14; Hebrews 1:3). And even as the physical world and its living creatures find their source and their subsistence in the Word of God, the Christian believer looks to the Word of God for the origin of his eternal life and for sustaining grace to live for Christ in a world that has been cursed because of sin, made subject to vanity, and to the degenerative processes related to the Second Law which would lead to utter dissolution apart from redemption of a wrecked universe by the grace of God (Romans 8:20-25).

3

The Primeval World

What was the world like in the beginning? Was it very different from what it is today? What about the plants and animals, the climate, the oceans and mountains? And how did all things begin—the earth and the creatures that inhabit it? Such questions about the ancient past have intrigued men of all eras. But is there any sure way of uncovering the answers to these questions about prehistoric times, that is, the times predating human works of history?

Two Approaches to the Evidence

Most scientists working in the fields of paleontology and geology believe that by studying the rock structures of the earth and the fossil remains of creatures that lived in the past, they can reconstruct an accurate picture of the world of long ago. And they believe that they possess valid scientific evidence for their view of the early history and conditions on the earth. It is important to remember, however, that they are dealing with questions of earth's prehistory which are actually not verifiable by the methods of experimental science. The evidence found in the rocks is merely circumstantial evidence; that is, its true meaning and significance depend upon what the total circumstances *may have been.* All of these circumstances are not known, nor can we by reason determine positively what the correct interpretation of any particular fact should be. Ultimate historical evidence always involves human eyewitness testimony or documents left by eyewitnesses, but no such testimony or documents are available for the early history of the earth.

One document, however, purports to give authoritative testimony about the early earth from a Person who was present. This document is the Bible, and its contents are to be classified not as scientific evidence but as divine revelation. Such revelation is either accepted by faith or rejected. Christians by faith accept the biblical revelation in all of its details, including its reports of early earth history. Thus the Christian student of origins approaches the evidence from geology and paleontology with the biblical record in mind, interpreting that evidence in accord with the facts divinely revealed in the Bible. On the other hand, the person who does not accept biblical revelation approaches the same evidence with different presuppositions, interpreting the observed facts in accord with the preconceptions which are basic to *his* thinking.

What two sets of *a priori* principles do the biblically and non-biblically oriented scientists bring to their studies of the earth's prehistory? Expressed in greatly simplified form they are as follows:

Biblical:

1. The earth and all "kinds" of living creatures were created in the space of six days, with providential arrangement for some variation within the kinds, but with impassable boundaries between the kinds.

2. The age of the earth is measured in thousands, not millions, of years, probably around ten thousand years. Evidence for a young earth is presented in Chapter 8 and in Appendix B.

3. The Flood of Noah brought about vast changes in the earth's surface, including vulcanism, mountain building, and the deposition of the major part of sedimentary strata. This principle is called "biblical catastrophism."

Non-biblical:

1. The earth and all living creatures came into being through extremely slow evolutionary processes without intelligent design or purpose.

2. The age of the earth and of life is measured in billions of years.

3. All the presently observed features of the earth's surface and crust were produced very slowly by essentially the same processes and at the same rates as are observed today. This principle is called "uniformitarianism."

It is obvious that two scientists interpreting the same observed data from geology and paleontology in accordance with two such contradictory sets of principles will very likely reach contradictory conclusions. However, we can still examine the evidence for ourselves and see which set of presuppositions more accurately correlates with the evidence. This is what we will now attempt as we look into the geological and fossil records.

Do Fossils Speak for Evolution or Creation?

We will be comparing two contrasting models designed to explain the evidence bearing on the origin of living creatures, both past and present. These two models make possible two entirely different predictions concerning the fossil record:[1]

1. According to the evolution model, the fossil record should contain finely graded sequences of fossils with intermediate types connecting all forms of creatures, living and extinct.

2. According to the creation model, the fossil record should reveal a systematic absence of intermediate types connecting all of the higher and intermediate categories of plants and animals.

Let us now consider the fossil record to see which prediction more clearly fits the actual evidence.

1. The supposedly earliest rocks containing every major phylum of life except the vertebrate sub-phylum are called Cambrian rocks. They are dated as being about 570 million years old.

2. The allegedly older Pre-Cambrian rocks are essentially empty of fossils. But where are the ancestors of the rich and varied assortment of Cambrian fossils? Paleontologists tell us that three-quarters of all evolution had to take place before the Cambrian, but where is the evidence? Instead of fossil evidence for evolution, we find a massive unfilled gap between all of the major phyla of life and the single-celled life forms from which they supposedly evolved.

3. Vertebrate fish supposedly evolved from invertebrates, yet in his authoritative book *Vertebrate Paleontology*, Harvard paleontologist Alfred Romer states that the fossil gap between the vertebrate fish and their unknown invertebrate ancestors is 100 million years.[2] And the theories about which invertebrate creature gave rise to the vertebrates are almost as numerous as are books on paleontology.

4. Amphibians supposedly evolved from fish, yet there is no fossil connecting-link, no creature with a half-fin-half-leg.

5. We are told that reptiles evolved from amphibians. While it is true that fossil amphibian skeletons rather similar to reptile skeletons have

been found, serious unanswered questions remain for the evolutionary view. For example, how could the simple gelatinous amphibian egg designed for incubation in water have gradually evolved into the complex amniotic reptile egg with its amnion and other membranes and specialized waste disposal system, all designed for incubation in air? There is no satisfactory explanation and no fossil evidence.

6. Mammals supposedly evolved from the reptiles, but once again there is an absence of needed transitional types. For example, all reptiles, living and extinct, have four bones on each side of the lower jaw and one

table 1. Uniformitarian Geological Time Scale

era	period	beginning of period (years before present)	assumed sequence of evolving life forms
Cenozoic	Quaternary	2,000,000	Modern man, plants, animals
	Tertiary	60,000,000	Modern birds, man from man-apes, mammals dominant
Mesozoic	Cretaceous	130,000,000	Pouched and placental mammals, flowering plants, extinction of giant reptiles
	Jurassic	180,000,000	First mammals, first toothed birds, reptiles dominant
	Triassic	230,000,000	First dinosaurs, mammal-like reptiles
Paleozoic	Permian	280,000,000	Reptiles displace amphibians, modern insects, evergreens
	Pennsylvanian	310,000,000	Reptiles from amphibians
	Mississippian	340,000,000	Winged insects, bony fish
	Devonian	400,000,000	First amphibians, insects
	Silurian	450,000,000	First land animals (arthropods)
	Ordovician	500,000,000	First vertebrates (fish), land plants
	Cambrian	570,000,000	Abundant marine invertebrates, all invertebrate phyla, trilobites abundant
Proterozoic (Precambrian)		2,000,000,000	Algae, microorganisms
Archaeozoic (Precambrian)		4,500,000,000	Origin of life (living cells from non-living chemicals)

bone in the ear, whereas all mammals have just one bone in the lower jaw and three in the ear. At any rate, the notion of bones gradually migrating from the jaw into the ear is difficult to accept. Staunch faith is required if one is to believe that the delicate mechanism of the human inner ear is the product of a long series of accidents. And would the hypothetical intermediate creatures have selective advantage, or would they even be able to hear?

7. Birds supposedly evolved from reptiles. The fossil *Archaeopteryx* is offered as the intermediate, but it is one fossil type in a period of alleged evolutionary change from reptile to bird spanning about 80 million years according to the evolutionary time scale.[3] And though *Archaeopteryx* does possess some reptilian characteristics, so do some modern birds, and the fact remains that *Archaeopteryx* was a fully feathered bird. In addition, the proposal that feathers developed slowly from reptile scales is supported by no fossil evidence whatsoever. Furthermore, the feathers of birds are efficiently designed structures which give no evidence of relationship to scales.

8. This brings us to the question of the origin of flight in general. In no case is there fossil evidence for the origin of flight, not in the case of birds, mammals (bats), reptiles, or insects. The origin of flight is a com-

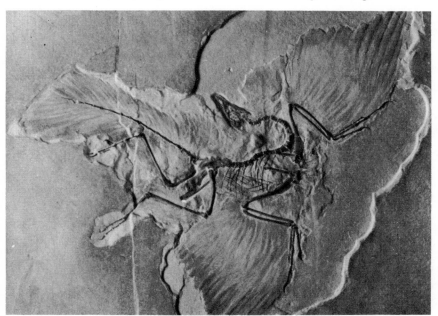

figure 3-1. The *Archaeopteryx* bird fossil shows fully developed feathers on wings, body, and tail. It was definitely a bird, although possessing a number of reptilian characteristics.

plete mystery as far as fossil evidence is concerned, and the evolutionary explanations devised thus far seem credible only when strong faith is exercised.

9. The absence of connecting links is especially noticeable in the fossil record of the more peculiar kinds of animals. For example, the *cetacea* (whales, dolphins, and porpoises), *sirenia* (manatee, dugong, and sea cows), *pinnipedia* (sea lions, seals, and walruses), turtles, kangaroos, bats, dragon flies, spiders, and other types are isolated in the fossil record. In each such group the fossils are all distinguished by the peculiar features necessary for their separate classification. Their evolutionary origins are represented by missing links and speculations.

In this connection the reader is invited to obtain, from a good library, Romer's book, *Vertebrate Paleontology*, cited earlier, and survey the charts which are distributed at intervals throughout the volume. The liberal use of dotted lines to show assumed courses of evolution between different groups of animals is quite apparent. These dotted lines signify the absence of intermediate fossils and/or the tentative character of the assigned connections. All of the charts contain many such dotted lines. The absence of intermediate forms is documented at great length in the book, *The Fossil Record*, which is listed in the bibliography for this chapter.

10. What evidence exists that man evolved from ape? All the alleged ancestors of modern man have been discarded, one by one. Neanderthal, now considered to have been an intelligent fellow, not bestial in appearance nor walking with an apelike posture, was found to have lived concurrently with modern man. *Pithecanthropus erectus* (so-called Java Man) was finally concluded by his discoverer, Eugene Dubois, to be an extinct giant gibbon and not a human ancestor. *Sinanthropus* (called Peking Man) appeared with some cooperation from Teilhard de Chardin, who in the opinion of some was implicated in deception connected with the Piltdown fossil man fraud in England some years before. The actual fossil remains of *Sinanthropus*, examined by very few people, mysteriously disappeared during the Sino-Japanese War, never having left China. The evidence was lost, and has never been found.

Validity of the African Australopithecene fossils so widely publicized by anthropologist L. S. Leakey was questioned late in 1972 by his son, Richard Leakey, who found buried in deeper strata a less ape-like skull. Richard Leakey suggests that the entire subject of human origins must now be reassessed. These questions will be considered in more detail in Chapter 5.

Let us consider now which prediction best fits the fossil evidence. Could one say from the preceding data that science has discovered finely graded fossil sequences with intermediate types connecting all the higher and middle categories of animals? Obviously not. Instead, there is a systematic absence of connecting links and intermediate types. The supposed evolutionary tree of life is really a bundle of disconnected twigs. We conclude that the fossil record reveals what one would predict on the basis of creation as recorded in the Bible. The first chapter of Genesis repeats the term "after his [their] kind" ten times.

Furthermore, the various creatures came from the hand of God fully formed and complete, distinguishable one from the other so that Adam named them, which also implies he classified them. Thus the fossil record agrees with the data from the Bible and from biology that life exists in distinct forms which are separated one from the other by genetic barriers. Each creature reproduces after its kind, and limited variation within the kinds occurs, but the boundaries of the kinds established by the Creator remain unbreached.

Geology—Gradualism or Global Catastrophe?

We are all familiar with some of the slow processes of change on the earth's surface. Streams and rivers erode their banks, waves wage unremitting war upon our coastal shores, sand and silt produced by these agencies of erosion are transported and deposited from year to year, and volcanic eruptions and earth movements called earthquakes occur from time to time. Some of these actions by natural agencies bring about quite astoundingly rapid changes in localized regions, but in general the changes we observe are quite slow, so that we only become aware of them after many years.

In mountainous areas and in places where rivers or man's construction activities have cut through the earth, we can often observe that the outer crust of the earth is built up of layers or strata of different kinds of rock. Having studied these structures for several centuries, scientists have concluded that except for lava flows and the granite cores of some mountain ranges, the rocks were for the most part formed of sediments deposited by water action. They have also found fossils of many kinds of creatures which were once living upon the earth.

For several hundred years scientists have been trying to determine what the rock structures and fossils reveal about the past history of the earth. As indicated earlier in this chapter, the evidence is circumstantial, and the interpretation depends to a great extent upon the presuppositions of the interpreter. Remember, the observed data of geology and paleontology have been interpreted from the standpoint of two mutually contradictory sets of presuppositions. That of materialistic evolutionists may be briefly characterized by evolution, vast ages, and uniformitarianism; that of the creationists by special creation, short time scale, and catastrophism. The view called *theistic evolution* is discussed in Appendix C. Geological evidence will now be assessed so that we may determine which viewpoint best accords with the observed facts.

The key question to keep in mind is whether the geological data is in better accord with the principle of uniformitarian action by processes and at rates observed on the earth today or with the principle of catastrophic action at rates unheard of today and perhaps by processes not presently observed.

Rock Structures and Earth History

We will first consider the types of rocks and rock structures which geologists have observed and the kinds of processes which must have been required to produce them. Dr. Henry M. Morris has published very useful compilations of this kind of data.[4]

1. In the southwestern states—Arizona, Utah, Colorado, New Mexico, Texas, and on into Kansas and Oklahoma—we encounter hundreds of thousands of square miles of flat, horizontal sedimentary strata, often thousands of feet thick. Similar vast strata are also found in other parts of the world. At no location on the earth today may the present production of similar deposits be observed.

2. Not only the structures formed by sedimentary rocks, but also the composition of the rocks bear witness to catastrophic deposition of most of the rocks in the earth's crust. Sandstones, shales, conglomerates, limestones, dolostones, cherts, and evaporites of the types found in the sedimentary strata are not observed being formed today. In fact, they must have been formed in the past by massive, rapid hydraulic and chemical processes continental and global in scope, such as man has never observed in the modern world.

The scale of water action required to grade the sand and muds that produced thousands of square miles of sandstone and shale strata is incomprehensible. The continent-wide maelstrom of violent oceanic currents which dumped hundreds of thousands of square miles of ungraded conglomerates across the United States and other parts of the world defies description. The ocean-sized reaction pots which rapidly precipitated the calcium carbonate, magnesium carbonate, and silica gel which formed the vast strata of limestone and dolomite and huge chert deposits boggle the mind of any laboratory chemist. And the huge beds of salt and gypsum evaporites, remarkably pure and free of organic material, must have been formed by rapid precipitation from concentrated geothermal solutions, rather than by slow evaporation in shallow seas, the usual uniformitarian explanation.

3. In the northwestern states of Washington, Oregon, and Idaho (and in many other places in the world) are hundreds of thousands of square miles of territory covered by thick flows of basaltic lava, which must have flowed out onto the surface of the land in veritable floods. Such massive vulcanism is presently occurring at no place on the modern earth.

4. Another type of igneous rock formation not being produced today includes the huge granite batholiths which form the backbones of many great mountain systems, and smaller intrusive rock formations such as dikes and sills. All of these structures apparently are products of past but not present earth activity.

5. Many of the major river systems of the world have great suboceanic river canyons which extend long distances from the present shorelines. Thus it would appear that the level of the oceans was in the past thousands of feet below the present level. This is corroborated by shallow water deposits located at midoceanic points as much as 10,000 feet below present sea level.

6. The large-scale folding, faulting, uplifting, and subsidences evidenced in the earth's sedimentary structures must have involved actions far greater in magnitude and rapidity than any seen today.

7. Major mountain systems are considered to be relatively young, yet still many millions of years old. But weighty evidence indicates that the Andes, the Himalayas, and others were pushed up thousands of feet in historic times.[5]

8. Extensive systems of deeply incised meanders cut by rivers in many parts of the world must have been produced rapidly at a time when the sedimentary layers were much softer than at present.

9. At many places in the world there are extensive areas in which the sedimentary strata are out of order according to the evolutionary theory of the order in which life evolved. An outstanding example is the so-called Lewis Overthrust which covers an area of some 13,000 square miles in the northern Rockies. Here whole mountain ranges composed of Pre-Cambrian rocks rest on top of Cretaceous rocks which, because of their fossil content, are dated as being at least 400 million years younger. The only explanation offered by uniformitarian geologists is that an overthrust pushed 800 trillion tons of old rocks some 35 miles over younger rocks.

However, no field evidence exists for such massive thrusting and sliding, which would have produced at the sliding surfaces a layer of crushed, ground-up fault breccia probably hundreds of feet thick. No thick layers of fault breccia are found at the interface of the alleged over-thrust. In any case, the laws of physics would not permit the sliding to occur since the frictional forces would be too great in comparison with the compressional strength of the rocks. Thus the actual facts at the Lewis Overthrust wipe out 400 million years of alleged evolutionary geological history.

figure 3-2. Dr. Clifford Burdick, consulting geologist, indicates the contact line at the so-called "overthrust" in the Empire Mountains 35 miles southeast of Tucson, Arizona. Dark Permian rocks overlie the lighter Cretaceous rocks. They have been classified Permian and Cretaceous on the basis of their fossil content. The wavy contact surface precludes thrust movement, and there is no layer of fault breccia (ground-up composite rock from the two layers) between the two beds. Thus, 100 million years of supposed geological history are wiped out, and the strata and fossils are out of order, "up-side-down," to the tune of about 150 million years. This field evidence, therefore, shows that the assumed evolutionary order of the fossils is invalid and that uniformitarian historical geology, which is dependent upon the fossil sequence, is likewise erroneous.

We have in our files, provided by Dr. Walter Lammerts, a compilation of references in the geological literature citing 500 or more examples of supposedly reversed strata. These usually pose difficult problems for uniformitarian historical geology, because in most cases field evidence for the supposed overthrusting is lacking, and the required distance of movement often is so great as to be incredible.

10. Coal deposits by their nature are both fossil materials and geologi-

cal structures. The most common evolutionary view of the origin of coal is that plant materials were collected and converted into coal in the same location in which they grew. Much evidence, however, supports the view that many or perhaps most coal deposits were transported by water to their present locations, then buried and transformed by pressure and heat into coal. Polystrate coalified tree trunks and snags, for example, are often found extending through several layers of coal and the intermediate rock strata. Fossil tree trunks as long as forty or a hundred feet have been found extending either vertically or diagonally across many sedimentary layers. A notable example was a 60-foot tree trunk having a diameter of five feet at the base, found at an angle of 40 degrees intersecting ten separate layers of coal in a coal mine at Newcastle, England.

Such evidence can only indicate a very rapid, catastrophic deposition of sediments. A tree would decompose to dust long before the passage of the millions of years required for uniformitarian deposition of forty or more feet of sediments and ten distinct layers of coal. Perhaps it can be added at this point that recent investigations have demonstrated that wood can be transformed to coal, and garbage into petroleum, in less than an hour by the application of pressure and high temperature.

Another important fact about coal deposits which makes the uniformitarian explanation difficult to accept is the large number of successive layers of coal which are found in many locations. In Nova Scotia up to 76 layers of coal are found, one above the other; in England and Germany as many as 80 and 100 layers, respectively. Supposedly, the historical geologists tell us, each layer represents a period during which the land surface sank to a low level and swamps and peat bogs formed. Then the collected vegetable materials were covered by sediments and the land level rose to complete a cycle. Many such repeated cycles produced the sequences of coal layers observed today.

But the imagination is severely strained by the assumption that the land rose and fell 80 or 100 times in a single location on the earth's surface. Furthermore, coal is almost entirely composed of trees, not of the kind of materials which are deposited in peat bogs. Finally, certain types of marine fossils are often found in coal deposits. The great weight of evidence points to rapid, catastrophic deposition of coal beds, rather than slow growth in position during millions of years.

11. Meteorites of various types are continually plunging into the earth's atmosphere from outer space, and some reach the surface. Supposedly this has occurred for billions of years with more falling in the earlier ages of earth history than at present. Yet no meteorites have been discovered in the deeper and supposedly very old sedimentary strata,

but only in the upper, recent strata.[6] Does this not strongly suggest that most of the sedimentary strata were laid down rapidly over a short period of time so that very few meteorites could be deposited in them?

12. Mount Ararat in eastern Turkey is almost certainly the place where the ark rested at the close of the flood year. It is not well-known that the geology of this massive mountain complex bears eloquent witness to the truth of the Genesis account of a global flood. Ararat is a volcanic mountain composed principally of lava flows and other types of volcanic material. Located at levels up to 14,000 feet above sea level are outcroppings of a peculiar rock called pillow lava. This rock is identified by the pillow-shaped masses in which it occurs and by the high glass content of its structure. These characteristic features are produced when molten lava is extruded under water and the very rapid cooling results in both the pillow forms and the production of uncrystallized glasses rather than the distinct crystals found in slowly cooled rocks such as granite. The high glass content causes the rock when broken to form characteristic curved fracture surfaces which are termed "conchoidal."

It is evident, then, that Ararat was submerged in water at least up to the 14,000-foot level. This is confirmed by deposits of sedimentary rocks on the mountain at the 13,500-foot level. These and other striking facts about the geology of the mountain and the surrounding terrain agree beautifully with the Genesis record of a global flood. Since water seeks its own level, the water which submerged Ararat must have covered the entire world. The geological observations were made by consulting geologist Clifford Burdick on two exploratory expeditions in 1966 and 1969.[7] These and several other recent expeditions have been made with the objective of searching for the actual remains of the ark which has reportedly been seen by over 100 people during the past century.[8]

All of the above structural features of the earth's crust are far better in accord with biblical catastrophism than with uniformitarianism. Numerous other features of geologic data refuse to fit into the mold of evolutionary geology, and the attempts to make them fit have led to many absurdities and contradictions in geology books. A large number of these facts have been dealt with in detail by Whitcomb and Morris in *The Genesis Flood* and by Reginald Daly in *Earth's Most Challenging Mysteries.* Let us now examine the fossil record to determine what the fossils suggest about the character of early earth history.

Fossils and Earth History

Once again the question we need to keep in mind is whether fossil evidence better accords with uniformitarianism or with catastrophism. It must first be pointed out that large-scale or even appreciable fossilization is not observed today. Only rarely are modern plants and animals preserved as fossils. Why? Because fossilization will practically never occur unless the plant or animal is catastrophically trapped and entombed. Without sudden entombment the creature is rapidly devoured by scavengers or decomposed by decay microorganisms. Therefore the very absence of fossilization in the present constitutes strong evidence that past processes in geology were catastrophic, for the sedimentary strata are rich in fossils of all kinds. Moreover, many features of the fossil record offer striking support for catastrophism. (See Footnote 4 for this chapter.)

1. The Cumberland Bone Cave in Maryland was found to contain remains of dozens of mammal species together with reptiles and birds. The types represented include creatures native to Arctic, temperature, and tropical zones, and both dry and moist habitats; yet the fossils are all mixed together in one cave.

2. The Baltic amber deposits have been found to contain fossil insect and plant remains which are native to all types of climatic zones ranging from near-Arctic to tropical. Competent zoologists have concluded that the Baltic amber fossils were the result of some worldwide cataclysmic process.

3. In the region of Geiseltal, Germany, are lignite beds which contain mixtures of numerous kinds of plants, animals, and insects native to all climatic zones and geographic regions in the world. The remarkable preservation of the fine structure and even the chemical content of the creatures is persuasive evidence of a very rapid and rather recent burial.

4. In the region of Lompoc on the Central California coast are huge diatomaceous earth beds containing millions of fossil fish, beautifully preserved and usually in attitudes indicating sudden, violent death.[9] Massive fossil fish beds are also found in Scotland.

5. In Sicily were found mass hippopotamus graves forming beds so extensive that the bones have been mined as a source of commercial charcoal.

6. In the far north of Alaska, Canada, and Siberia large numbers of mammoth tusks, and through the years even frozen carcasses of mammoths and other animals, have been found. Some islands north of Siberia are reportedly packed with jumbled masses of fossil animal bones and vegetation.

7. Throughout the world there are vast sedimentary formations containing billions of fossils, sometimes packed together in high concentra-

tion. These suggest anything but slow, calm conditions of deposition.

8. "Ephemeral markings" is the term given to the preserved imprints produced on the surface of sand or mud by the action of waves, raindrops, or crawling creatures such as worms. Such markings are quickly removed from the surfaces of sand and mud by subsequent water or wind action.

Preserved ephemeral markings are rare in recent geological deposits, but they are widespread throughout the remaining geological strata. Since all evidence indicates that some kind of sudden covering and preservation is required to produce fossil ephemeral markings, the only conclusion is that the greater part of the geological strata are connected with rapid deposition processes, not with the slow processes envisioned by uniformitarian geologists.

9. In fact, with minor exceptions, all fossils require rapid deposition and burial. There is no place on the earth today in which production of fossils by slow deposition of sediments can be observed. When plants and animals die, unless they are rapidly buried, they are quickly consumed by scavengers. The entire fossil record points to catastrophic, global flood action.

The foregoing features of the fossil and geological records all seem to be in agreement more with the catastrophic than with the uniformitarian concept of geological processes of the past. Thus, in this respect, fossils corroborate the structural data given previously and lend themselves readily to the framework of biblical catastrophism. One final category of fossil evidence remains to be considered briefly, that of fossils found completely out of the sequence predicted by evolutionary throty.

Do All Fossils Appear in Evolutionary Order?

Evolutionary biologists, zoologists, and paleontologists have arranged living plants and animals with fossils in morphological sequences (that is, in series according to their forms). These sequences show gradually increasing complexity, from single-celled to many-celled, from invertebrate to vertebrate fish to amphibians to reptiles to birds and mammals, and finally to man.

Evolutionists contend that the possibility of arranging creatures in such a sequence gives evidence for evolutionary relationship. But it is also claimed that the order in which the fossils are actually found in sedimentary strata agrees with the evolutionary theory—the least complex types, for example, the invertebrates, being found on the bottom, the more complex in the upper rock strata.

Actually, the picture is far more complex than most textbooks and newspaper articles ever indicate; there are many gaps and reversals in the published strata sequences. The so-called geological column of sedimentary strata supposedly totals about 100 miles in thickness and is said to correspond to several billion years of earth history. However, only tiny fractions of the column are ever found at one location on the earth. The theoretical column is pieced together from many different places all over the earth so that the fossils in the strata correspond to the order in which they supposedly evolved. A number of fossil finds, however, are embarrassingly out of their proper places in the evolutionary geological column. Six examples will suffice to illustrate the problem.

1. In recent years fossil pollen grains of many different species of trees have been found in the rocks of the lower levels of the Grand Canyon, even in the Pre-Cambrian rocks.[10] But Pre-Cambrian rocks are dated as being older than 600 million years and were supposedly deposited hundreds of millions of years *before* the pollen-bearing plants evolved.

2. European and Russian scientists have reported numerous instances of fossil pollen in all of the strata down into the Cambrian.[11]

3. Fossils of many kinds of woody stemmed plants have been discovered in the geological column in rocks assumed to represent periods predating by many millions of years the supposed time of their evolution.[12]

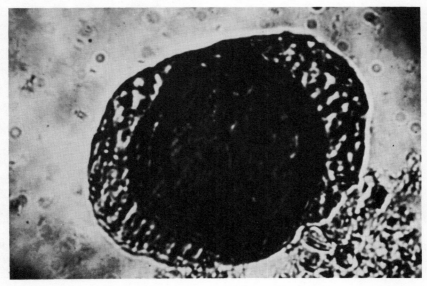

figure 3-3. Photomicrograph of one of many specimens of fossil pollen grains discovered by Dr. Clifford Burdick in Grand Canyon rocks at all levels of the canyon wall, including the Pre-Cambrian Hakati shale in the lower levels of the canyon. According to evolutionary theory and historical geology, this fossil pollen is located several hundred million years too early in the rock and fossil record.

4. Both man and dinosaur tracks have been discovered and thoroughly validated and identified in limestone strata along the Paluxy River in Texas. But dinosaurs supposedly became extinct almost 100 million years before man evolved.[13]

5. In 1968, near Antelope Springs, Utah, what appear to be five human sandal prints were found in Cambrian rocks. Several of these prints have closely associated trilobite fossils in the same rocks, and one sandal print has several trilobites embedded in the print itself. But trilobites are a principal index fossil used to identify Cambrian strata. According to evolutionary chronology, man did not appear on the scene until a half billion years after trilobites became extinct. If these prints prove to be valid, historical geology has another serious problem to solve.[14]

figure 3-4. This sandal print discovered by William J. Meister, Sr., near Antelope Springs, Utah, contains embedded trilobite fossils. Trilobites supposedly evolved and became extinct hundreds of millions of years before man appeared on the earth. Is this print valid?

6. "Living fossils" are occasionally discovered, animals which supposedly became extinct many millions of years ago and therefore left no fossils in later geological deposits. Yet they are found living on the present

earth. The most notorious living fossil is the coelacanth deep water fish. This creature was thought to have been extinct for over 60 million years when a specimen was captured live off the coast of Africa.[15]

The data assembled in this chapter from paleontology and geology seem to harmonize more fully with the biblical record of the creation and global flood than with the materialist theories of evolution and uniformitarian geology. This is not to say that no difficult questions remain for creation-oriented scientists who are concerned with developing a scientifically viable apologetic for the biblical Christian faith.Many questions *are* unanswered, but evolutionary theorists face as many and far more profound difficulties in supporting and defending their interpretation of the observed data.

Fossils and Strata—A Creationist Interpretation

Since creationists are sharply critical of evolutionary and uniformitarian theories concerning early earth history, can they project a constructive, alternative interpretation of strata and fossils? The answer is *yes*. Nevertheless, the creationist interpretation is no more capable of verification by experimental test than is the materialist interpretation. The following, however, is an interpretation in conformity with observed scientific facts and also with the divinely inspired revelation contained in the Bible. See Appendix A for a more fully developed Creation Model.

Some basic assumptions of a creationist interpretation of early earth history are the following:

1. The creation of all things took place in six days around ten thousand years ago.

2. The antediluvian world was probably characterized by uniformly mild climate, high average humidity, perhaps a high-level envelope of water vapor, smaller oceans and lower mountains than presently exist, and much more extensive cover of vegetation than is seen in the modern world.

3. The global Genesis Flood was the chief agent in the production of the greater part of geological strata and other features of the earth's surface. These include:

a. The rise of sea level above the highest mountains during the Flood may have been brought about by a combination of factors including: (1) condensation of the postulated water vapor canopy as rain (windows of heaven opened); (2) subterranean water released from the earth's crustal rocks (fountains of the deep opened); (3) floors of the oceans may have risen relative to the dry land surface; and (4) additional water from outer space may have been deposited on the earth by divine miraculous agency.

b. The inundation of the entire surface of the earth in a period of only forty days, and the water's subsidence after a year in a similarly short time produced vast tidal waves and stupendous currents which scoured the land surface, eroding vast volumes of rock.

c. The resulting sediments were deposited to produce the major sedimentary structures observed on earth today.

d. The Flood was accompanied by vast volcanic and mountain-building activity.

e. Extensive catastrophic glaciation occurred during and after the Flood.

f. Sedimentary deposits classified as Pleistocene and also some classified as Cenozoic probably were mostly laid down in the post-Flood era.

4. The factors determining distribution of fossils in the sedimentary strata were:

a. The association together of particular assortments of plants and animals in ecological communities.

b. Geographic locations of particular plants and animals.

c. Relative mobilities of different animals.

d. Relative densities, sizes, and other properties of particular plants and animals.

e. The physical principles of water transport and deposition, a subject which is only imperfectly understood and which defies exact mathematical analysis.

Pre-Cambrian strata   Several types of formation occur in the strata which have been classified as Pre-Cambrian, including rocks such as limestone, shales, and conglomerates. Either they contain no fossils at all or only a few remains of algae, bacteria, and perhaps worm tubes. In fact, because the Pre-Cambrian rocks contain so few fossils a theoretical "time sequence" for such rocks has never been worked out. Radiometric dating has proven of little value to evolutionary paleontologists working on this problem, because good correlations between the sedimentary and the radiometrically datable igneous rocks are scarce.

Moreover, the results of radiometric dating have often proved to be erratic. Recent discoveries of fossil pollen grains in Pre-Cambrian rocks have complicated the picture. Sometimes Pre-Cambrian rocks are found above as well as below fossil bearing strata. The creationist interpretation assigns most underlying igneous (crystallized from a melt) rocks such as granite and basement rocks to the period of creation, whereas most sedimentary rocks are assigned to the period of the biblical flood.

Cambrian rocks   The rocks classified as Cambrian contain numerous
fossils of many different kinds of invertebrate marine creatures. One particular community represented in the Cambrian fossils, called the *Olenel-
lus fauna*, is found in various places all over the world. It consists of
sponges, jellyfish, corals, starfish, worms, brachiopods, clams, and trilobites. Trilobites, important index fossils used to classify rocks, are flat
bottom-feeding crustaceans with jointed bodies and many legs. Com-
prising hundreds of species, most trilobites were small, but some were as
large as modern crabs. In the creationist interpretation, the Cambrian
fossils represent marine communities of living creatures, most of which
are now extinct, but some of which were quite similar to modern types.

Carboniferous strata   The rock strata classified as Carboniferous contain many stratified deposits of coal, though coal is contained in strata
other than Carboniferous. Coal represents the largest fossil assemblage in
the world—literally billions of tons. In New Brunswick the Pennsylvanian
strata (not all coal) are 13,000 feet thick. Coal results when plant remains
are compressed and heated by the weight of overlying sediments. Most of
the fossils making up the coal have lost their identity, but around the
edges recognizable specimens can be found. Fossils in the sedimentary
rock strata between the coal layers help complete the picture.

The communities which were trapped under the overlying sediments
must have been enormous forests. Cone-bearing (conifer) trees called
Cordaites were like pines except, instead of needles, they bore leaves six
feet long. Some of these trees were 100 feet high, others were like our
modern tree ferns, and some were like nothing growing today (seed ferns,
for instance). Some were related to our little club-mosses and horsetails
but grew as large as trees. A few of the trees had structures that looked
like small cones on the ends of the branches. These "cones" contained
spores instead of seeds.

No fossil bees or butterflies have been found in the remains of these
spore-bearing forests, but the large plants provided food and shelter for
many other insects. The giant cockroaches averaged larger than modern
tropical species, although some present-day roaches are as large as the
fossil varieties. Strange spiders, most of them apparently lacking spinnarets, stalked cockroaches and other insects. Scorpions scurried among
the ferns searching for tasty spiders. Dragon flies existed with wing spans
up to two feet. And some of the amphibians, including salamanders,
weighed as much as 400 pounds. In addition, there were some reptiles

and also some fish of modern freshwater types. Sea shells and starfish are sometimes found, indicating that the ocean flowed over the coal forests at some time.

As suggested earlier in the chapter, there is considerable evidence to support the view that most of the coal deposits were not formed in the place where the forests actually grew. Rather, it would appear that the plant material was moved into place by water action, covered rapidly by deep sediments, and transformed into coal in a short time by the influence of the great pressure and resulting high temperature. This fits the creationist interpretation of sedimentary strata formation by the biblical flood.

Mesozoic strata The fossils found in rocks classified as Mesozoic represent a community which included most of the same families of plants and animals still in existence today, particularly the reptiles, such as snakes, turtles, lizards, alligators, and crocodiles. Fish and mammals also lived in these communities.

The most prominent members of the Mesozoic community were the dinosaurs. There were hundreds of different kinds, in all sizes and shapes. Some were huge, many over fifty feet long; others were no bigger than a pet cat. Early discoveries of dinosaurs were thought by scientists to resemble lizard bones of enormous size. Hence the name *dinosaur* is derived from two Greek words, *denios* meaning terrible and *sauros* meaning lizard. Some evidence has led scientists to suggest that dinosaurs were actually warm-blooded and therefore are not to be classified as reptiles. Not all dinosaurs lived on dry land; many remained submerged most of the time in coastal waters or swam in the warm seas, and others could fly.

Dinosaurs are divided into two large groups (orders). One order is called the ornithischian or bird-hip. Bird-hip dinosaurs have deep sockets for the upper leg bones and a strong attachment to the spine. Stegosaurus, Camptosaurus, Ankylosaurus, and Triceratops are examples of the ornithischian order of dinosaurs. The order of reptile-hip dinosaurs is called saurischian. Allosaurus, Brontosaurus, Diplodocus, Compognathus, and Tyrranosaurus are all examples of the saurischian order. Let us consider several of the better known kinds of dinosaurs.

The saurischian Diplodocus, the longest of the dinosaurs growing up to 87 feet in length, was nevertheless smaller than the modern blue whale which reaches 100 feet in length. The dinosaur Brachiosaurus was much heavier but not as long as Diplodocus. Apparently spending most of its time in the water feeding on plants, Diplodocus featured a small head carried on a very long neck, its long tail trailing behind. Fossils are found in the western United States.

Stegosaurus, like all the armored dinosaurs, was of the bird-hip order, ornithischia. About twenty feet long, with a small head and brain, Stegosaurus walked on all fours. Its back legs were much longer than its front legs, as was the case with most bird-hip dinosaurs, and this caused its back to arch high in the air. Sail-shaped protective plates stood up along the spine. Fossils have been found all over the world—in Wyoming, South America, England, Asia, and Africa.

Triceratops ("three-horns-on-the-face") was one of the largest of the horned plant-eaters, measuring twenty-four feet in length. Its nose resembled a parrot beak, and two horns projected forward from above the eyes. An immense frill-shaped bone on the back of the skull made the head appear very large. Triceratops was heavy, powerful, and slow-moving, somewhat resembling a modern-day rhinoceros. Fossils have been discovered in North America.

Tyrannosaurus (Rex), the "king of the lizards," was the most fearsome of all the dinosaurs, measuring twenty feet high and fifty feet long and armed with powerful jaws set with teeth six inches long. The forelegs, however, very short and spindly, were probably of little use to him. Thought by many to have been a ferocious carnivore, recent studies suggest that Tyrannosaurus was actually herbivorous, as were other dinosaurs. Fossils of this creature have been found in Europe, North America, and South America.

Cenozoic Strata

Cenozoic strata are those in which are found fossil remains of many extinct mammals. Just as in the case of the extinct reptiles of the Mesozoic strata, a fantastic variety of all types and sizes of mammals have been uncovered in the Cenozoic strata. These are generally extinct species but readily classifiable into the same groupings as the modern mammals. Many of the extinct mammals are most bizarre by modern standards. It seems impossible to imagine why chance evolution should be able to produce so many different kinds of mammals. In view of the difficulties with evolutionary theory, creation by a purposeful Creator appears the more reasonable explanation. The largest mammal was the Baluchatherium which stood eighteen feet high at the shoulder and was twenty-five feet long! This creature, classified with the rhinoceroses, must have weighed some twenty-five tons.

Evolution and extinction—why? Fossil remains of several thousand kinds of extinct reptiles have been discovered as well as even larger numbers of mammals, plus vast numbers of species of all the other types of animals. Many of them, such as those just described, were immense, some very small, others very bizarre. Several questions come to mind in relation to these creatures.

First, if they were the product of evolutionary development, can the theory of evolution provide a rational, detailed explanation of why and how they evolved? The answer is that the evolutionary explanations are very incomplete and unsatisfactory. What, for example, is the adaptive advantage of a plant-eating mammal eighteen feet high and weighing twenty-five tons? The reality of the assumed history of evolution is accepted by faith. It is not possible to devise experimental tests which potentially could falsify the theory. Unverifiable explanations can always be imagined for inconsistencies or gaps in the fossil record. In the words of Birch and Ehrlich, "Our theory of evolution has become . . . one which cannot be refuted by any possible observations. Every conceivable observation can be fitted into it. It is thus 'outside of empirical science' but not necessarily false. No one can think of ways in which to test it."[16]

A related question is whether or not the evolutionary time scale affords enough time to make the alleged evolutionary changes seem plausible. Again, the immense number of supposed mutations and the time required for natural selection to operate would appear to demand much more time than the currently accepted age of the earth makes available.

Finally, what happened to all of these creatures; why did they become extinct? For a century baffled theorists of evolution have framed numerous speculations in fruitless attempts to explain this mystery. But no particular explanation seems to satisfy all of the experts. The mystery remains. But it is no mystery to those who believe that dinosaurs and other extinct creatures were destroyed in a cataclysmic global flood. Creation scientists conceive that each of the communities represented in the fossil record was quickly overwhelmed and buried by the Flood of Noah.

From the fossils of creatures buried at the time of the Flood some limited knowledge can be gained of the conditions on the earth before the Flood. Evidence from fossils indicates that the antediluvian world was largely tropical in climate. Global atmospheric conditions were probably quite different from the present, being more uniform and characterized by higher humidity and moderate temperatures. Relatively few deleterious gene mutations had accumulated in the gene pools of populations of the various kinds of creatures, compared with today, thousands of years later. This relatively smaller "genetic load," of bad mutations, in conjunction with the different atmospheric conditions and the possibly much lower incidence of cosmic radiation, permitted much longer life-spans for man and some other creatures than are normal in modern times.

According to this view, the post-Flood climate was greatly altered to approximate modern conditions. This, together with the large quantity of mutations accumulated subsequent to the Flood, brought about the shortening of human life-span and the gradual extinction of some life forms which populated the earth immediately after the Flood. The extensive glaciation of the polar regions, large remnants of which still exist, occurred probably during the closing part of the Flood year and in the period immediately following. Gradually as glaciers receded and the surface effects of the Flood disappeared completely or were altered by weathering, erosion, and sedimentation, and by volcanic activity and earth movements at the much slower modern rates, the earth was repopulated and postdiluvian human history unfolded as it is recorded in the Bible, in the data of archeology, and in secular histories.

Conclusion

The creationist reconstruction of early earth history as evidenced in the fossil and strata records has been only lightly traced in this chapter, and creation scientists have much work to do in filling out the picture. The greater part of the scientific community has for more than a century approached this subject with evolutionary and uniformitarian presuppositions, and their conclusions agree with their assumptions. Perhaps this is the time for the advance of science by a study of earth history based on biblical presuppositions.

"I have more understanding than all my teachers: for thy testimonies are my meditation. I understand more than the ancients, because I keep thy precepts. . . . Through thy precepts I get understanding: therefore I hate every false way." (Psalm 119:99, 100, 104)

4

Life—Miracle, Not Accident

What is Life?

Biology is the science devoted to the study of living things. By observing plants and animals in their natural environment and also under experimental conditions, biologists are able to discover and understand the characteristics of living things. It would seem that any scientific discipline would include a precise definition of the object of study, but complete agreement on the definition of life has never been attained, primarily because scientists are not capable of discovering the source of life.

One way of defining life is to list the essential functions which appear to be common to all living creatures. A generally accepted list of essential life attributes and functions would include the following:[1, 2]

1. Stable, complex structure
2. Growth
3. Metabolism
4. Homeostasis
5. Response to environment
6. Reproduction
7. Coded genetic information

Stable, complex structure as a property of living things is fairly obvious to everyone, but the degree of complexity has only become apparent in the several decades since the advent of molecular biology. Later in this chapter some of these findings, outstanding triumphs of modern science, will be described.

Growth is easy to understand since it is a process which we have observed both in ourselves and in other living things. No matter how small or large, whether plant or animal, all living things grow in some way, though not necessarily in the same way.

Metabolism is the name given to the entire complex of chemical reactions used by plants and animals as they appropriate energy, food, oxygen, and water from the environment, using them to power life functions and provide building and repair materials for their bodies.

Homeostasis means literally, "staying the same." This refers to the unique capacity of living organisms to maintain their bodies in a state of chemical structure, composition, and energy content quite different from their surroundings. Thus a living organism will have within its body higher or lower concentrations of certain chemicals than exist in the surroundings, a higher or lower temperature, perhaps, and always a higher content of free energy. A living organism uses energy from its surroundings to maintain itself in a condition which is not in chemical equilibrium with the outside world. With death equilibrium is soon established as the structures of the organism degenerate.

Response to environment is a very general term which includes both apparently very simple and also exceedingly complex activities. For example, most plants are in some way phototropic or light seeking. Bacteria are attracted by some chemicals and repelled by others. Female fireflies flash response signals to the flashes of male fireflies. Human beings respond to symbolic communications of ideas contained in words transmitted in written or verbal form.

Reproduction is one of the most important definitive characteristics of living things. Many different methods are used by organisms to reproduce, including seeds, eggs, spores, and cellular division. By these means living things are able to bring additional members of their species into the world.

In every organism all of the properties and functions are defined and regulated in accordance with coded information contained in the DNA molecules of the genes in the cell nuclei and apparently also in DNA contained in at least one other kind of cell structure, the mitochondria. Some scientists propose that essential coded information is also carried in some unknown manner in the general structure of the cell, in the cytoplasm.

Cellular Life

Microscopic examination of living systems, beginning with Leeuwenhoek and Hooke in the seventeenth century, revealed that practically all living things except the non-cellular slime molds are composed of tiny units called cells. In 1839 Theodor Schwann suggested that all organisms are composed of cells, and Virchow in 1858 proposed the doctrine that living cells can come only from previously existing cells.

Cells vary greatly in size among different plants and animals, but generally they are quite small and can only be studied with the aid of a microscope. Units of measurement useful in microscopy are as follows:

1 centimeter (cm) = 0.4 inch

1 millimeter (mm) = 0.1 cm

1 micron (μ) = 0.0001 cm = 10^{-4} cm

1 nanometer (nm) = 10^{-9} meter = 10^{-7} cm

1 angstrom (Å) = 1/100,000,000 cm = 10^{-8} cm

The average plant cell is about 0.005 cm in diameter, the average animal cell about 0.001 cm or 10 microns. Bacterial cells range in size from 5 microns down to the smallest types which cannot be viewed with a light microscope. Some cells are large enough to be seen with the naked eye— for example, insect or bird eggs, and the juice-filled cells which make up the sections of citrus fruits.

The cell is the smallest unit of life. In some animals, such as the amoeba or paramecium, one cell acts as a complete organism, taking in food and metabolising it, growing, and reproducing. In another more complex organism, such as man, there may be trillions of cells of many different types, each type forming a tissue with special tasks to perform. Using powerful electron microscopes, scientists have discovered that even one-celled organisms are highly complex systems. The one cell of an amoeba, for instance, can duplicate the primary functions of other living things, while the specialized cells of more complex organisms may each perform only one function.

The Structure and Composition of Cells[3, 4]

The cells of plants, animals, fungi, and the one-celled organisms called protista share many similarities. The outer cell membrane encloses the protoplasm which comprises most of the material of the cell. The protoplasm is made up of the nucleus, surrounded by the nuclear membrane, and the cytoplasm. The nucleus contains the information which controls the cell, and the cell organelles (little cells) contained in the cytoplasm

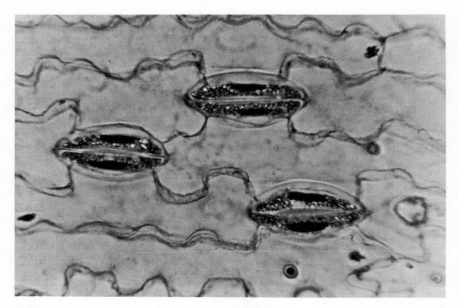

figure 4-1. Photomicrograph of surface layer cells of a lily leaf at 500X magnification. The lip-shaped structures are stomata (Greek *stoma*, mouth) composed of two guard cells with large, dark nuclei. The guard cells separate to form openings through which water, oxygen, and carbon dioxide diffuse. Evolutionary theory fails to explain the chance origin of any cell, let alone highly specialized guard cells and stomata.

carry out the functions which enable the cell to live and reproduce.

The common intestinal bacterium, *Escherichia coli*, illustrates the fantastic complexity of cells. Only 2 microns (slightly less than 0.0001 inches) long, *Escherischia* contains about 30,000 tiny chemical factories called ribosomes which manufacture 2,000 to 3,000 different kinds of very complicated protein molecules used by the cell. This tiny cell also contains about 2,000 other different kinds of molecules, large and small, which take part in the internal operations of the cell.

The average cell in the human body is roughly ten times as large and far more complex, linked with trillions of other cells in an amazing design to form the physical body of the being called man. These cells in man and the plants and animals contain many parts which make up their complex structure.

Some of the cell structures and organelles include:

1. Double-layered cell membrane (permits certain substances to enter or leave the cell, but blocks passage of other substances).

2. Endoplasmic reticulum, an intricately folded, double-layered membrane spread through much of the cytoplasm within the cell (apparently provides channels in its folds and convolutions for transport of

substances between different parts of the cell).

3. Ribosomes, mostly attached to endoplasmic reticulum (assembly plants for the manufacture of new protein molecules).

4. Lysosomes (vesicles containing digestive enzymes).

5. Mitochondria (convert the chemical energy of sugar into other forms immediately useable by the cell).

6. Golgi bodies (package cell products in membrane sacs for transport to proper places in the cell).

7. Nucleus bounded by double-layered nuclear membrane (contains chromosomes and nucleolus).

8. Chromosomes (complex bodies composed or protein and DNA molecules which carry the genetic information of the cell).

9. Nucleolus (manufactures ribosomes from RNA and protein molecules).

10. Centrioles formed of nine bundles of three microtubules each (organize formation of the spindle which appears when the chromosomes are duplicated in cell division).

11. Chloroplasts in plant cells (location of chlorophyll and other pigments which couple radiant energy in photosynthesis).

All living cells possess protoplasm as their essential substance. Protoplasm is made up of many simple chemical substances such as water, inorganic ions, simple carbohydrates (sugars), amino acids, lipids (fat-like substances), and nucleotides. The carbohydrates, amino acids, and nucleotides are largely combined to form long chains called polymers. Two types of carbohydrate chains are called starch and cellulose. The amino acid polymers are called proteins. The nucleotides combine to form the long deoxyribose nucleic acid molecules (DNA).

The functions of some of the components found in protoplasm may be familiar to the reader. Carbohydrates are consumed to provide energy for heat and movement. Fats (simple lipids) store energy and are combined with proteins in cell membranes. Proteins are used by living things for growth and repair of tissues and as enzymes (biological catalysts) to speed up and control chemical reactions in the cell. Nucleic acids help to pass on an organism's characteristics to its offspring.

The fact that all living things are made of certain basic, simple, building-block compounds, and that these substances work in the same general way in all organisms, could lead a biologist to two different conclusions. One who assumes a materialistic origin for life might say that this is evidence that all living things evolved from one common ancestral organism. A believer in the biblical record of creation would say that it provides evidence that the Creator inaugurated a careful plan which makes it possible for living things to work together with other creatures living in their environment. Intelligent planning would result in much similarity and parallelism between life systems because the most effective and efficient designs would be used as basic models.

It should be added, however, that while there are many chemical and structural features common to all forms of life, there are also many differences which are difficult to explain on the basis of common ancestry. For example, while the majority of organisms use the same system of enzymes to metabolize the sugar glucose, there are also numerous variations of this scheme. The many variations in biochemistry and structure of living things would suggest separate creation of types, while the common features would suggest a common Creator.

The most fundamental difference between plants and animals is that plants have cells which contain chloroplasts, whereas animals do not. Chloroplasts are tiny structures containing the green pigment chlorophyll. This complicated molecule, in association with other pigments, absorbs the sun's energy and enables the plant to use the energy to transform carbon dioxide gas and water from the air and soil into simple carbohydrates (sugars) and oxygen gas. The sugars produced in this photosynthesis are combined to make larger carbohydrate molecules, and the excess oxygen gas is released into the atmosphere.

Animals cannot make their food in this way, but must depend upon plants or other animals for food. Plants take the sun's energy and store it in high-energy food substances that animals can use.

Living Things Are Classified[5]

The differences between the various kinds of living things form the basis for the system of classification used by biologists to name and distinguish them. Classification promotes organization, clarity, and conformity in scientific investigations. To classify means to arrange things in groups and give them names.

Living things are usually classified by their structure according to obvious external differences in structure, hidden internal differences, or even subtle differences in cell structure. Taxonomists supply Latin names for each organism because Latin as a language is not used in everyday speech and therefore does not change. The meanings of the Latin terms afford the precision necessary in scientific communication and investigation.

The modern system of zoological classification stems from the eighteenth century work of the Swedish scientist Linnaeus. He believed that all things were designed and created by God, and that his system of classification was simply a logical means whereby man could better know and understand the Creator's handiwork. With the increase of knowledge Linnaeus's system has been greatly modified and enlarged. Cells are classified into two types: prokaryotic cells, which have no nuclear membrane, and eukaryotic cells, which have nuclei enclosed by membranes. All living things are then classified into five kingdoms:

1. Kingdom Monera: Prokaryotic single-celled organisms including the bacteria and blue-green algae.

2. Kingdom Protista: Eukaryotic single-celled organisms including protozoans, algae, diatoms, and non-cellular slime molds.

3. Kingdom Fungi: Eukaryotic unicellular organisms which sometimes exist as continuous, non-cellular filaments containing many nuclei.

4. Kingdom Plantae: Eukaryotic many-celled and unicelled forms using photosynthesis as their main source of nutrition.

5. Kingdom Animalia: Eukaryotic many-celled organisms which are not capable of photosynthesis, including marine invertebrates, fish, reptiles, mammals, birds, insects, spiders, etc.

A kingdom is divided generally into two or more major groups, these into smaller groups, and so on. The names, then, of the ranks of classification from larger to smaller groupings are kingdom, phylum, class, order, family, genus, and species. Most biological scientists consider that the correct or "natural" system of classification is a consequence of and evidence for a real historical process by which all creatures evolved by chance from one or a few original single-celled organisms. As was indicated earlier, however, an arrangement of animals in a graded series of bodily forms or internal structures does not establish genetic relationship. Only actual breeding experiments or eyewitness observation of the original process could provide scientific verification for evolution, but this kind of evidence is not available to evolutionary theorists.

Bible-believing students of the biological sciences possess a guide for their interpretation of the available data, the biblical record of divine creation contained in Genesis, which states ten times that the kinds were created to reproduce each after its own kind. They find that the sum of scientific information fits the biblical record in many respects better than it does the materialist theory of origins.

For example, the fact that living things can be put into groups and classified establishes distinct differences between one kind and another. The kinds are distinct, but each organism can make limited changes to fit the environment in which it lives without changing the kind of organism it is. For example, a particular kind of bird may have diversified into several different varieties. Careful study would provide evidence for the relationship of these varieties. Perhaps such differentiation has extended in some cases to the species level from an original kind. The actual extent of variation within kinds and the boundaries of the kinds would be fruitful subjects for scientific investigation by biblical creationists. Massive amounts of genetic evidence exist for the reality of impassable genetic boundaries. Furthermore, although there were undoubtedly a number of different original kinds of birds, and although the kinds may have diversified into many species and varieties, birds are readily classified as birds.

If all organisms had come from one common ancestor by evolutionary change, one would expect to find one chain of life going on and on. It would not be possible so readily to classify species and genera, either of living kinds or of fossils. There would be species starting to change into other kinds of animals or plants, and proto-organs just beginning to take on their role as genuine organs. But this is not observed. The various kinds of living plants and animals are separated by impassable boundaries. For example, one cannot discover reptiles starting to evolve feathers and attempting to fly, nor is there fossil evidence that reptiles evolved feathers and became birds.

The beautiful manner in which each creature is adapted to its place in nature is strong evidence for intelligent, purposeful design. In the Christian view, similarities between different creatures are the result of a plan for each creature which provides it with the organs and capabilities required for life in its particular environment. As an example, each organism requiring vision possesses the type of eye which is adapted to give vision of just the correct kind for that creature.

Living Things Work Together[6]

Not only do plants and animals have their parts carefully organized to form a complete organism, but all living things in the world are grouped and arranged in order to work together. They depend upon each other and their environment. Organisms live under the surface of the earth, on the surface, in the waters, and above the surface in the air.

The complex web of living things which exists in the earth's outer layer is called the biosphere. This layer extends about five or six miles above and below sea level. The biosphere as a system receives from the sun a continual flow of radiant energy. This energy drives the atmospheric activities such as wind currents, storms, and rain, and is then radiated out into space as long wavelength infrared radiation. A tiny fraction of one percent of the solar energy reaching the biosphere is captured by photosynthetic plants. Energy from the sun powers all of the life activities of the biosphere, and some of it is temporarily stored in the tissues of plants and animals in the form of chemical free energy. This energy, used to power life processes or released when the organisms die and are decomposed, is finally transformed into heat in accord with the Second Law of Thermodynamics discussed in Chapter 2.

Therefore we say that the biosphere is a steady-state system through which energy flows from the solar energy source to the outer space heat sink. The living organisms capture some of the energy flow and hold it for a while, thus maintaining themselves in a steady energy state, an elevated free-energy state. Non-living chemical systems can capture energy from the flow in a somewhat analogous manner, but only with a small fraction of the efficiency, maintaining a much smaller difference in free energy content from the environment.

In addition, the living organisms continually reproduce more copies of themselves, each a system of vast chemical and structural complexity. Living organisms of the biosphere are unique in possessing this reproductive capability. All the evidence points to intelligent, purposeful design of the biosphere.

For purposes of study, the immensely complex biosphere may be thought of as an aggregate of many ecosystems. An ecosystem is a fairly self-contained combination of living organisms and their environment through which energy flows and in which various vital minerals move in cycles. A pond, swamp, or meadow is an ecosystem. A properly stocked aquarium or terrarium is a man-made model of larger natural ecosystems. Some of the important elements or minerals which circulate in an ecosystem include carbon, oxygen, water, nitrogen, phosphorus, and certain trace elements.

The living creatures inhabiting an ecosystem are called a community, and the members of each species in the community make up a population. The place and function of each species in an ecosystem is its ecological niche. No individual organism in a population could succeed in living by itself, for each one depends upon living and non-living forms of matter for the energy and materials it needs to live. Organisms, populations, communities, and ecosystems which make up the whole biosphere are all organized into a very detailed chain of dependence upon each other.

The Pyramid of Producers and Consumers[7]

The green plants are the primary *producers* in the ecosystem, for they capture the sun's energy in high-energy biomolecules which they and the *consumers* in the system can use. The consumers may be classified as herbivores (which eat plant materials), carnivores (which eat herbivores and carnivores), supercarnivores (which eat other carnivores), and the decomposers (bacteria, fungi). At each consumer stage, about ninety percent of the food energy is either not assimilated or is used for life processes rather than being stored. Because of this inefficiency each population annually consumes food equivalent to many times its own weight.

Since plants provide food for many insects and animals, a very large number and mass of plants is necessary. The energy stored in each level of consumers is reduced to roughly one-tenth that stored by the members of the preceding level below. This is illustrated in the diagram of the ecological energy pyramid (a pyramid of biomass would be similar in shape, for the stored energy is proportional to the dry weight or mass of the plant or animal material). Note that the primary producers, the plants, generally form the large base, whereas each of the successive levels of consumers is increasingly smaller in stored energy and biomass.

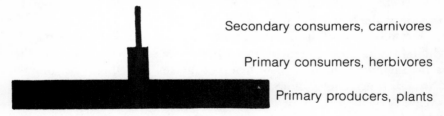

Secondary consumers, carnivores

Primary consumers, herbivores

Primary producers, plants

figure 4-2. Pyramid of biomass in grasslands. The base is the great mass of grass, shrubs, and trees. Next come the herbivores such as antelope, zebra, and wildebeest, and finally the carnivores such as lions, hyenas, and wild dogs. The decrease in total mass of living things at each successive consumer level is required by the inefficiency with which a consumer stores the energy contained in the food consumed.

For the first example of such an ecosystem pyramid, consider the African veldt where large quantities of grass and shrubs grow. Great herds of many different kinds of herbivores—antelope, buffalo, wildebeest—roam the plains, feeding on specific kinds of vegetation. The carnivores include lions, hyenas, wild dogs. There are also scavengers such as jackals and vultures, and finally the carrion-consuming insects and the decomposers in the soil.

The ocean presents excellent examples of communities of living things. Here the primary producers are the phytoplankton, microscopic, single-celled plants in the surface water layers which absorb sunlight and produce the basic food supply for the entire community. The microscopic zooplankton are tiny animals which feed on the phytoplankton.

Small fish, tiny crustaceans and other invertebrates feed on the plankton. Larger fish feed on the smaller, and so the food chain extends to the supercarnivores such as sharks and swordfish.

The actual complex of food chains in any ecosystem is much more complicated than the brief sketches given above, but the principles of interdependence, energy flow, material cycles, and the pyramid relationships are, with variations, common to them all. When the complexity and balance of the biosphere and the beautifully adapted and unique environmental conditions on the earth's surface are considered, one is impressed with the reality of an intelligent master plan in nature.

The Creator designed nature so that no single plant or animal could produce too many of its own kind. If too many of one species survive, the balance of nature is upset. For example, excessive numbers of porcupines can damage a forest, and they will multiply beyond the sustainable limit if suitable predators are scarce. In northern forests the most successful predator of porcupines is the fisher. This animal has been hunted almost to extinction in some areas, with resulting increase in the porcupine populations and unacceptable damage to the forests. Now the fisher is being protected and the porcupine populations are coming under control. Thus a dynamic balance of nature preserves the natural order for the benefit of all the species.

Many interesting interrelationships exist between different kinds of animals, kinds of plants, or between plants and animals. Sometimes one organism cannot survive or even reproduce without another as part of its environment. Many illustrations of this are to be found among the pollen-bearing plants and the pollenating insects, where special design characteristics make a particular insect necessary or specific for a particular plant. In all of these amazing details and in the balance of nature we see the wisdom and handiwork of God, the Creator of all things.

Environment and Heredity

Two factors decide most of the characteristics of the organism, heredity and environment. Heredity is the transmission of an organism's characteristics to its offspring. Organisms also develop certain characteristics as they respond to their environment. Hereditary traits may be passed on from one generation to another, but environmental traits cannot.

One-celled animals and plants can reproduce by dividing themselves into two new organisms. The amoeba, for example, reproduces in this manner. When it becomes a certain size, its cell nucleus and cytoplasm divide and form two amoebas. A more complex, many-celled organism, the hydra, can form a bud which eventually breaks loose to become another individual.

Many plants and animals develop sex cells, known as egg cells and sperms. When sperms encounter egg cells, one of the sperms enters an egg cell (fertilization) and the substance of the two is combined. Each fertilized egg cell produces a new organism.

Ordinarily the characteristics of one generation are inherited by the next, like begetting like. But though this is generally true, numerous exceptions may be observed in all populations. For example, a trait of parents may disappear in their children and reappear in the grandchildren. Or an entirely new trait may suddenly appear and prove to be inheritable. Plant and animal breeders have for thousands of years selected their stock to develop more desirable strains or varieties. Until the nineteenth century, however, nothing was known about the laws and mechanisms responsible for these observations.

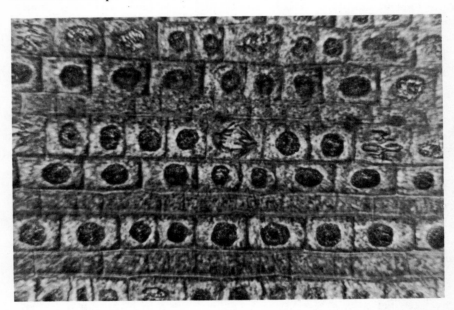

figure 4-3. Photomicrograph of onion root tip cells at about 800X magnification. Several cells are elongated, with the chromosomes separating in the process called mitosis, which produces two identical sets of chromosomes in the course of cell division.

Mendel's Laws[8]

Between 1856 and 1864 Gregor Mendel conducted experiments which led to the discovery of the cardinal principles of heredity. He worked with pea plants in his garden, carefully observing and recording the characteristics of successive generations of pea plants which resulted from the crossing of different kinds. He discovered a mathematical relationship evident in the characteristics of the plants making up the different generations. The basic characteristics he followed were shape, color, and size. Mendel noticed that some pea plants were tall, some short; some peas were round, some wrinkled; some were green, some yellow.

Mendel found that if he crossbred a round pea with a wrinkled pea, the first generation gave him round peas. If he crossed a yellow pea with a green pea, the first generation gave him yellow peas. The second generation of offspring showed a ratio of three round peas to one wrinkled pea, three yellow peas to one green pea. He reasoned that the characteristics for round peas and wrinkled peas (shape), and yellow peas and green peas (color), were stored in the "memory" of the peas. The characteristics that showed up in the first generation Mendel called dominant, the hidden characteristics, recessive.

Mendel's research led him to draw the following conclusions:

1. There are definite hereditary units which are responsible for the transmission of characteristics. Mendel called them factors. Now we call them genes.

2. There are two of each type of factor in the mature organism.

3. When the factors differ, only one will be expressed (dominant) while the other will remain latent (recessive).

4. The factors segregate unchanged into the gametes so that each gamete (egg or sperm) carries only one factor of each kind.

5. There is a random union of gametes which results in a predictable ratio of characters in the offspring.

A careful study of the accompanying chart will reveal why crossing pure round-yellow peas with pure wrinkled-green peas results in a first generation which is all round-yellow, whereas the second generation has the different kinds in this ratio: 9 round-yellow to 3 round-green to 3 wrinkled-yellow to 1 wrinkled-green.

Mendel's law works for all organisms. This is why a person might have eye color like one of his grandparents instead of his parents. Most variations within kinds can be explained by this concept. Secondary effects are produced by mutations (discussed below). Several other genetic processes occur which only result in reshuffling of existing genetic information.

With this view of the law of heredity we begin to understand a little of the process by which the Creator of all life chose to insure the fulfillment of His command that His creatures reproduce each one after its own kind.

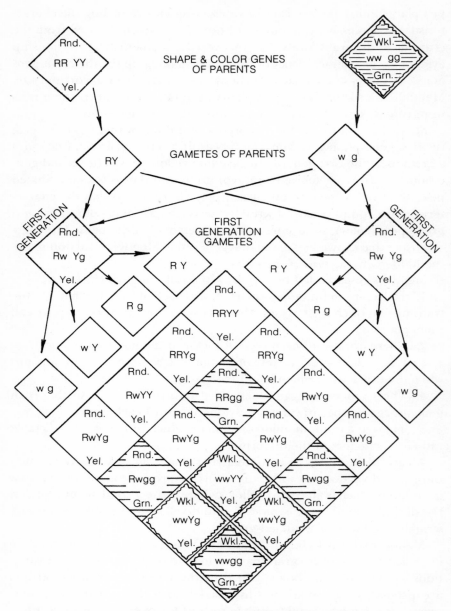

SHAPE & COLOR GENES
OF PARENTS

GAMETES OF PARENTS

FIRST
GENERATION
GAMETES

FIRST
GENERATION

FIRST
GENERATION

ALL POSSIBLE 2nd GENERATION GENE COMBINATIONS

figure 4-4. Mendel's law illustrated. The letter symbols for genes of the peas are as follows:
R = round (dominant), w = wrinkled (recessive), Y = yellow (dominant), g = green (recessive). The "gametes" are the sex cells (pollen or eggs).

The kinds were established in the beginning and the genetic boundaries set. The basic genetic process provides for limited variation within kinds, and other processes produce further changes. But human observation and reproducible experiment have yet to demonstrate more than trivial changes compared with those required by evolutionary theory. The facts fit the picture found in the opening chapters of Genesis.

The actual molecular structures and designs by which the Creator carries out His purposes in ordaining the genetic law will be our next object of study. These discoveries, resulting from several decades of intense scientific research, constitute one of the most striking accomplishments in the history of science. Such knowledge leads the Bible-believer to glorify the Creator for His great wisdom. He is amazed that the unbelieving scientists can so easily assume God out of the fantastically complex systems of molecular genetics which they have so recently discovered and which still are shrouded in much mystery and a web of unanswered questions. Let us go on now to a consideration of the basis of genetics in the chromosomes and the molecular structure of the gene.

Genetics

The orderly operation of Mendel's law in heredity suggests that there must be a very exact mechanism which acts when the germ cells of the parents combine to form a fertilized egg. What is the actual basis of heredity? The biological research of the past two decades which has answered this question is one of the great stories in the history of science. This research reached its climax in the work of scientists who carried the understanding of heredity down to the molecular level. What did they find inside the nucleus of the cell?

That the factors governing heredity called genes are contained in the chromosomes was a long established fact. It was further well established that the genes are arranged in order along the length of the chromosome. Furthermore, each type of organism possesses in its body or somatic cells an even number of chromosomes which are paired, each member of a pair containing the genes for the same characteristics of the organism— for example, the genes for blue or brown eye color, short or tall height, straight or curly hair, etc.

The two chromosomes of a pair may, for example, both have the gene for blue eyes or for brown eyes, or the two chromosomes may have different genes, one for blue and the other for brown eyes. The gene for brown eyes in dominant over the blue gene. Therefore, if a person possesses either one or two genes for brown eye color, actual eye color expressed in the individual will be brown. Only if the eye color genes are both the recessive blue gene will the individual be blue-eyed.

How is it that different descendants of two parents have different combinations of genes for a particular characteristic such as eye color? This is determined partly by the process called meiosis, which produces the germ cells of the parents. These germ cells contain only one-half of each of the pairs of chromosomes possessed by the ordinary body cells. For example, human body cells each contain 23 pairs or a total of 46 chromosomes. The egg of the female and the sperm of the male, however, contain only 23 chromosomes, one from each pair. Therefore, if the body cell chromosome pair of the parent contains both brown, both blue, or one brown and one blue gene, the germ cells which contain only one member of each chromosome pair will have, respectively, a brown, a blue, or either a brown or a blue gene with equal probability.

When the fertilization process occurs, the germ cells from the male and female parents combine, each chromosome pair of the descendant receiving one chromosome from each parent. Depending upon the gene makeup of the two parents, the descendant can have either two brown, two blue, or one of each kind of gene for eye color. The eye color expressed will be determined by the dominant gene possessed by the descendant. The probabilities for the different combinations are indicated in the chart on page 76.

The Building of a Gene

Research over the past two decades has revealed much about the structure of the gene. A great deal has been learned about the function of the gene at the molecular level. Molecular genetics is a most complicated subject which affords powerful support for the biblical creation model. We will now devote considerable space to an explanation of this subject to enable the reader to have some appreciation of the exquisite precision and forethought of our Creator God in designing the atoms and the structures of living things composed of atoms so that all would fulfill His sovereign will. The following explanation is framed in an outline form and amply illustrated to aid in understanding this marvelous handiwork of God.

Replication of DNA—the foundation of genetic inheritance

1. Each chromosome contains one or more molecules of deoxyribonucleic acid (DNA). In order that each daughter cell may have the same genetic information, chromosomes and therefore DNA must be repli-

cated when cell division takes place:
   a. to multiply cells (mitosis)
   b. to produce sex cells (meiosis)
   2. The DNA molecule is a chain of four kinds of units called nucleotides connected by strong chemical bonds:

nucleotide name	symbol
Deoxyadenosine-5'-phosphate	A
Deoxythymidine-5'-phosphate	T
Deoxyguanosine-5'-phosphate	G
Deoxycytidine-5'-phosphate	C

Thus, a portion of a DNA molecule may be represented, for example, by
-T-A-T-C-G-G-T-A-C-   ("-" = strong bond)

   3. Because their structures enable them to fit together, like a key in a lock, certain nucleotides have specific mutual attractions, A for T, and G for C. Each of these pairs form two or three of the type of weak bonds called hydrogen bonds. These bonds correspond to the parts of a key which fit specific parts of a lock.
   The two members of a pair are said to be complementary nucleotides: A·T and G·C ("·" = hydrogen bonds)
   4. DNA occurs in most cells in a two-chained or two-stranded form. The corresponding positions in the two strands are occupied by complementary nucleotides, so the strands attract each other and fit together, held by hydrogen bonds. The two strands twist around each other, so this form of DNA is called a "double helix." The double helix may be represented by

         -T-A-T-C-G-G-T-A-C
          · · · · · · · · ·
         -A-T-A-G-C-C-A-T-G-

   5. When DNA is replicated in the cell, the two strands partially separate and serve as templates on which the complementary strands are constructed. The nucleotides A, T, G, and C are arranged in the proper order by the formation of hydrogen bonds with their complementary nucleotides in the DNA strand. They are joined together with strong bonds formed under the control of the enzyme DNA-polymerase. This is a protein molecule consisting of a chain about 1,100 amino acid molecules. It travels along a DNA strand superintending the linking together of the complementary nucleotides to produce a complementary DNA strand. Several other enzymes are also involved. When DNA replication is completed, there are two complete sets of DNA double helices for the two cells which result from the cell division. The new DNA chains are built

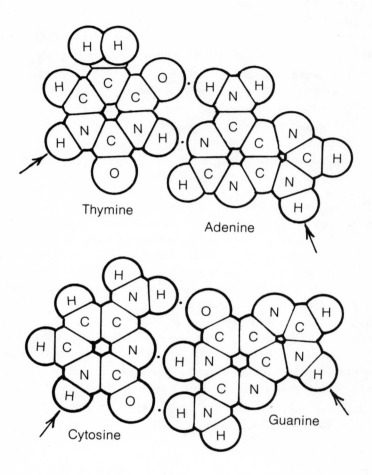

figure 4-5. The nitrogen bases which are combined with phosphoric acid and deoxyribose to form the nucleotides are planar molecules. Shown here is the lock-and-key fit of the two pairs, thymine-adenine and cytosine-guanine, held together by the weak force of hydrogen bonds (represented by single dots). A hydrogen bond can be formed between a nitrogen and an oxygen atom, between two oxygen atoms, or between two nitrogen atoms, by means of a hydrogen atom which is attached by a strong bond to one of the two atoms. Note that thymine and adenine each have two hydrogen bonding sites which can fit together, whereas cytosine and guanine each have three sites which are differently arranged in space. Therefore, the thymine "key" can fit only the adenine "lock," while the cytosine "key" can fit only the guanine "lock." The arrows indicate the point at which each nitrogen base attaches to deoxyribose in the DNA strand.

figure 4-6. The deoxyribose (top) and phosphoric acid (bottom) molecules are not planar but three-dimensional. Thus they are represented here by means of ball models so that the structures can be seen. The angles in space formed by the bonds from the deoxyribose molecule and from the phosphorus atom (P) are such that, with proper rotation of the bonds, a spiral or helical backbone for the DNA strand is formed. The twist and diameter of the spiral is just right to hold the A-T and C-G hydrogen-bonded pairs like a stack of flat pancakes up the center of the two-stranded DNA double helix. A nitrogen base (A, T, C, or G) attaches to the deoxyribose carbon atom at *A*. The deoxyribose attaches to two phosphate group (PO₄) oxygen atoms at *B* and *C*. The connections of two deoxyribose molecules to the phosphate are at *D* and *E*.

up at rates of from hundreds to thousands of nucleotides per second. The probability of error at a particular point is estimated to be as low as one in 100 million or one in a billion. High accuracy is, of course, vitally important for inheritance. The achievement of this accuracy at such high rates is truly amazing.

6. The nucleotides are brought into the DNA synthesis process in the form of energy-rich triphosphate compounds. The formation of each of these involves a dozen or so chemical steps, each one catalyzed by a different specific enzyme molecule made up of hundreds of amino acid molecules.

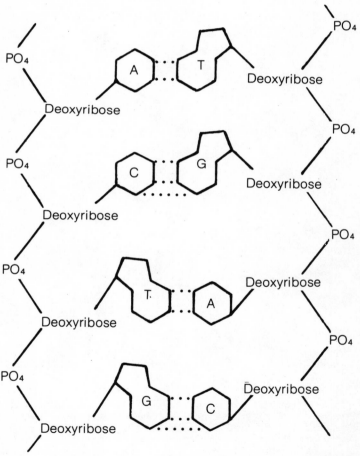

figure 4-7. The phosphate-deoxyribose backbones of two DNA strands hold their attached nitrogen bases in proper position so that complementary bases A and T or C and G on opposite strands can form hydrogen-bonded pairs. The coded information in a gene is contained in the sequence of the nucleotides which act as letters in a four-letter alphabet. Each phosphate-deoxyribose-nitrogen base unit is called a nucleotide.

figure 4-8. A model showing the actual shape of the DNA double helix as presently understood.

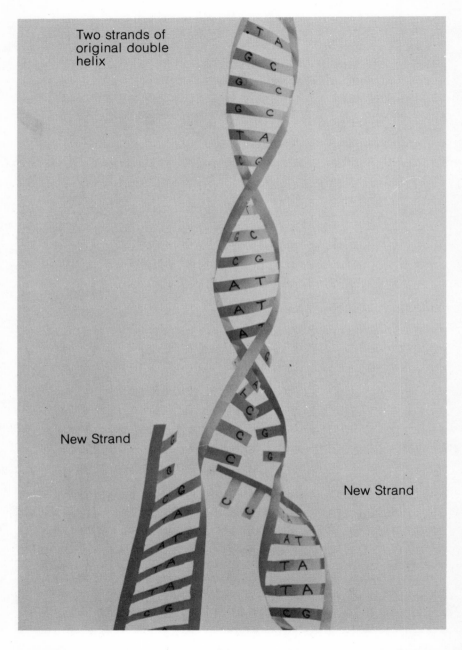

Two strands of original double helix

New Strand

New Strand

figure 4-9. When the two-stranded DNA helix is replicated prior to cell division, the two DNA strands partially unwind and separate in a process that is only vaguely understood. The two old strands serve as templates on which the new strands are formed.

This abbreviated description of the process by which the DNA molecule is copied introduces us to the fantastic complexity of structures and activities in the cell connected with inheritance. We can begin to appreciate in some small degree the infinite knowledge and power of God revealed in the biblical creation account: "And the LORD God formed man of the dust of the ground, and breathed into his nostrils the breath of life; and man became a living soul" (Gen. 2:7).

Transcription of RNA upon DNA templates

1. The genetic information contained in the nucleotide sequence of DNA is not directly translated into the amino acid sequences of protein molecules. Instead, DNA serves as a template upon which a similarly constructed RNA (ribonucleic acid) molecule is formed.

2. The RNA molecule is a chain of nucleotides very similar to DNA, except that for the sugar deoxyribose is substituted ribose, and uridine is substituted for thymidine. Thus the four RNA nucleotides are:

nucleotide name	symbol
Adenosine-5′-phosphate	A
Uridine-5′-phosphate	U
Guanosine-5′-phosphate	G
Cytidine-5′-phosphate	C

3. Hydrogen bonded pairs are formed as follows:

Nucleotides in DNA chain: A T G C

Nucleotides in RNA chain: U A C G

Thus DNA can serve as a template to direct the formation of a precisely ordered complementary RNA chain.

4. When RNA is produced in a cell, normally one gene at a time, or a small group of closely related genes called an operon, is transcribed from the DNA chain. A gene is a section of DNA chain containing on the average from 600 to 1,800 nucleotides. The principal enzyme involved is RNA polymerase. This is a complex protein molecule formed of six separate, folded amino acid chains containing a total of about 4,700 amino acid molecules. One of these chains, actually itself a protein molecule called the sigma-factor, reads a start signal on the DNA chain. Then there is an entirely separate protein, the rho-factor, which stops the transcription when one gene or operon has been copied from DNA to RNA.

For each gene, just one of the two complementary DNA chains is transcribed to RNA. Some unknown mechanism determines the correct chain to transcribe. The process of transcription may be represented as follows:

DNA double helix {
-T-A-T-C-G-G-T-A-C-   The "+" chain to be transcribed

· · · · · · · · ·

-A-T-A-G-C-C-A-T-G-   The "-" chain not to be transcribed

+ A, U, G, and C, catalyzed by
RNA polymerase and controled by
↓ sigma- and rho-factors

RNA chain-A-U-A-G-C-C-A-U-G-

This RNA is called "messenger RNA" (mRNA), because it transmits the instructions in a DNA gene to the places in the cell where protein molecules are being constructed.

RNA in the synthesis of proteins

1. The four nucleotides—A, U, G, and C—contained in the mRNA chain serve as letters in a special alphabet. The letters of this alphabet are used in a code which contains three-letter words called "codons." Using a four-letter alphabet, there are 4x4x4 = 64 possible three-letter words or codons. Scientists have established that of the 64 possible codons, 61 are code for particular amino acids of the 20 amino acids used in proteins. The remaining three codons serve as "stop" signals. Thus for each of the 20 amino acids there are from one to as many as six codons. The code is therefore said to be redundant, because some of the amino acids are coded by more than one codon.

2. If we examine our sample portion of an mRNA molecule and compare the nucleotide sequence with the codons for the different amino acids, we will find that it contains three codons for three different amino acids:

A - U - A - G - C - C - A - U - G -
codon for   codon for   codon for
isoleucine   alanine   methionine

Thus this sequence of nine nucleotides in the mRNA molecule codes for the insertion in a protein molecule of the three amino acids isoleucine, alanine, and methionine, in that order.

3. But how is the coded information in the mRNA molecule actually translated into a newly constructed protein chain? The answer to this question is as yet only partially understood, but current knowledge indicates that this translation is accomplished by a complex and very efficient process involving the action of many very complicated and highly specific enzyme molecules, which are protein molecules that are themselves coded

for in the DNA and were constructed by the very same process of translation from mRNA to finished protein molecule.

Before continuing our story of protein synthesis, let us take an overview of the sequence of processes which leads from the DNA in a cell to DNA in new cells to mRNA to newly constructed protein molecules. Observe that this is a kind of manufacturing flow chart in which all of the stages fit into a cyclic system. All stages are dependent upon other stages. DNA is required for the manufacture of protein and protein is required for the manufacture of DNA. In fact, protein molecules (enzymes) are required in every one of the stages. Yet the design information for construction of each enzyme is stored in the DNA molecules.

Moreover, each of these molecules, DNA, mRNA, and enzymes, are very complex, large molecules. The average protein molecule is a chain of 200 to 600 amino acid residues which is coded for in one gene in the DNA molecule. Since the codon for one amino acid consists of three nucleotide "letters," the average gene contains 600 to 1800 nucleotides. Some enzymes are much larger than the average. For example, the two enzymes which superintend the replication of DNA and the transcription

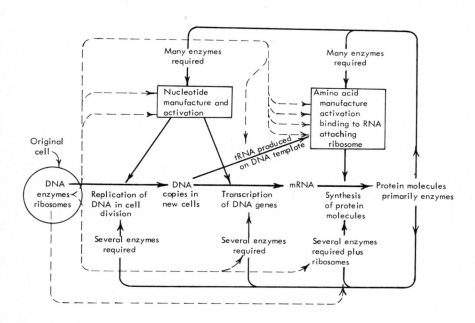

figure 4-10. Flow chart, greatly simplified, showing the interdependent factors involved in replication of DNA, transcription to RNA, and translation of the genetic code in the production of enzymes (protein molecules).

from DNA to RNA, called DNA polymerase and RNA polymerase, contain about 1,100 and 4,700 amino acid residues, respectively. RNA polymerase is particularly complex, consisting of six separate peptide chains which fold up into unique shapes and then fit together to form the complete enzyme molecule.

The Psalmist was truly speaking wisdom when he said, "I will praise thee; for I am fearfully and wonderfully made: marvellous are thy works; and that my soul knoweth right well" (Psalm 139:14). Do not the facts of molecular biology powerfully support the biblical assertion that God designed and created all living things? Yet materialist scientists zealously search for some hypothetical scenario for the purely chemical origin of molecular genetics by chance, without any intelligent design or purpose. The creationist is fully justified in rejecting such theories because they are contrary to the Scriptures, arising from a materialist philosophy or faith, and are scientifically unfounded, not capable of being corroborated by the methods of experimental science.

Building a Protein Molecule

Let us return now to the synthesis of proteins in living cells. The mRNA molecule transcribed from a DNA gene contains the instructions for arranging the amino acids in the chain of a specific kind of protein. But the actual construction of the protein molecule is carried out by an exceedingly complex cellular constituent called a ribosome, of which there may be thousands in one cell.

Ribosomes are constructed of some 55 different protein molecules combined in a very specific structure with a roughly equal weight of special kinds of RNA molecules called ribosomal RNA (rRNA). It is the complex ribosome which attaches to an mRNA molecule, moves along its chain of codons, and constructs a protein molecule in accordance with the information contained in the codons. Each codon, you will recall, orders the attachment of a particular amino acid molecule at a particular point in the protein chain.

But how is the codon command translated into the addition of the proper amino acid to the chain? There are no known specific attractions between amino acid molecules and the nucleotide codons of mRNA. The solution of this problem is provided by special RNA molecules called "transfer RNA" (tRNA). Transfer RNA molecules are relatively small, containing only about 77 nucleotides. There are one or more special tRNA molecules for each of the twenty amino acids found in proteins. At one end of the tRNA molecule is an anti-codon for the amino acid it is designed to transfer. The amino acid molecule is activated by high-energy ATP and then attached to the other end of the tRNA by a strong bond formed under the direction of a special enzyme which recognizes and operates only for one amino acid and its tRNA molecule.

Once the tRNA is attached to its amino acid, its anti-codon for that amino acid is attracted to a corresponding codon in the mRNA molecule. The ribosome moves along the mRNA strand, building a protein chain in accordance with the instructions contained in the codons of the mRNA. Molecules of tRNA with their attached amino acids are attracted by their anti-codons to corresponding codons in the mRNA molecule. When the ribosome comes to a particular codon, it binds the growing protein chain to the amino acid. This action is catalyzed by a special enzyme, as is the removal of the tRNA molecule. Thus the protein chain grows by this stepwise process at the rate of 20 to 40 amino acid residues per second.

It should be emphasized that the foregoing, including the diagram, gives a highly simplified and incomplete picture of a most complex network of cell activities which are only partially understood. In particular, the exact structure and mode of operation of the ribosome in protein synthesis are almost entirely unknown. The ribosome is so complex that its three-dimensional structure will probably never be completely elucidated.

So we see that there is much mystery still remaining about protein synthesis in living cells. Yet enough is known about this most complex process to make clear the fact that cycles of operations are involved all of which are in some way dependent upon the others. So which came first, DNA or protein? Furthermore, each protein synthesis is controlled by a promoter-repressor system or some other means which certainly would be unnecessary without the synthesis process. Yet it is difficult to imagine how a process to synthesize an enzyme would be useful without a control mechanism to turn it on and off at the proper times.

A Library in a Molecule

As we close this discussion of molecular genetics, let us ask how much information can be carried by the DNA molecules in a cell.[10] The DNA of the intestinal bacterium, *Escherichia coli*, contains roughly three million three-letter codons. Thus, to describe the amino acid sequences of the proteins of this bacterium, plus other information contained in the DNA, would require three volumes of 1000 pages each. And this still would not describe the actual structure of the cell independently of a previously existing *E. coli* cell.

Human DNA contains about two billion codons. Printed as three-letter words, these would fill a library of 2,000 volumes of 1,000 pages each, with 1,000 words on each page! And this still, as far as actual evidence is concerned, would not describe the actual structure of the human body, apart from a previously existing living cell. The original fertilized cell from which the individual organism develops comes equipped in advance with the DNA plus many essential enzymes, ribosomes, and other necessary organelles, as well as the original structure of that cell. Without any of these factors preexisting, the individual will not develop.

The Materialist's Dilemma

The most vexing dilemma facing materialist scientists rests exactly on this point: Life rides on complex protein molecules the design of which is coded by DNA molecules which depend upon those same protein molecules for their production. How could one originate without the other? Furthermore, the production processes and the control mechanisms are so interrelated that one could not be useful without the other. How could such a system originate except as a complete, integrated system? Finally, how could the code and the coded messages originate spontaneously from chaos?

If one's philosophy is materialism, he must believe materialistic answers exist for these questions. Thus far scientific search for such answers has proven futile. But if one's philosophy is biblical theism, the Genesis record of creation provides the answers, and the data of molecular biology lead the Bible-believing student of science to give honor and glory to God the Creator.

"Known unto God are all his works from the beginning of the world" (Acts 15:18). "The works of the LORD are great, sought out of all them that have pleasure therein" (Psalm 111:2).

Mutations[11]

What is a gene mutation? It is the alteration in any way of the sequence of nucleotides in a gene in the long DNA molecule. This can result from the alteration of just one of the 18- to 54,000 atoms that make up the average gene. The types of mutations which have been observed include changing one nucleotide to another nucleotide or to another kind of compound, adding one or more nucleotides, or deleting one or more nucleotides. If such a mutation occurs, the code message is changed, and the protein manufacturing system of the cell produces a protein molecule which is different from the original design.

As a consequence the protein will function differently in the cell or may not function at all. The cell may function differently, poorly, or not at all. The tissues constructed of the mutated kind of cell may be distorted or non-functional. The organism may be weakened in some way, die, or never achieve life. The mutation is correspondingly said to be either deleterious or lethal.

Gene mutations occur accidentally by natural processes in living organisms and can likewise be induced in the laboratory by the influence of chemicals or radiation. They are detected by their effect upon the bodily form or structure of plants and animals, upon their behavior, and upon their internal chemistry. In nature, mutations are relatively infrequent, but they do occur. What is their effect upon plants and animals? Have mutations been observed to improve the organisms, or are they normally deleterious or lethal?

In reply to these questions it can be affirmed that the vast majority of mutations are either deleterious or lethal. The mutated individual is either weaker than the wild variety or cannot live. Theodosius Dobzhansky, a renowned geneticist, believes that less than one percent of all mutations are favorable, and biologist Julian Huxley has suggested a figure of only one out of a thousand. Dobzhansky says, "Most mutants which arise in any organism are more or less disadvantageous to their possessors. The classical mutants obtained in Drosophila (fruit fly) show deterioration, breakdown, and disappearance of some organs." To be specific, some of the mutations observed in Drosophila include absence of eyes, change in size, shape and veining of wings, and changed eye color. In human beings, mutant genes cause several kinds of color blindness, defective enamel and other abnormalities of the teeth, hemophilia, and other undesirable traits.

Evidence from horticulture reinforces the principle that mutations are normally weaker than the parent. Mutant rose varieties produced by neutron radiation, while possessing certain esthetically desirable traits, were always found to be less vigorous than the original stock. This is generally the case in both horticulture and animal husbandry. The stock is bred for traits which the breeder considers desirable, and a few of these traits result from gene mutations. Under human supervision on the farm, the new varieties are successful. However, allowed to breed wild, the plant or animal always tends to revert to the wild variety.

In nature some mutations die out because they cannot reproduce themselves. The seedless orange is a mutant which man has learned to save by growing new seedless orange trees from cuttings. The grower cuts a limb from a seedless orange tree and grafts it to a regular orange tree. Without this help, however, the seedless orange tree would have died out without reproducing itself.

Genetic research with bacteria has provided the greatest amount of data on mutations, because bacteria are easy to grow and investigate. Some mutant forms are more viable under specific conditions—for example, in the presence of antibiotics. Bacterial strains resistant to antibiotics have made life difficult for the medical profession in recent years. There is always the tendency, however, to revert to the wild strain in the absence of the special conditions.

Enzymes by Mutation?

That genetic variations including mutations do occur in populations of organisms is a fact which we can all observe. But the changes which occur are always variations on a preexisting theme, and they are limited in scope. The horse continues as horse, the fruit fly as fruit fly, *E. coli* as *E. coli*, etc. Recalling the enzyme and control systems involved in protein synthesis, consider whether mutations could originate them.

The bacterium *E. coli* uses the enzyme β-galactosidase to split the milk sugar, lactose, into its two constituent sugars, galactose and glucose which the bacterium can digest. When glucose is already present, it fits into a special slot in the enzyme and changes the enzyme's shape so that it cannot split lactose and so produce an excess of glucose. When glucose is absent, the enzyme is left free to split more lactose.

If random mutations were responsible for the design of this system, the lactose-splitting function certainly had to evolve first. Then if glucose were plentiful, the enzyme system would make the cell inefficient by continually producing large quantities of excess glucose from lactose. The most likely change to occur by mutation and be selected would be a single mutation to destroy the lactose-splitting function, a result easily accomplished by any one of many possible changes in the gene for β-galactosidase.

This would surely happen long before the complex series of mutations could occur to produce the clever and complicated control system described above. Then if glucose again became scarce, the enzyme would have to be re-evolved, or the bacterial strain would perish. Hopefully, upon re-evolving, by trial and error mutations, it would also by accident have the control feature incorporated. Does this sound like science fiction?

Or perhaps we might hypothesize a long period of fluctuating glucose supply with fluctuating lactose-splitting capacity for the enzyme, not total destruction. And in the meantime a lengthy succession of random mutations affecting the backside of the enzyme molecule finally produces a slot into which glucose can fit to deactivate the enzyme. The whole scheme is completely speculative and highly unlikely to the point of incredibility. This is the same type of reasoning which Darwin made popular with *The Origin of Species*, full of assumed conditions, processes, and imaginations. And when one's speculations have been recorded, the origin of the initial lactose-splitting enzyme remains unexplained, as does also the origin of the fantastically complex set of enzyme systems for the metabolism of the glucose produced by the lactose-splitting enzyme.

Indeed, just as it is not possible to deal independently with the origins of an enzyme system and its control mechanisms, it is also not possible to consider any enzyme system or function of DNA or RNA entirely independently of the whole cell and the entire organisms. The observed facts are most reasonably understood in terms of created design systems, rather than as products of mutation and natural selection.

Recent Enzyme Research

The reports of recent work with an *E. coli* strain lacking the enzyme β-galactosidase indicate that under special conditions the strain could undergo a series of five mutations which restored the ability to digest lactose. It is reported that a floating or inactive gene was transformed by the mutations so that it could code for the production of an enzyme possessing some ability to metabolize lactose.[12] This is interpreted as the production of new genetic design information by means of random mutations and natural selection. However, more research will be required to determine exactly what has happened in this case. One important question is, Was the floating gene one that was originally designed to code for the production of the enzyme but deactivated by a few deleterious mutations?

Another recent investigation dealt with a bacterium which is able to extract needed nitrogen from a two-carbon compound called acetamide. Mutant strains were obtained in which the enzyme responsible for the nitrogen metabolism has been modified so that it is able to use the four-carbon compound butyramide, a five-carbon compound, valeramide, and the even larger molecule, phenylacetamide.[13] Apparently the enzyme molecule has been modified so as to lengthen a groove into which the longer-chained amides can fit. But the basic function of the enzyme, i.e., the use of amides as a source of nitrogen and/or carbon, remains the same. Furthermore, the authors point out that the special bacterial strains which they have developed in the laboratory, because they lack certain essential characteristics, could not survive in a natural ecosystem. Thus the natural evolutionary origin of the altered enzymes was not demonstrated.

Summary of Mutation Effects

The fact is that scientists, after many years of work with fruit flies and other kinds of organisms, have not yet succeeded in transforming one kind of creature into another kind. For example, the bacterial strains discussed above are still classified as the same species. Ernst Mayr of Harvard, an international authority, in his 1970 book, *Populations, Species, and Evolution*, deals only with types of variation which are trivial compared with what is required by evolutionary theory. Even some scientists who believe in evolution admit that the limited changes observed are not a scientific basis for postulating the evolution of all forms of life, ever upward from simple to complex, by means of gene mutation and natural selection.

The fossil evidence of the numbers and kinds of extinct life forms, together with the historical evidence of the gradual extinction of many kinds of plants and animals, suggests that the natural process is "devolution" rather than evolution. The total diversity of genes in the world of living things is decreasing, not increasing. Every species or variety that becomes extinct represents a disappearance of genes from the world. Many species are facing extinction today, largely as a result of man's dislocations of the natural order. Every species, including man, is accumulating an increasing "genetic load" of mutated genes which are unfavorable. Natural selection operates to weed out damaged genes, but when they become established in the population, the effect is degenerative.

This degenerative course in nature is to be expected from the exquisitely complex organization of the genetic information contained in the DNA molecule. Accidental changes in the DNA molecules of any creature's germ cells will almost always be disruptive and destructive, or at best neutral. The proposal that random, accidental changes in the nucleotide sequence of the DNA molecule, that is, gene mutations, could be responsible for the innovative design of new and improved cell chemistry, new cells, tissues, organs, or organisms is comparable to suggesting that a defective television set could be improved by firing a bullet into the solid-state circuitry. The fact that one bullet might accidentally jar a loose connection back into contact could not possibly overcome the fact that the next ten thousand bullets will certainly totally destroy the television set.

The observed genetic degeneration of natural populations agrees with the biblical record of the divine curse which was imposed upon the entire creation as a consequence of Adam's sin. The original creation was perfect, and this included the original gene pool of every kind of living creature created by God. When the curse of Genesis 3 became effective, degenerative influences immediately began to affect every creature. That the consequences have not been even more disastrous can be attributed both to the marvelous design of the mechanism of inheritance and to the gracious providence of God.

Where Does Life Come From?[14]

Philosophers and scientists have for centuries speculated about the possibility that life can originate apart from reproduction by existing life. Greek and Egyptian scholars thought that mice, frogs, or worms came up from the ground. Some scientists in the past have believed in the idea of spontaneous generation, that life could suddenly appear. It was thought, for example, that pond water produced frogs. One man reported that he had found a way to develop mice through spontaneous generation, placing some wheat, cheese, and dirty rags together in a jar. After a time, he found that the jar contained mice. No doubt the experiment would have proven negative had he put a lid on the jar.

The spontaneous generation view was popular until the excellent work by Francisco Redi, an Italian gentleman of science who began a study of maggots. People of his day believed that maggots sprouted spontaneously from meat. This would not have been actual *spontaneous* generation, for the cells in the meat had been living material, but it would have been on the order of spontaneous generation, having entailed the rapid conversion of one creature's substance into another complex creature.

Redi showed that meat left open to the air was soon infested with maggots, whereas maggots did not appear in meat loosely covered with a cloth. This led subsequently to the discovery of the life cycle of the fly which lays eggs on the meat. The eggs hatch into the larvae form which are called maggots. The cycle closes when the maggots are transformed into a new generation of flies. These findings resulted ultimately in the rejection of the concept of spontaneous generation for large creatures.

When Leeuwenhoek discovered microscopic organisms and their universal presence became known, many thought they arose by spontaneous generation. Scientists observed that almost any sterilized nutrient medium left exposed to the air soon was filled with millions of microorganisms. Louis Pasteur demonstrated, however, that the organisms were introduced into the system riding on air-born dust particles. He established this by placing nutrient broth in a "Pasteur flask," a flask connected to the air only through a very narrow, sharply curved tube. Air-born dust and bacteria were trapped in the sharp bend, and the broth remained sterile indefinitely although the air had free access to it. Only the bacteria on the dust were excluded. Pasteur's work permanently settled the question of spontaneous generation. All scientists agree that it is not occurring in the present world.

Spontaneous Generation in a Primeval World?

Even before interest in theories of organic evolution became widespread, astronomers and philosophers were speculating about how the solar system and the earth originated. Not believing the Bible, they presumed that random physical processes were responsible. Various forms of condensing gas-dust-cloud nebular theories have proven the most popular. (See Chapter 6.) These theories, combined with observations of the gases that exist in space, have led to speculation about the primeval atmosphere of the earth.

In order to construct a plausible scheme for the chemical origin of life, it was necessary to show how the small building blocks of life, the biomonomers such as amino acids, sugars, and nitrogen bases, could have formed. (The nitrogen bases are the central constituents of the nucleotides, A, T, U, G, and C.) Some of these biomonomers can be produced from a mixture of such simple gases as water vapor, methane, ammonia, and hydrogen if radiant or electrical energy is supplied, as shown by biochemist Stanley Miller in 1953.[15] However, the presence of oxygen gas results in the destruction of the biomonomers. Therefore, it is reasoned, the original earth atmosphere must have been a reducing atmosphere, essentially free of oxygen.

The Russian scientist, A. I. Oparin, began such speculations in 1924, concurrently with the British biologist, atheist, and Communist, J. B. S. Haldane.[16] Oparin continued to develop his theories of spontaneous generation during the thirties and forties while also becoming a principal supporter of the now-disgraced Russian Lamarkian biologist, Lysenko.[17] Western scientists still revere Oparin as the father of their faith in abiogenesis (the generation of life without preexisting life). They continue the struggle to make their theory seem reasonable, but all is speculation because they cannot repeat the past earth history and spontaneous generation which they hypothesize. One cannot be sure what the early earth was like. There is no conclusive evidence for a reducing atmosphere on the earth at any time. Some scientists consider that the weight of evidence is against the idea. Nevertheless, much research is in progress designed to establish a possible course for the origin of life by spontaneous generation.

The most widely accepted scenario has electrical discharges providing energy to produce simple energy-rich compounds and amino acids in an ancient reducing atmosphere. Sugars and nitrogen bases which are constituents of nucleotides were formed in the oceans. Since the hypothetical reducing atmosphere would be transparent to solar ultraviolet radiation which would destroy these biomonomers, the initial reactions are now supposed by some to have occurred in the lower atmosphere so that the products could diffuse down to the oceans quickly.

It has been suggested that brown tars formed in the atmosphere and coated the oceans, preventing the ultraviolet light from penetrating the waters. Then, in the oceans or other bodies of water, the biomonomers finally linked up in chains to form biopolymers—DNA and protein molecules—which are the basis of life chemistry.

This all may sound plausible to one who desires to believe, and it is true that reactions have been demonstrated experimentally which produce many of the necessary biomonomers under the hypothetical primeval earth conditions. Nevertheless, plausible syntheses have yet to be discovered for many important biomonomers, as well as biopolymers, and there are numerous theoretical difficulties yet unsolved.

Some of the problems for theories of abiogenesis under the conditions postulated in the primeval earth are the following:[18]

1. No satisfactory syntheses discovered for:
   a. Five of the twenty necessary amino acids
   b. Fatty acids
   c. The sugar ribose
   d. Nucleosides (nitrogen base + sugar) and nucleotides (nucleoside + phosphate)
   e. DNA and RNA
2. Many of the necessary compounds are rather unstable, making it difficult to explain how adequate concentrations could accumulate.
   a. Sugars (notably ribose)
   b. About half of the twenty amino acids
   c. Several of the nucleosides
   d. DNA and RNA

So while chemical reactions can be demonstrated which might possibly produce an ocean full of many interesting compounds connected with life, according to present scientific knowledge many essential compounds would be absent. As indicated above, the formation of the long polymers, DNA and RNA, is a very difficult problem. The synthesis of protein molecules deserves separate comment.

Proteins by Chance—Faith in the Impossible

The early schemes pictured an ocean of dilute amino acids reacting a sufficiently long time for the amino acids to link up to form long protein chains in the equilibrium reaction mixture. But much free energy must be added to make a protein chain. Therefore at equilibrium the concentration of a particular protein chain of 100 amino acid residues would be only one molecule in every 10^{32} universes! Consequently it was necessary to seek some non-equilibrium situation in which activated molecules react to form the polymers.

Recent research showed that if an amino acid is combined with adenylic acid to form an aminoacyl adenylate, this product when shaken in aqueous solution with Montmorillonite clay adsorbs on the clay particles and polymerizes to form chains containing up to 56 amino acid residues.[19] This is the closest approach thus far to spontaneous production of protein-like molecules in aqueous solution, and it would seem to offer hope that a simple enzyme molecule of, say, 100 amino acid residues could form spontaneously. But there are serious problems. The first problem is that there is as yet no known plausible way in which aminoacyl adenylates, the necessary building blocks, could form spontaneously in the ancient oceans.

The second problem is one of statistical probability. Let us assume that a set of conditions is found under which mixed amino acid chains (called peptide chains) containing 100 amino acid units can form. To get the life process started, it would be necessary to produce such a chain that would be a protein with the properties of an enzyme to, for example, catalyze the synthesis of itself according to the information coded in a DNA or RNA molecule. Using the twenty commonly occurring amino acids, any one of the twenty kinds can be placed in each of the 100 places in the molecule. Therefore, the total number of different 100-unit protein molecules which can be constructed is equal to 20 multiplied by itself 100 times, or $20^{100} = 10^{130}$. This is the number "1" followed by 130 zeros.

Let us explain this using a hypothetical protein chain just three units long. Let us assume that there are just two different amino acids, A and B, which can be put in the three positions in the chain. Then the possible different chains would be A-A-A, B-A-A, A-B-A, A-A-B, B-B-A, B-A-B,

A-B-B, and B-B-B. This is a total of eight different amino acid sequences reading from left to right. This total number can be calculated by multiplying together the numbers of different amino acids that can occupy the three positions in the chain. That is, $N = 2 \times 2 \times 2 = 2^3 = 8$. This is why we said that for a 100-unit chain with 20 different amino acids the number of different chains would be $20^{100} = 10^{130}$. The final change from the base 20 to the base 10 will simplify the following calculations.

Now it is known that in an enzyme molecule which performs a specific function, a certain amount of variability is allowable in the amino acid sequence without destroying the enzyme activity of the molecule. Variability in cytochrome *c* molecules, which are important enzymes found in all living things, seems to *average* about 2.7 different amino acids at each position, but 35 of the 104 positions in the amino acid chain are invariant (See Chapter 7). Let us make a generous assumption that in our hypothetical evolving enzyme molecule, an average of five different amino acids may fit into each position in our hypothetical 100-unit amino acid chain. Then the total number of enzymes that could be produced having the desired enzyme function would be $5^{100} = 10^{70}$.

We may now calculate the probability that for any new 100-unit protein molecule constructed by random process, the result would be an enzyme molecule with the desired activity. This probability will be

$$P_{\substack{\text{success in} \\ \text{one trial}}} = \frac{\text{total number of active 100-unit enzymes}}{\text{total number of 100-unit proteins}} = \frac{10^{70}}{10^{130}} = \frac{1}{10^{60}} = 10^{-60}.$$

This is a very small probability of success in any one trial construction of a protein molecule by chance. But the evolutionary argument is that even with such a small probability, given sufficient time, the number of trials will be so great that success is inevitable. Let us look at that argument.

Let us assume that one percent of the earth's atmospheric nitrogen is converted into 100-unit protein molecules. This would be about 95 pounds of protein per square foot of the earth's surface, or a total of about 1.2×10^{40} protein molecules. Let us repeat this process annually for one billion years, a total of 1.2×10^{49} trial constructions of a 100-unit protein molecule. The probability of at least one success, i.e., forming one active enzyme molecule in N trials will be

$$P_{\substack{\text{at least one} \\ \text{success in} \\ \text{N trials}}} = 1 - P_{\substack{\text{all failures} \\ \text{in N trials}}}$$

$$= 1 - (P_{\substack{\text{failure in} \\ \text{one trial}}})^N = 1 - (1 - P_{\substack{\text{success in} \\ \text{one trial}}})^N$$

Now we substitute in this formula the numerical values

$$P_{\substack{\text{success in} \\ \text{one trial}}} = 10^{-60}$$

$$N = 1.2 \times 10^{49}$$

The result is

$$P_{\substack{\text{at least one}\\\text{success in}\\\text{N trials}}} = 1 - (1-10^{-60})^{1.2 \times 10^{49}} = 1.2 \times 10^{-11} = \frac{1}{80\text{ billion}}$$

See Appendix D for development of these formulas.

Now let us visualize what this means. It means that to have just one chance in 80 billion of finding at least one accidentally formed active enzyme molecule, one would have to search through 260 trillion tons of fresh protein muck every year for one billion years! The probability of finding two of the active molecules would be about 10^{-22}, and the probability that they would be identical would be 10^{-70}. And could life start with just a single enzyme molecule? Furthermore, what is the probability that an active enzyme molecule, once formed, could find its way through thousands of miles and millions of years to that randomly formed RNA or DNA molecule which contains the code for that particular enzyme molecule's amino acid sequence, so that new copies of itself could be produced? Zero for all practical purposes.

In our probability estimate, the assumptions have all been made so as greatly to favor the successful production of our hypothetical enzyme. Nevertheless, even under the most favorable imaginable conditions the calculated probability of success is still effectively zero. Thus we see that in the real world time is *not* the "hero" who can make the impossible chemical origin of life possible.

Since it is clear, then, that complete enzyme molecules coupled with their coded DNA molecules could not come into being by chance, the theorists are forced to look for some rudimentary interaction between the amino acids and the nucleotides which make up the protein and DNA or RNA chains. They hope to find some simple interaction involving only a very few amino acids and nucleotides which could be the basis for the initial process which started coupling DNA- or RNA-coded information to the sequence of amino acids in a growing protein chain.

Professor Melvin Calvin of the University of California at Berkeley stated in his book, *Chemical Evolution* (1969), that a long-term university experimental program had been initiated to solve this problem.[20] But five years later Professor Stanley Miller at the La Jolla campus and Leslie Orgel of Salk Institute lamented in their very honest and informative book, *The Origins of Life on the Earth* (1974), that this is still the most fundamental unanswered question: "We clearly do not understand how the code originated. New ideas that can be tested experimentally are needed."[21]

In the absence of experimental demonstration that nucleotides can recognize amino acids, except through the complex mechanisms and structures available in living cells, any claim that such recognition is possible or that it did, indeed, occur in the distant past is a declaration of faith, not a scientifically supported conclusion. As we have shown, the chance chemical origin of the most fundamental process of the living cell is fantastically improbable. What of the origin of a complete living organism? Thermodynamicist Harold Morowitz estimates the probability for the origin of the smallest likely living entity by random processes.[22] He comes up with the value $10^{-340,000,000}$, i.e., the fraction $1/1000000 \ldots \ldots$ a total of 340 million zeros. Yet Dr. Morowitz and his fellow evolutionary scientists still believe that it happened!

A rather different approach to the chemical origin of life has been developed by a school of Russian investigators.[23] Karl Trincher in his book, *Biology and Information* (1965), examined the thermodynamic properties of living cells and of man-made cybernetic devices. A cybernetic device is a machine which performs complex useful functions in accordance with programmed information. He observed the following essential differences between living systems and such non-living machines:

1. The living cell exists and functions at temperatures such that its structure is thermally labile. This means that the heat motions of its atoms and molecules at those temperatures are capable of destroying the structure of the cell. Therefore, the living cell must simultaneously carry on two different sets of functions, a set of useful life functions, and a set of reconstruction activities which continually rebuild the cell structures being broken down by heat motions of the molecules.

2. If the cell ceases to operate, its structure is soon destroyed by heat motions.

3. No non-living cybernetic machine can operate at temperatures which cause its parts to break down or liquify.

4. Non-living machines do not immediately disintegrate if they are turned off and stop working.

From these and other differences between living and non-living systems Trincher concluded that we cannot artificially produce living cells by physical and chemical processes now known to science. He further concluded that when the non-living world came into existence—billions of years ago, in his opinion—at the same time living matter came into existence, perhaps even a complete biosphere of primordial organisms, and this occurred by processes unobservable in the present world. It would appear that even the scientists in Marxist Russia are being pushed to the brink of admitting divine creation.

Reflection upon the chemical and theoretical difficulties just reviewed, combined with some understanding of the complexities of the DNA-

RNA-enzyme cycles of the smallest living organisms, allows only those who possess strong materialistic faith to believe that chemical abiogenesis actually occurred. A more reasonable faith—better in agreement with the observed characteristics of living organisms—is faith in the biblical account of creation of all things by an omnipotent, omniscient, purposeful Creator.

Life in a Test Tube?

But have not recent experiments demonstrated the creation of life in a test tube? No, these experiments have only involved the use of selected parts of living cells to perform in a test tube certain basic functions of the cell. Drs. Ochoa and Kornberg mixed DNA and certain enzymes from living cells with the high-energy coupling agent, adenosine triphosphate, and the four nucleotides, A, T, C, and G. They found that the DNA was duplicated.[24]

More recently Dr. Khorana was able to synthesize the DNA gene for the transfer RNA of the amino acid, alanine, in yeast cells. He then mixed this artificial gene, containing 70 nucleotide units, with the four nucleotides A, U, C, and G, plus enzymes and the coupling agent. He obtained tRNA identical with that produced in yeast cells.

But it is plain that neither of these experiments produced life in a test tube. They merely duplicated outside of the cell basic processes which living cells carry on all the time. Furthermore, patterns and enzymes found in living cells were used. Moreover, these two processes are just two out of many thousands of chemical processes which are continually being carried on in living cells. Reexamine the diagram on page 87 which gives a highly simplified picture of just a small fraction of the chemical processes required for the life of a cell. Perhaps many parts of the chemical process networks of living cells will be reproduced experimentally in the years to come, copied by teams of very intelligent scientists using millions of dollars worth of complex scientific equipment. But this hardly encourages one to believe that the original living cells originated by chance without a designer and Creator. Just the opposite.

Mechanism in Biology: A Materialist or Theistic Concept?

Scientific discovery in the nineteenth century, leading to continually expanding knowledge of the natural world, caused many to believe that the demonstrated ability of the human mind to uncover, understand, and predict the structures and processes of material things, living and inanimate, was proof that all things including living organisms were essentially mechanisms entirely explainable in terms of physics and chemistry. The reasoning behind this conclusion which is widely held today stems from the belief that man-made machines are entirely explainable in terms of physics and chemistry. After all, the argument goes, any scientist or engineer understands the physical laws which are operative in his instruments or machines. Are these not, therefore, entirely explained by physical law? In like fashion, biochemists are able to understand the chemical and physical laws operative at many levels of complexity in living organisms, even down to the function of individual molecules. Is not this proof that life can be reduced to pure chemistry and physics?

The error of this "reductionist" view of biology has been made clear in the writings of the eminent physical chemist and philosopher, Michael Polanyi.[25] He observes that a machine or mechanism designed by man provides, by its designed structure and form, those boundary conditions which determine or control what will be accomplished in the machine through the operation of the laws of physics and chemistry. Thus, although physical law can explain the operation of a mechanism designed by man, what it cannot explain is the origin of the design and the translation of the original design blueprint into the original copy of the machine. This is because the design originated in the creative imagination of man, which is not reducible to physics and chemistry.

Moreover, at least the original copy of the machine was produced by craftsmen who could read and understand the design information. Similarly, while the chemistry and physics of many cell functions are understood, the design and origin of the living cell are not explained by physics and chemistry. As Polanyi says, "Physics is dumb without the gift of boundary conditions, forming its frame; and this frame is not determined by the laws of physics."

A specific example is afforded by the design information carried in DNA molecules. Although the chemical structure and the chemical bonds and other interactions involved in the functioning of the coded DNA molecule are at least partially understood, chemistry cannot explain the origin or content of the design information carried by the DNA. A parallel is provided by a book or newspaper. The physics and chemistry of paper, ink, and printing presses are rather well understood. But chemistry and physics do not to the slightest degree explain the origin or content of the news and editorials carried by the printed symbols on the newspaper.

Polanyi's conclusion is that "life transcends physics and chemistry." We would extend his conclusion. Just as the structural organization of man-made machines was the product of the mind of intelligent man and cannot be reduced to physics and chemistry, so the machine-like structural organization of living organisms must also have its source in a purposeful intelligence. Contrary to the common view of nineteenth and twentieth century materialists, mechanism in biology points not to purposeless evolution, but to intelligent, purposeful design—to creation.

Conclusion

Science can never discover the truth about the origin of life. It will never be possible to say, truthfully, "Science has now *proved* the special creation of all things at the beginning." It will always be equally impossible to say, truthfully, "Science has *proved* that all things have evolved from non-living material by chemical reactions, mutations, and natural selection." Genesis 2:7 tells of the source of life: "And the LORD God formed man of the dust of the ground, and breathed into his nostrils the breath of life; and man became a living soul."

Science cannot observe, experiment, and report what happened at the very beginning because those events were not observed by man and cannot be repeated by man. Repeatability is a necessary part of scientific verification. For this reason, each person must reach his own conclusion in answering questions about the origin of life.

Scientists can improvise models designed to fit as many as possible of the observed facts. The two models which have been suggested are the evolutionary model and the special creation model. Of these two, we believe that the special creation model as reported in the Bible better fits the known scientific facts. The idea that the whole universe came into being at some time in the past because a Creator made it is not only the simplest and easiest to understand, but also the most reasonable.

5
Man in His World

Man Is Different[1]

Man is different from all other creatures because he asks questions about his world and the things in that world. He uses language to ask these questions and also to find and express the answers. Man is the only cultural creature, for he alone depends upon the transmitted wisdom gained by past generations to guide and help him in the present. He alone preserves his present intellectual accomplishments and uses them in planning for the future. In all activities which characterize and distinguish man as man, he uses symbols in thinking, writing, and speaking. This special ability which separates man from the animal world is referred to by anthropologists as the ability to symbolize.

A symbol is a form that expresses meaning arbitrarily attached to it by a number of individuals. Thus, when a child's father makes the sound of "no," both father and child know what he means, for they speak the same language. A Dakota Indian father would use the sounds "sni" to express a similar negative meaning to his son, but both would understand what he meant. Only human beings communicate with each other using names to indicate specific objects and other types of words to represent actions and ideas.

All men use language and other symbols to understand their world. But since all people do not live in the same place, and their ancestors neither shared the same experiences nor spoke the same languages, they have developed different understandings of the world in which they live. Anthropologists would say that they possess different cultures. The Yir Yoront people in Australia feel they understand correctly the meaning of events occurring in their society because they believe these are reoccurrences of similar events experienced in the world of their ancestors a long, long time ago. Thus a man whose name is "Dog-chases-iguana-up-a-tree-and-barks-at-him-all-night" and is a member of the Sunlit Cloud Iguana Clan believes that his ancestor had that name and belonged to that clan. In addition, everything that happens in his life does so because it occurred in the life of his ancestor.

It seems that man has always had a curiosity about himself and his world, and for many groups such as the Yir Yoront their mythological world-view serves to satisfy this human need. It provides them with an *a priori* perspective by which they interpret the objects and events which they observe around them. They believe that their whole world is living and that it is understood by becoming a living part of it. Like many others, the Yir Yoront find that their roles in life, their values and goals for the present and the future are stated clearly in the teachings, both formal and informal, which stem from their religion.

Science and the Study of Man

The biblical record of pre-Flood civilization contained in the fourth chapter of Genesis tells of a rather highly-developed technology. It is even possible that foundations of a scientific understanding of natural phenomena were also laid in that early era. The Jewish historian Josephus states that Cain invented a system of weights and measures thousands of years before the founding of Greece, and that the godly descendents of Seth studied the movements of the heavenly bodies. Much of the culture, technology, and scientific knowledge of that former age must have been carried through the Flood by Noah and his family. The sudden or seemingly rootless appearance of highly developed civilizations in the post-Flood archaeological record of some 3000 years before Christ is in agreement with this view as will be shown later in this chapter.

There is considerable evidence that the ancient Babylonians and Egyptians possessed the knowledge of mathematics and astronomy and put this knowledge to practical use in the construction of the pyramids and other great civil engineering projects, as well as in a program of accurate mapping of the earth's surface. Nevertheless, the pagan religions introduced false ideas into the post-Flood cultures, with the probable result that man's understanding of the natural world was corrupted by mythology.

It was the Greek natural philosophers of the sixth century before Christ who imparted to western civilization the foundations of a rational way of understanding the natural world. It is true that they believed in a beginning of nature that was separate from the Infinite and Eternal, but they very sensibly did not try to make the order of nature explain how it came into existence.

To these early Greeks something in nature like a storm was not to be understood as the anger of a god, but as an impersonal force that could be seen. The observer must be objective. That is, he must keep himself and his desires from influencing what he sees. Today this way of viewing our world is an important element of what is called the scientific method.

The Scientific Method

The "scientific method" is an expression with some variable meaning which refers to the processes by which people called scientists systematically increase their knowledge and understanding of the natural world or find the solutions to specific problems. Let us discuss the scientific method under three stages.

Stage one ideally begins with learning all one can about a particular subject of interest. A good scientist must be a good observer who collects information carefully. He also studies reports of observations made by other scientists. The terms "raw data" or "brute facts" have sometimes been applied to the primary observations or measurements made in scientific investigation. Actually, however, there is no such thing as a "brute fact." All data in science is mixed with the theories, opinions, prejudices, assumptions, and interpretations held by scientists. It is sometimes difficult to perceive new or significant information because these other things cloud the mind of the observer.

Stage two ideally involves studying and reflecting on the information which has been collected and attempting to discover some common pattern or elements which suggest a hypothesis. A classic example of this procedure may be found in Kepler's years of trial and error fitting of different hypothetical orbits to the observational data which had been painstakingly collected over a previous span of years by Tycho Brahe. He finally hit upon the three descriptive laws of planetary motion which are known by his name.

In reality, however, there is no single mode of origination of scientific hypotheses. It may be a single unusual, or surprising, or perhaps very common fact that sets the scientist thinking. He will try to come up with some idea that can explain the facts that interest him. Or he may have a vague hunch or a flash of intuition, a wild new idea which is really "far out." A suitable scientific hypothesis may come from any source whatsoever. Usually considerable factual knowledge and mature reflection underlie the formation of such a hypothesis, but a junior high student or a science fiction writer might stumble on an idea which revolutionizes the understanding of a scientific problem. A good scientist is able to break his thinking free from old assumptions and theories. He is an independent thinker.

In any event the quality of a scientific hypothesis is not determined by its source or mode of formation, which depend upon the mysteries of creative human imagination and cannot be subjected to logical analysis. What criterion, then, determines the quality of a scientific hypothesis? The criterion is testability or falsifiability.[2] A good hypothesis must be capable of being subjected to tests which, depending upon the results, may either falsify the hypothesis or leave it standing. The more potentially falsifiable consequences a hypothesis has, the greater is its value as a scientific theory, the greater is its content of information about the real world. The fewer the potentially falsifiable consequences, the poorer an idea is as a scientific hypothesis. If there are no possibly falsifiable consequences, the hypothesis is not scientific. It is in the realm of metaphysics, i.e., of philosophy or religion.

The third stage, which is the essence of the scientific method, follows from the falsifiability criterion. The hypothesis must be subjected to the severest possible critical testing to see if it can be falsified, i.e., disproved. First, the logical consequences of the new hypothesis are deduced. Predictions are made that certain things must or must not occur under certain conditions if the hypothesis is true. Then experiments or tests are carried out to see if the predictions are correct. If the hypothesis passes one or a series of such tests, it stands as corroborated, but not "proved."

A single test may disprove a hypothesis but it cannot prove it to be correct. A given series of tests may corroborate the hypothesis, but subsequent experiments under different conditions may disprove it. Therefore, there is no absolute knowledge in science. There is only progress—hopefully—toward a more complete and accurate understanding of the natural world. But at any time current scientific opinion may be overthrown by new observations, by better theories.

Indeed, the deeper physicists delve into the structure of matter, the more mysterious reality becomes. The forces that hold the atomic nucleus together, for example, may be described by quantum mechanical equations, but their origin and ultimate nature remain unknown to science.

Is there, then, any source of absolute truth if science cannot attain to it? The only channel of absolute truth is divine revelation. "Known unto God are all his works from the beginning of the world" (Acts 15:18). And in connection with the mystery of the nuclear forces just referred to, God reveals their origin to be Jesus Christ: "And he is before all things, and by him all things consist" (Colossians 1:17). This ultimate knowledge of the universe could not be discovered by scientific research, nor can it be subjected to experimental test. It had to be revealed by the Creator and it must be received by faith.

The scientific method can be strictly applied only to the present observable world. The experimental sciences such as physics, chemistry, and genetics, are based upon direct experimentation in the laboratory. And the experiments can be repeated as often as desired. Astronomy, on the other hand, is an observational science the objects of which are very remote and cannot be controlled under laboratory conditions. Also, some of the observations of astronomy cannot be repeated. In biochemistry the chemical structures and events inside of microscopic cells are studied. Thus the data of biochemistry is often indirect, for the objects being studied are too small to see. However, the experiments are controlled and repeatable in the laboratory. In science if the tests are indirect or the data is limited, we are cautious about accepting the conclusions. More data is usually sought on which to base firmer conclusions.

In the case of such sciences as geology and paleontology, the rocks and fossils are objects which can be examined and tested in the laboratory or out in the field. But the events that produced the rocks, and the lives of the creatures that left the fossils were far in the past. The actual events of earth history were not seen by scientists, nor can they be repeated. Scientists believe that by studying the rocks and the fossils they can tell something about the past events and the creatures when they were living. However, the rock and fossil data are susceptible to many different interpretations which depend upon the presuppositions of the interpreter. Furthermore, since hypotheses about prehistory are not subject to falsification as are the theories of the experimental sciences, there is a much stronger tendency to accumulate *ad hoc* hypotheses to shore up evolutionary theories whenever new data does not seem to fit them.

Finally, in connection with the applicability of the scientific method, the validity of viewing man merely as an object in nature arises. In science man tries to observe and record in a detached way, looking at nature with an open mind, without letting his own feelings affect his observations. Is it possible, however, for man to examine himself as impersonally as he would a rock or flower? Possible or not, it almost seems as if underlying the evolutionary explanation of man's origin is an actual desire to understand him as merely a part of nature. Thus man is assumed to be simply another part of nature which was brought into being by changes in natural conditions which existed before man appeared.

Is completely objective scientific study of man possible? It is true that study of the human body, for example, has led to large advances in medicine. But this kind of progress of knowledge is entirely apart from, and has probably actually been hindered by, the assumption man is merely an evolutionary development in nature, fully explainable in terms of the laws that govern atoms, electricity, and magnetism.

A Modern Myth

Come with us, if you will, through the looking glass into the strange country of Evolutiana. The landscape we view is wild and barren. No sign of life can be seen. The atmosphere is suffocating, without ozone, and one breath makes us feel giddy. We quickly don our oxygen masks and start to explore the rough terrain. Look, there's a pool of water. Stooping down, we look into its depths. It is not pure water but seems to contain dissolved chemicals which are filtering down out of the atmosphere. We examine the pool using the super-microscope from our portable laboratory, which magnifies a hundred million times to enable us to see atoms and molecules.

We observe no living organisms, only the mad dance of trillions of various molecules colliding, combining, breaking up, recombining in other myriad forms. There are some larger molecules forming, too. Say, look at that large molecule of several thousand atoms. It has just reproduced itself. Now there are two of them ... three ... four! We watch, spellbound, as the strange new kind of molecule multiplies. The new molecules seem to be able to break up smaller molecules in the pond and appropriate their atoms to build copies of themselves. Now there are several other kinds of large molecules which are doing the same thing and are linking up with the first kind. They are making larger and larger globs of molecules. The globs are dividing to make copies of themselves. Look, there is a living cell! They are dividing, too.

Soon the pond is filled with the newly evolved cells. Some of the cells when they divide are a little different from the parent cells. The chemicals in the pond are getting eaten up. How will the cells survive? Oh, some of them are green. See, they are catching light from the sun and are making sugar molecules and other kinds of molecules from the minerals dissolved in the water. Look there, the brown cells are eating the green cells. Isn't this exciting? We are seeing life and different species, and plants and animals, and an entire ecosystem evolve right before our eyes.

Say, aren't those some clumps of cells? Yes, and they are developing tails and fins and are swimming around the pool. Some of them are changing their fins into legs. One is crawling out on the bank. He is crawling around the pool. Look, now he is standing up, straighter and straighter. It's an animal. No, now it's a man—I think. He's walking around the pool. He's stopped. He must be thinking. Now what is he doing? Why is he stooping down in the mud? Look, he has taken a microscope out of his pocket and is studying the little squiggling things that are trying to climb out of the pool in his footsteps.

If this fantasy sounds absurd to you, come back with us through the looking glass into the world that God created. Here we can shake off the befuddling effects of the atmosphere of Evolutiana that must have gotten to us. We can see the folly of a theory which pictures impersonal causes bringing into existence personal beings who are concerned with understanding the impersonal causes which produced them.

Creation and the Study of Man

A creationist reasons that the world of nature must have been produced by an intelligent Creator independent of the forces or causes found in nature. Otherwise nature could not have had a beginning. A creationist is one who chooses to believe that the world of nature and of man *did* have a beginning. To say that there was no beginning would also be a matter of choice, so at this point a choice is the basis for belief rather than scientific data or proof. When the evolutionist says that all events in the past took place in the same way as events we observe today, he has made a choice that makes any real idea of the origin of the world of nature impossible, because nothing can create itself. Many technologically unsophisticated peoples have met this problem by understanding their world to be without a beginning.

As one well-educated Dakota Indian said, "You see, we Indians lived in eternity." In contrast, the scientist who believes the biblical creation account does not try to discover by science *how* the world and the things in it came to be. As a scientist he limits his investigations to the events and order that he can see, record, or measure in some way. He recognizes that such extraordinary order and design as scientists have discovered could not have formed itself.

The scientist tries to learn about the world he sees by asking "how" questions. He observes what happens in laboratory experiments and seeks to explain the "how" of these events. The historian can only observe the world of the past from some distance in time. He is also interested in how things happened, but in terms of particular events, such as the bombing of Pearl Harbor or the assassination of President Kennedy. These events can happen only once in time. The historian asks at least two other questions—"when" and "why." The latter question is the "why" of moral, religious, sociological, and other factors of history. If the scientist asks the questions "when" or "how" about some supposed prehistoric event, he must recognize that, apart from historical evidence, i.e., eyewitness testimony, the evidence he adduces in support of any answers to his questions will be circumstantial. This is because his answers are interpretations of the evidence which, if wrong, cannot be conclusively falsified by experimental test. Consequently the answers are unscientific, even though some of the evidence may have been obtained by scientific means.

The historian studies past events through written records of these events. The archaeologist investigates the events of prehistory through the objects that man in the past has made. These items, usually found buried in the ground, are called artifacts. The questions and methods of the historian and the archaeologist tell us much about man that the "how" questions and methods of natural science do not. But man asks still other questions, such as "What is man?" and "Who am I?" The subjects of learning pursuing these problems are usually labeled "Humanities." Such disciplines as philosophy and religion pursue these questions and develop different methods from those of science and history. Closely related to the question of "What is" is the question of "Coming to be." Philosophers speak of these kinds of questions as existential because they concern the problems of existence.

Since creationists and evolutionists are agreed that man has not always been, they both must meet the problem of origins. The creationist does not try to offer a scientific explanation of origins for two reasons. First, it would not be logical to explain how nature came into being by the things that he now sees in nature, for this would be saying that things made themselves, an obvious impossibility. Second, creation means that a Creator exists outside of nature.

When the evolutionist asks the difficult question "How?" concerning origins, he is compelled to pursue his question by using only the things he can perceive. Since he did not and cannot observe these kinds of events in the past, he must go outside the scientific method and use the eyes of his imagination along with his physical eyes. He sees what is closest in appearance to man and then imagines how a similar ape-like animal became man. He explains the entire living world as developing from less complex to more complex. He collects fossils of extinct animals and, arranging them in sequences by form, adduces the sequence as evidence for an alleged historical process of evolution from simple to complex. He must even imagine how life "could have"come into being from the non-living.

The evolutionist's search for origins begins in nature but cannot lead beyond nature; therefore he can find no first or real origin. The creationist sees origins as necessarily beyond nature; therefore his concern begins and ends with the Creator who, he believes, brought all things—man and his world—into being. His "how" questions are asked only regarding the world which he observes, the real world of science.

Can a Scientist Be Mistaken?

Like all human beings, a scientist is fallible. Yet the scientific method keeps him from making errors that he otherwise might make. If he bases his findings only on repeatable, carefully observed data, he will not build his ideas concerning his world on flying saucers that he has dreamed about. A scientist may err in his observation, but since the same experiments and tests can and are performed by others, these mistakes will be discovered sooner or later, and corrected.

Errors in the works of scientists are a result of a number of things:

1. Bias on the part of the scientist. Not entirely objective, he wishes to prove something as true to others. This kind of bias may very well result in a person's "seeing" flying saucers, for example.

2. The scientist may not have enough data. A few more experiments, properly designed, may bring to light new data which would falsify his theory.

3. Knowledge about a certain subject may not have been developed to the point where one is able to do the necessary experimentation. For instance, not enough is yet known about cancer to develop a scientific cure or preventative, and because of this many suffering and dying people reach out to "try" "unscientific" cures.

4. When the scientist attempts to answer the questions of history or speculate concerning the origins of man and nature, he may fall into the error of equating metaphysics with science. Falsifiability is the criterion which separates science from metaphysics. Theories about origins are

not subject to falsifying tests. Therefore, when a scientist asserts an explanation of origins, he is asserting a theory of metaphysics, not science.

5. Deliberate deception stemming from actual moral turpitude can result in false information finding its way into the scientific literature. The classic example was the falsification of sketches of embryos a century ago by German biologist Ernst Haeckel. He was later forced to admit his dishonesty in print in a scientific journal. His excuse was that others had done similar things.

Science Is Self-Correcting

If the rules of the scientific method are carefully followed, they will prevent the scientist from asking improper questions and also aid him in amending his incorrect answers. The progress of science offers clear evidence that mistaken ideas are being corrected. Medical science, at the time of our first president, treated Washington's tonsilitis by a method called "bloodletting." Making cuts on the body and letting them bleed so weakened the President that he finally died as the result of this scientifically wrong treatment. The findings of science have corrected this mistaken idea so that bloodletting is no longer practiced.

Even more recently we can see how scientists were in error because of incomplete information. They described in great detail canals on the planet Mars and claimed they had gathered information which proved plant life could be found there. (It must be remembered that the evolutionist would expect life to develop wherever conditions are favorable, and he therefore would wish to find life on other planets in support of this theory.) Our space probes have shown that Mars is a cratered planet, much like our moon in appearance, with none of the conditions necessary to support life as we know it. Our mistaken ideas, at least about Mars, have been corrected by the scientific observation made possible by the instruments of space exploration.

Is This Really Science?

The key chapter in Darwin's *The Origin of Species* is Chapter IV on natural selection. In the 1958 Mentor edition this chapter occupies forty-four pages. On these pages Darwin used the language of speculation, imagination, and assumption at least 187 times. For example, pages 118 and 119 contain the following phrases: "may have been," "is supposed to," "perhaps," "if we suppose," "may still be," "we have only to suppose," "as I believe," "it is probable," "I have assumed," "are supposed," "will generally tend," "may," "will generally tend," "if," "if . . . assumed," "supposed," "supposed," "probably," "It seems, therefore, extremely probable," "We may suppose."

In 1956 W. R. Thompson, a Canadian entomologist of international repute, was sharply critical of Darwin's "logic" in the *Origin*. In the introduction to the centennial edition of Darwin's book he wrote: ". . . Personal convictions, simple possibilities, are presented as if they were proofs, or at least valid arguments in favor of the theory. . . . . The demonstration can be modified without difficulty to fit any conceivable case. It is without scientific value, since it cannot be verified; but since the imagination has free rein, it is easy to convey the impression that a concrete example of real transmutation has been given." "Darwin did not show in the *Origin* that species had originated by natural selection; he merely showed, on the basis of certain facts and assumptions, how this might have happened, and as he had convinced himself he was able to convince others."

It would seem high time for the self-correcting features of science to be applied to the theory of evolution. Perhaps if the members of the scientific community were to do this, they would suddenly find themselves set free from an intellectual bondage which has greatly hindered scientific progress. The new freedom might result in unimagined advances in human understanding of the Creator's handiwork, which is the objective of true science.

The Origin of Civilization

Language and "primitive" cultures   Many of our ideas about ancient man have been based on tribes of people found in North America, South America, Africa, and other parts of the world. Early anthropologists called these peoples "primitive" because they used crude stone tools, could not write, and lacked a state form of government like ours. These "stone age" cultures were offered as models of what early man must have been like. There is considerable evidence, however, that some of these tribes are actually the degenerate posterity of ancient nations which enjoyed high levels of culture and civilization.

Such is the case with tribes in Yucatan and in Peru whose ancestors were the proud Mayas and Incas. So while it is true that tribes living in any era with backward technology might well be expected to develop cultures having certain characteristics related to their technology, it is not necessarily safe to draw conclusions about the culture of ancient peoples based upon today's "primitive" cultures.

The scientific study of language, called linguistics, now demonstrates that tribal peoples whom we consider to be rather uncivilized use languages with rules of grammar as strict and complex as ours. For example, English has only one verb for "to be," together with many tenses. The Dakota Indian child soon learns that if he is to be understood, he must use the correct one of eight different words meaning "to be." One of these means "to be" in a specific place when a certain thing happened. Another form is used only with living things. Still another means being temporarily in a place, another being permanently in a place. The sex of the speaker also forms a part of the Dakota grammar.

Scientific data from the languages of many tribal peoples reveal form as highly developed and structured as our own. This suggests that while language has obviously changed with time, it has not necessarily been evolving upward from primitive simple language. The biblical view is that man has had complex language from the beginning of the race.

The Model for the Evolution of Civilization[3]

Since the evolutionist portrays man as having evolved or developed from ape-like animals, he must find some way of explaining how he developed his way of life and finally became civilized. By civilization we mean a way of living that includes such things as writing, a central government as in a democracy or a kingdom, metal tools, agriculture, and domesticated animals.

For many years evolutionists taught as fact that for about one million years man lived very much like our plains Indians, hunting and gathering and using tools such as hammers and arrow points made of stone. Then, perhaps by accident, he found that the seeds from some of the wild plants could be collected and sowed. In this way, man became a farmer and began to live in one place instead of foraging about for food. Farming gave him an increased amount of food, and he greatly augmented his numbers.

He then moved from the Zagros Mountains down into the Tigris-Euphrates River Valley, where his food production increased still more. Men began to use the river to help raise even more food because of the enlarging population. The use of the river for irrigation led to construction of great canal networks and made necessary many more rules and regulations, primarily to guarantee equity of food supplies and other goods to all the people. As the story goes, early religious leaders, called shamans, then became political leaders. Writing had to be invented to keep records, and thus civilization evolved in this valley.

We see then that the cultural evolution model for the origin of civilization envisages successive stages of human cultural development: 1. advanced animal; 2. paleolithic, stone age, or hunting and gathering beings; 3. agricultural village dwellers; and 4. city-state civilization. Three major transitions supposedly occurred, 1-2, 2-3, and 3-4.

Cultural Evolution—The Facts

This evolutionary picture of the development of civilization seems quite logical, but is it based upon factual evidence? Do the data of paleontology and archaeology support this theory? Documentation for the first alleged transition—from animal to stone-age man—will be considered in the closing section of this chapter, but let us review at this point the supposed transition from the hunting and gathering stage to the agricultural village stage by quoting two evolutionary archaeologists.

Leslie White states in his book, *The Evolution of Culture,* "We have no adequate records of how, when and where this new type of adjustment became necessary and took place."[4] Henri Frankfort says, "We do not know [how] the change from old to new, from Old Stone Age to New Stone Age came about, for nowhere has a series of continuous remains covering the transition been recognized."[5] In other words, the factual evidence for the evolutionary transition has not been discovered. That it took place is, therefore, a matter of faith, not historical evidence.

Is there, then, factual evidence for the third alleged cultural transition, that from agricultural villages to city-state civilizations? Archaeologist Robert Adams proposes that rather than large-scale irrigation creating the need for more complex social organization and thus producing cities, " . . . the beginnings of large-scale canal networks seem clearly later than the advent of fully established cities."[6] In fact, the evidence indicates that irrigation came 1000 years after the appearance of civilization. Adams further indicates that economic factors did not cause shamans to evolve into priests and governors, but that "the first clear-cut trend in the archaeological record is the rise of temples" and that perhaps the religious influences brought people together in more complex social structures.

Adams also reports that in southern Mesopotamia, "the major quantitative expansion of metallurgy and of the specialized crafts in general came only after dynastic city-states were well advanced," that technology was "less a cause than a consequence of city growth."[7] The actual evidence, therefore, does not support the view that agricultural village cultures slowly evolved into city-states.

What, then, was the source of civilization? Thorkild Jacobsen reports that in the Mesopotamian River Valley, a long succession of similar patriarchal family village cultures came to a close suddenly with the advent of the Protoliterate Period. "Overnight, as it were, Mesopotamian civilization crystallizes. The fundamental pattern, the controlling framework within which Mesopotamia is to live its life, formulate its deepest questions, evaluate itself and evaluate the universe for ages to come flashes into being complete in all its main features."[8]

A similar pattern is evident also in the case of the civilizations in the Indus Valley and in the Nile Valley. Civilization appeared suddenly in each of these three ancient centers, brought in by newcomers. C. Leonard Wooley says, "It is safest for the time being to regard the two civilizations (Indus and Mesopotamian) as offshoots from a common source which presumably lies somewhere between the Indus and Euphrates Valleys, though whether the center from which this culture radiates so far afield is to be found in the hills of Baluchistan or where, we have no means of knowing yet."[9]

The evidence points to the ancient Sumerian people as those who brought civilization to the Mesopotamian River Valley. They brought with them metallurgy, art, and the potter's wheel, as well as writing, all in a highly developed state indicating, in Wooley's opinion, at least a thousand years of cultural development before they appeared on the plains of Babylonia. These facts are not in accord with the evolutionary view of the origin of culture, but do they fit the biblical record? The answer is *yes*. It is an established fact that Sumer is the biblical Shinar, to which, according to Genesis 11, men migrated, took counsel together to build a tower and a city, and then were divided by a supernatural intervention that confused their tongues.

The earliest cities found in archaeological excavations—such as Erech, Kish, Ur, and Lagish—are cities mentioned in the biblical record. This record also gives us a genealogical sequence that reaches back to the Flood, at which time an old civilization was destroyed. From this point, genealogy connects with Adam, whose son Cain is the father of the civilization that was destroyed at the Flood. The description of this civilization in Genesis 4 speaks of cities, metallurgy, domesticated animals, and musical instruments; it is not unreasonable to assume that writing was also known. Thus the Bible points to a long history of civilization prior to our earliest observation of it in the Mesopotamian Valley and the other two river valleys.

It may be reasonably concluded, therefore, that the factual data of archaeology relative to the origin of human culture and civilization is in agreement with the biblical record but fails to support the evolutionary view at the most critical points. The data may be reasonably interpreted in accordance with biblical presuppositions. Although the historical veracity and truth of the Bible do not rest upon such foundations, archaeology affords a large body of data which attests to the correctness of the scriptural picture of human origins.

Fossil Men and Physical Anthropology

In Chapter 3 it was demonstrated that the general body of fossil evidence can be interpreted in accord with biblical presuppositions and in support of the biblical record of creation and the Flood. But what about fossil men? Do not fossils declare a gradual progression from ape-like creatures to modern man? This is the impression given persistently in newspaper reports and superficial accounts in school textbooks. Critical examination of the actual data, however, once again reveals that the facts do not actually support the ape-to-man thesis.

Fossils can be classified in accordance with several different types of information, the most important being the following: 1. skeletal form, 2. geological strata in which fossils are found and the flora and fauna fossil content of these strata, 3. radiometric dating of fossils or strata, 4. associated cultural remains, and 5. geographical location. These types of information provide only circumstantial evidence relative to prehistory and to any theories of prehistory such as the theory of human evolution from lower forms. Therefore the data must be interpreted, and the conclusions arrived at will depend upon the presuppositions of the interpreter.

The vast majority of researchers in human paleontology have approached the subject with the materialistic presupposition that man has evolved from lower forms of life. We will consider the evidence for fossil man from the viewpoint of the biblical revelation of creation and the Flood. First, the five kinds of information used to classify fossil man will be described and analyzed. Then a biblical creationist interpretation will be outlined.

The Fossil Evidence: Five Kinds Used to Classify Fossils

Classification by fossil form   Fossils which are either definitely human or allegedly ancestral to man may be roughly classified according to their forms into five groups.

a. *Modern types:* These are fossils which in their form fall within the range of variation of modern man. The skull shape is relatively round

table 2. Important Humanoid Fossils (Selected)

fossil, parts found	form or type	stratum	age assigned	cultural remains
Skull 1470 (Leakey) frag. braincase & facial bones, few teeth, distantly located leg bones	Less ape-like than Homo habilis	Pliocene	2.8 MY (radio on rocks)	No
Homo habilis frag. braincase	Less ape-like than Zinjanthropus	Pliocene	1.7 MY (radio on rocks)	No, except for so-called stone choppers
Zinjanthropus 400 frags. of skull	Quite ape-like	Pliocene	1.75 MY (radio on rocks)	No. Same as above.
Calaveras frag. braincase and most of facial bones	Modern	Pliocene, 140 feet deep	Several MY (by stratum)	No
Castenedolo frag. braincase	Modern	Pliocene, 6½ feet deep	Several MY (by stratum)	No
Olmo frag. braincase	Modern	Pliocene 50 feet deep	1 MY + (by stratum)	No
Saccopastore skull	Neanderthal	Early Pleistocene	0.76 MY (radio on rocks)	No
Australopithecus africanus skull	A small, quite ape-like creature	Early Pleistocene		No

Sinanthropus (Pekin Man) frags. of skulls and some skeletal bones	Rather ape-like	Middle Pleistocene	0.5 MY (by stratum)	No definitely connected cultural remains
Pithecanthropus erectus (Java Man or Homo erectus) braincap, femur (?), frags. of several other skulls	Rather ape-like	Middle Pleistocene	0.5 MY (by stratum)	No
Swanscombe skull cap	Modern	Middle Pleistocene	0.6 to 0.25 MY (stratum)	No, except for stone tools in same gravels
Fontechevade skull	Modern	Middle to late Pleistocene	0.22 MY (stratum)	Yes. Stone tools
Steinheim skull	Neanderthal	Middle Pleistocene	0.2 MY (stratum)	No
Keilor skull	Modern	Late Pleistocene	8,500 to 150,000 Y (radio, stratum)	
Omo two braincases plus frags.	Modern	Late Pleistocene	More than 35,000 Y	No
Spy skull	Neanderthal	Late Pleistocene	35,000 to 70,000 Y (radio, stratum)	Yes
Monte Circeo brain case and facial bones	Neanderthal	Late Pleistocene	35,000 to 70,000 Y (radio, stratum)	

figure 5-1. Important fossil skulls referred to in the text and in the Table of Important Humanoid Fossils.

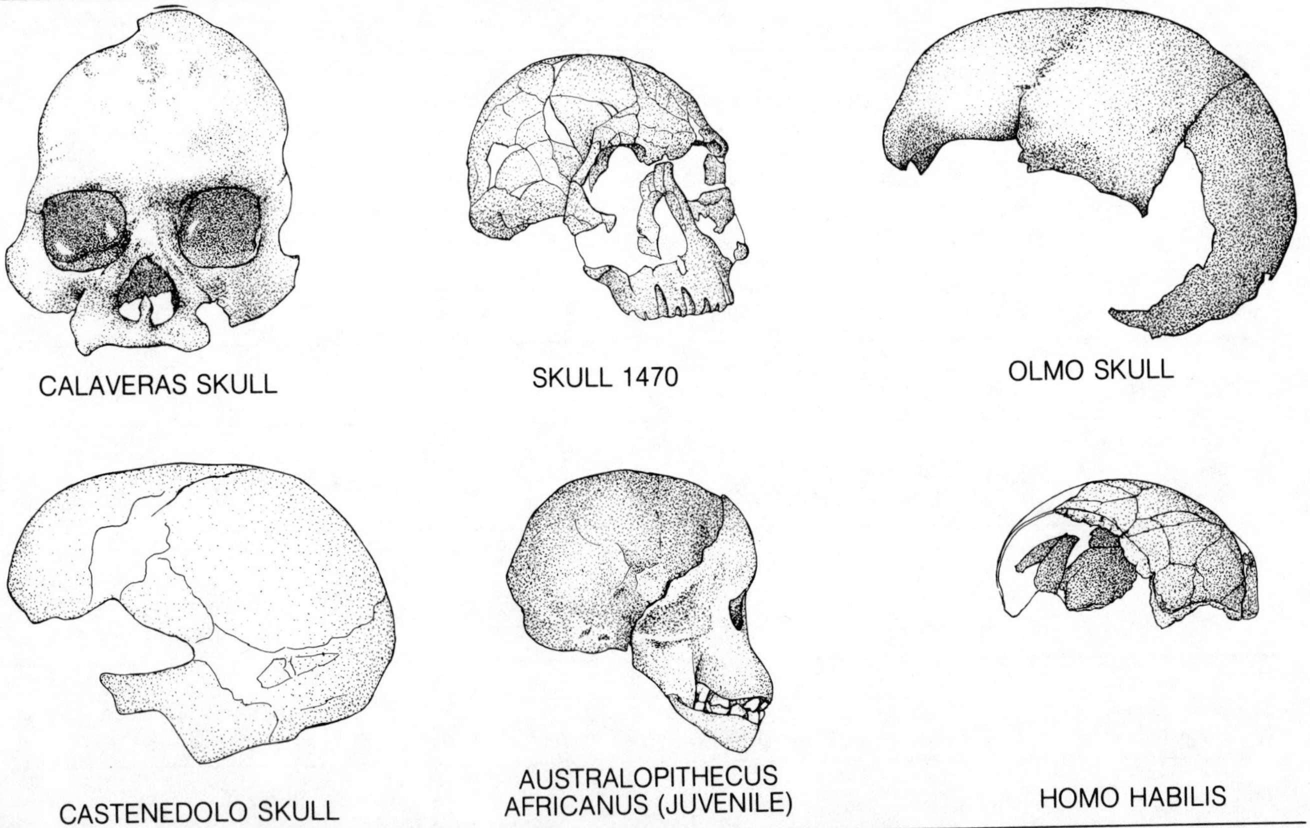

OLMO SKULL

HOMO HABILIS

SKULL 1470

AUSTRALOPITHECUS
AFRICANUS (JUVENILE)

CALAVERAS SKULL

CASTENEDOLO SKULL

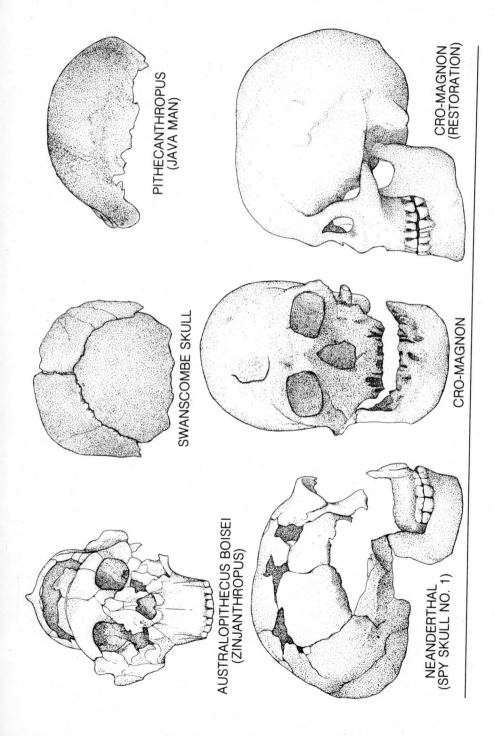

PITHECANTHROPUS
(JAVA MAN)

SWANSCOMBE SKULL

AUSTRALOPITHECUS BOISEI
(ZINJANTHROPUS)

CRO-MAGNON
(RESTORATION)

CRO-MAGNON

NEANDERTHAL
(SPY SKULL NO. 1)

with high forehead and crown, and the chin is prominent.

b. *Neanderthal types:* These types are characterized by skulls which, while actually averaging as large as or slightly larger than the modern average in brain capacity, are nevertheless materially different in form, being longer, with sloping brow, and very prominent to massive ridges above the eyes. The Neanderthal skeleton, powerfully built, is quite similar to that of modern man. Neanderthal walked just as upright as we do, contrary to earlier views of anthropologists based upon a skeleton that was badly deformed as a result of disease.

c. *Pithecanthropus types:* The term means "ape-man." This type of fossil is characterized by skulls with very heavy brow ridges above the eyes, low sloping brow, and a long low shape, compared to the higher, rounder shape of modern man's skull. The brain capacity averages much smaller than that of modern man. The teeth are in general more man-like than ape-like, though larger than man's.

d. *Australophithecine types:* The term, meaning "southern ape," includes degrees of ape-like character of skull and skeleton. The teeth have varying degrees of man-like or ape-like character in different specimens.

e. The most recent find by Richard Leakey, called 'Skull 1470' (1972), which has more man-like form and larger brain size than *Australopithecus.*

Analysis of Fossil Finds

The largest number of fossils are of Neanderthal type, and these are quite plentiful. Among the skull and skeletal remains of Neanderthal are the most complete human fossils that have been discovered, other than the Cro-Magnon skeletons, which are essentially identical to modern man. *Pithecanthropus* and *Australopithecus* fossils are much fewer in number. Complete skeletons are very rare, and the fossil remains are in general quite fragmentary. Most fossil skulls are fragmentary; the facial portion is usually missing, being the most fragile part. Some fossil finds consist only of a few teeth and perhaps fragments of a jaw bone.

Interpreting Fossil Forms

Historically anthropologists have generally based their studies of human fossils upon evolutionary presuppositions. They have therefore labelled fossil types differing from modern norms as "primitive," attempting to arrange fossils in sequences according to form so as to demonstrate an evolutionary progression from primitive to modern forms. The tendency has been to draw more conclusions from fossils than the data really permit and to state speculation as though it were fact. Deductions which may *not* be conclusively established on the basis of the form of fossil remains are the following: a. the intellectual, moral, or spiritual attributes of the creature; b. the possession of the ability to speak; c. the nature and appearance of the fleshy body parts; and d. genetic relationship to other creatures, fossil or living.

It is possible, however, to infer with some assurance considerable information from the bones of a fossilized creature, depending upon how complete the remains are. The capacity of the skull has a general but not absolute relationship to intelligence. The form of bones of the hand— rarely recovered as fossils—indicates something of manual ability. The pelvis indicates whether or not the creature had erect posture. Other inferences drawn from skeletal form are less sure. The form and wear of the teeth give indication of dietary habits. The form of jaw bones may suggest whether or not speech was possible, but any conclusion from fossil remains as to the possession of speech is highly speculative.

Classification by strata and the associated flora and fauna Most of the human fossils have been found in strata classified as Pleistocene, supposedly dating over the past one to three million years. However, some modern forms have been discovered in Pliocene or Tertiary strata which are dated earlier than the Pleistocene. The three notable examples of human bones of modern form found in such supposedly ancient strata are the Castenedolo, Olmo, and Calaveras fossils. These are included in the table on pages 120 and 121. These finds contradict the postulate that the form sequence of the fossils should parallel and agree with the sequence of the strata.

Supposedly the more primitive forms should in general be deeply buried in the sequence of strata, with more modern forms closer to the surface. This is not always the case, as the three examples referred to above demonstrate. The tendency has been to question the authenticity of fossils which do not fit into this pattern. Thus the Castenedolo, Olmo, and Calaveras fossils, all carefully documented, have been relegated to dusty museum closets and forgotten by the anthropologists because they do not fit into the accepted evolutionary scheme of human origins. Sir Arthur Keith, British scientist and dean of anthropologists in the first quarter of this century, in his book *The Antiquity of Man,* described in great detail the Castendolo, Olmo, and Calaveras fossils. He told how these fossils would have been accepted as genuine had they not so radically contradicted the ape-to-man dogma which rules the minds of most anthropologists.

It will be seen from the Table of Humanoid Fossils that other fossils classified as modern in form are found in a non-evolutionary sequence in the strata. Likewise, Neanderthal type remains tend to be scattered rather widely through the strata sequence. Furthermore, Neanderthal fossils span a range of skull types distributed in the strata in such a way as to indicate that Neanderthal degenerated with the passage of time into *less* modern forms.

There seems to be some disagreement in scientific literature between observed facts and interpretation in the case of the Swanscombe fossil, or basically modern skull type. The gravel stratum in which this fossil was found is reported to contain fossil animals connected with what is called the "second inter-glacial period." The date given to this assortment of fossil animals is about 600,000 years B.C., but such a date placed Swanscombe entirely too early in the accepted sequence of fossil man types, at a time in their proposed history when man supposedly had evolved only to the *Pithecanthropus* level. Therefore, Swanscombe is generally placed at about 225,000 years ago, where he fits a little more comfortably with current theory.

Australopithicene fossils also do not seem to fit into a sequence with other fossils from "primitive" to more man-like form. Two fossils found by L. S. B. Leakey in East Africa, called *Homo habilis* and *Zinjanthropus,* were located in rock strata at close to the same level, yet the latter is much more ape-like in form. The Potassium-Argon date of the stratum containing *Zinjanthropus* is 2.03 million years, but the stratum just below tested a quarter of a million years younger than the stratum above! But this reversal is ignored and several such dates are averaged to give *Zinjanthropus* an age of 1.75 million years.

It is interesting that animal bones nearby at about the same level were dated at 10,000 years by the Carbon-14 method, but supposedly they were placed there as a result of erosion and later deposition. The Africa "Skull 1470," announced by Leakey's son, Richard, in late 1972, has been assigned an age of 2.8 million years as compared with the 1.75 million year alleged age of the *Homo habilis* and *Zinjanthropus* fossils. However, this fragmentary fossil skull appears less ape-like than *habilis* and possesses a somewhat larger brain capacity.

In his June 1973 report Richard Leakey alleges that this fossil "leaves in ruins the notion that all early fossils can be arranged in an orderly sequence of evolutionary change."[10] He then proposes that several different kinds of early man were living at the same time, suggests that the ones formerly nominated by his father as human ancestors were only dead-end varieties, and implies that man actually evolved from the creature *he* has discovered.

Developments such as these with the Leakey finds are typical of the history of fossils put forth as man's ancestors. In fact Skull 1470 was superceded just two years later in 1974 by a find of teeth and jawbones made in Ethiopia. These fossil remains are said to be definitely human, yet they are dated by the evolutionary scientists at four million years. The finders assert, "All previous theories of the origin of the lineage which leads to modern man must now be totally revised."[11] Where does such a statement leave the evolutionary dogmatists of just three or four years ago?

The *Pithecanthropus* fossils, remains of creatures now usually classified as *Homo erectus,* were originally dated at 500,000 years old, but on the basis of a find made in the Olduvai Gorge in East Africa it is proposed that *Pithecanthropus* was also around as early as a million years ago. The two principal types have been known as *Pithecanthropus erectus* or Java Man and *Sinanthropus* or Peking Man. In neither case is there clear evidence that the creature was anything more than an animal.

Eugene Dubois, the original discoverer of a Java Man fossil in 1891, finally decided in 1936 that the fossil skull cap actually belonged to a giant extinct gibbon. The femur discovered some time after the skull cap and buried about forty feet away is of modern human type. The geology of Java is exceedingly complex and confused owing to the heavy rains and tropical climate combined with frequent volcanic eruptions. The geology of the area in which the original Java Man skull was found has been critically examined by two later expeditions in 1906 and 1931, and Dubois' analysis of the fossil-bearing strata refuted. Dubois' first find in Java was the very large-brained Wadjak skull, classified as *Homo sapiens,* which he secreted for thirty years before reporting it to the public. This, of course, was dishonest and constituted a scientific fraud. It has been suggested that the Java and Wadjak skulls may well have belonged to contemporary creatures, so the Java skull could hardly have belonged to an ancestor of *Homo sapiens.* [12]

The Peking Man fossils were reportedly found beginning in the late 1920's at the site of an ancient lime furnace about twenty-five miles outside of Peking, China. Over a period of almost twenty years, often-conflicting reports of fossil man finds and also a few plaster casts of skulls emanated from China. None of the actual fossil bones ever left China, and few outsiders were allowed to examine them. Two internationally recognized French authorities, Abbé Breuil and Marcellin Boule, were able to study the fossil remains and also the discovery site. Their conclusions were that the so-called Peking Man was actually an animal and that the discovery site was a lime burning furnace where true man prepared lime for construction purposes.

It was reported that modern-type human skulls were found associated with *Sinanthropus* fossils. This, together with the fact that the *Sinanthropus* skulls generally were pierced and their bones crushed, led to the speculation that *Sinanthropus* was merely an animal which sometimes served as food for a human being who worked in the lime kiln.

Several informed sources have claimed that Peking Man was largely a fraud on a par with the Piltdown fossil found in England in 1912 and formally exposed as a fake in 1953. It is interesting and perhaps significant that a principal sponsor of the Peking research, Teilhard de Chardin, was also implicated in the Piltdown discovery. In any event, with the evidence gone and the witnesses dead, Peking Man becomes a somewhat mythical stage in the supposed evolution of man.[13]

Classification by radiometric dating of fossils   Fossil bones do not lend themselves to radiometric dating for several reasons. They often do not contain sufficient carbon to make Carbon-14 dating practical. A new chemical dating method based upon the slow change of amino acids in the bone proteins from the L to the D form is only considered reliable when the history of the conditions to which the bone has been subjected are known or when the method can be calibrated against the Carbon-14 method applied to other fossils in the same stratum. Therefore, fossil bones are usually dated by reference to the radiometric dating of the rock stratum in which they are found or by reference to the assemblage of fossil animals in the rocks. Various methods of radiometric dating are often not in agreement, and it is not uncommon for results fitting an accepted view of prehistory to be accepted while other results are rejected.

The table of fossil finds is generally arranged according to the accepted radiometric dates that have been assigned to the various fossils. It can be seen that the sequence of fossil data according to form does not fully agree with the sequence of radiometric dates. It can also be noted that fossils not fitting the accepted sequence are sometimes ignored or rejected, and unsatisfactory dates have a way of being adjusted. The problems of radiometric dating will be considered in some detail in Chapter 8.

Classification by associated cultural remains   Man is the only cultural being. Thus associated cultural remains should serve to distinguish human from animal fossils, provided that it is possible unmistakably to connect the fossil with the cultural material. Stone tools and evidences of the controlled use of fire are the principal cultural remains used by anthropologists to identify fossil men and to distinguish among their varying cultures.

Many fossils have no associated cultural remains, and often there is no necessary connection between a fossil and stone implements found near-by. Assemblages of stone implements and fire sites located in ancient living floor areas reveal many things about the culture of ancient races of men, but these are often found without any human fossils. Some of the modern type human skulls have been uncovered with no associated cultural remains. On the other hand, Neanderthal and Cro-Magnon fossils have sometimes been found with extensive cultural remains, including even their paintings on cave walls and indications of their worship and burial practices which reveal that they believed in life after death.

In particular, the *Pithecanthropus* and *Australopithecus* fossils have been found with either no or very few associated cultural materials. There is no way to be sure that the crude stone choppers reportedly found in association with *Homo habilis* and *Zinjanthropus* were either made by them or used by them. The anthropologists continue to promote and continually modify varied opposing theories related to these questions.

Classification by geographical location The Bible pictures the human race radiating from the Middle East after the Flood, and this is confirmed by much evidence from archaeology. What can we learn from the geographical location of human fossils? The fact is that the greater part of the fossils are found far removed from the Middle East. Particularly, the more "primitive" or less modern forms have generally been found in the more inaccessible areas and in the extremes of the Eurasian and African land masses, e.g., Western Europe, South Africa, and Southeast Asia. As was reported earlier, Neanderthal fossils tend to be distributed so as to suggest that Neanderthal degenerated in time to a form more "primitive" and less modern. There is also evidence that modern types moved in on the more primitive forms and displaced them, driving them into extinction and occasionally intermarrying with them. The origins of these invaders are not clear from the fossil remains.

Biblical Interpretations of Fossil Man Data

What conclusions can be drawn from the remains of fossil man and what interpretation developed which accord with the biblical record of creation and the Flood? First, let us suggest some general conclusions from the fossil record and then offer an overall interpretation which fits with the biblical data.

1. The fossil record does not support the thesis that ape-like creatures slowly evolved upward through increasingly man-like beings until modern man arrived on the scene, for "modern" and "primitive" types were apparently contemporary with one another.

2. *Pithecanthropus, Australopithecene,* and other similar fossils were probably simply animals. The slight cultural materials found near some of them were probably the products of human beings who left no fossils in those sites.

3. Neanderthal was undoubtedly true man, intelligent and possessing a spiritual nature. There is evidence that Neanderthal was a degenerate and degenerating type, evolving not upward, but downward.

4. The fossils with skulls more similar to the average of modern types probably represent true man, even in the cases where no associated cultural materials were found.

Now we will offer an integrated interpretation of the biblical data and the fossil data which is adapted from the writings of Arthur C. Custance.[14]

1. In the beginning, some 10,000 years ago, God created all things in the space of six days, and all very good. Soon our first parents sinned, and by their disobedience all mankind was plunged into a state of sin and rebellion against God. The creation for man's sake was subjected to a curse and to vanity (Genesis 1, 2, 3).

2. The effect of sin and of the curse upon mankind was immediately degenerative and cumulative, both spiritually and physically (Genesis 3, 4, 6; Romans 5).

3. Nevertheless, there was rapid development of culture and technology in the period from creation to the Flood (Genesis 4).

4. Because of the sinfulness of the fallen human race the Creator brought judgment upon them by a global, catastrophic Flood (Genesis 6, 7, 8).

5. The family of Noah carried much of the culture and technology into the post-Flood world, so that civilization was able to blossom rapidly at the center of human culture in the Middle East. Much archaeological evidence points to this part of the world as the cradle of civilization, also indicating that civilization and technology arrived suddenly from unknown sources.

6. Cursed and rebellious peoples spread out rapidly in forced migrations shortly after the confusion of tongues at Babel, radiating from the Middle East. They moved out in small groups to establish outposts ever farther from the center (Genesis 10, 11).

7. As a result of the combined effects of sin and the curse and of crude living conditions, promoted by the more rapid genetic variation which is

characteristic of small population groups, the pioneer populations tended to degenerate rapidly, both physically and culturally, as they radiated farther from the center of human origins in the Middle East. This explains the larger number of "primitive" fossil types found in more inaccessible and more distant parts of the Eurasian land mass.

8. Subsequent waves of peoples from the Middle Eastern center swept over the degenerate tribes, forcing them either into immediate extinction or out into more remote areas, where their degeneration was accelerated. With their final extinction or reabsorption, the stage was set for modern history.

Conclusion

The attributes and powers of man cannot be explained on the basis of a purely materialistic process of development from chemicals to cells to animals to man. Man is a spiritual and personal being who must have had a spiritual and personal source. In this chapter we have attempted to coordinate the information from archaeology, paleontology, and the Bible to show that the scientific data can be interpreted in accordance with biblical revelation. There are problems remaining with this interpretation, but there are equal or greater problems for those who insist upon the materialistic interpretation.

The Christian investigator in science, history, or prehistory has important advantages over those who are committed to a materialistic conception of origins. The Christian who believes in the biblical account of creation does not try to find in the world of nature the answer to the questions of how and when all things began. Origins are problems of philosophy and religion, not of science and history. As a scientist the creationist is able to search for knowledge and go as far as the observable data permit. As an historian or prehistorian, he can study the past as far as written records and the remains of man's works permit him to go. He does not try to imagine materialistic processes of origin and thus introduce vain philosophy or pseudo-science into his scientific or historical research, for he has the advantage of divine revelation concerning the creation of all things. Therefore, the Christian student of science and of man can pursue the facts, confident that the final judgments of true science and history will entirely concur with the biblical record.

6

Design in the Universe

The Psalmist often rejoiced in the powerful revelation of the wisdom and knowledge of the infinite, personal Creator God. "O LORD our Lord, how excellent is thy name in all the earth! who hast set thy glory above the heavens . . . When I consider thy heavens, the work of thy fingers, the moon and the stars, which thou hast ordained . . ." (Psalm 8:1, 3).

Everywhere as we have considered the scientific evidence, we have seen the órder, the design, the coordination which speaks of intelligent, purposeful design. In this chapter we will briefly span the vast range of space from the nucleus of the atom to the distant galaxies to observe the underlying order of the physical universe and the facts that support the biblical record of creation.

The Design of the Atom[1]

The modern history of the atom may be said to have begun in 1808 when John Dalton published his Atomic Theory. He proposed that all matter is composed of tiny indivisible particles called atoms, the atoms of various elements differing from each other, but all the atoms of a given element being identical. Ninety different naturally occurring elements have been discovered on the earth. In 1897 J. J. Thompson discovered the electron and in 1902 Ernest Rutherford showed it to be a part of the atom. Rutherford also discovered the nucleus of the atom in 1911 and the proton in 1914. The neutron was discovered in 1932 by James Chadwick, and thus was completed the disclosure of the three basic particles of which all atoms are composed—the electron, proton, and neutron. Their properties are indicated in Figure 6-1.

Scientists are always looking for patterns in the facts which they find, patterns which will lead them to an understanding of the underlying order and laws responsible for the observed facts. With the finding of the nucleus it became apparent that the atom consisted of a central, tiny but massive, positively charged nucleus to which light, negatively charged

table 3. Basic Atomic Particles

name	mass	charge	where found in atom
electron	9.11×10^{-28}g	1	in outer electron cloud
proton	1.673×10^{-24}g	+1	in nucleus
neutron	1.675×10^{-24}g	0	in nucleus

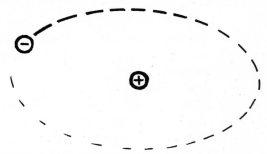

figure 6-1. Original simple concept of the atomic orbit of an electron.

electrons were bound by electrostatic attraction. It was proposed that the electrons travel around the nucleus in circular orbits like planets orbiting the sun (Figure 6-1). But according to classical electromagnetic theory, a charge moving in a curved path radiates energy, so it was reasoned that an electron moving in an atomic orbit around the nucleus would gradually dissipate its energy and fall from its orbit into the nucleus (Figure 6-2).

Excited atoms do in fact radiate their energy, but not gradually. They emit packets or photons of radiation having definite wavelengths corresponding to definite amounts of energy. For example, sometimes the excited atoms in a glowing gas give off light which, when passed through a narrow slit and a prism, is dispersed into an emission spectrum, a band of different colors of light containing bright lines of particular colors or wavelengths (Figure 6-3). For a given gas these spectral lines are arranged in characteristic, precise patterns along the spectrum according to wavelength (Figure 6-4).

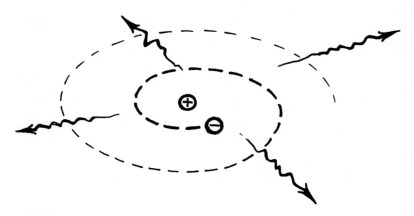

figure 6-2. According to classical physical theory an electron moving in an orbit would gradually radiate its energy and fall into the nucleus.

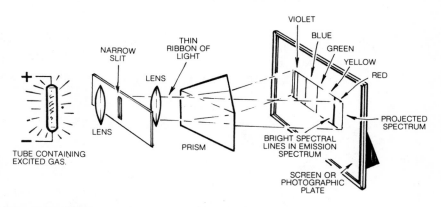

figure 6-3. Schematic diagram of a prism spectroscope.

It was these patterns that led physicist Niels Bohr to propose that the electrons in an atom orbit the nucleus in elliptical paths which have definite energies. As long as an electron remains in a particular orbit, it radiates no energy. This new idea of Bohr was a radical departure from the classical theory described earlier. He proposed that only when an elec-

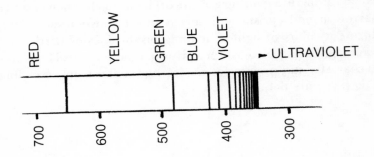

figure 6-4. The visible light line spectrum of hydrogen atoms, called the Balmer series.

tron jumps from a higher energy to a lower energy orbit is energy radiated, the exact amount corresponding to the difference in energy level of the two orbits. These discrete amounts of energy are the quanta of radiation which correspond to the exact wavelengths of light that produce the sharp lines in the emission spectrum of a gas.

Bohr's initial rudimentary theory of the atom was later replaced by the quantum mechanical or wave mechanical theory of atomic structure upon which the modern understanding of the atom is based. An electron in an atom is no longer considered to be moving in a simple orbit. Rather, its exact location and velocity at any time is unknown, but its probability of being found at any point is known. Thus the electron is spread out in a probability cloud which has a wave-like character around the nucleus. These electron probability clouds have interesting shapes which are described precisely by the mathematics of quantum mechanics (Figure 6-5). When an excited atom undergoes a transition from one electron

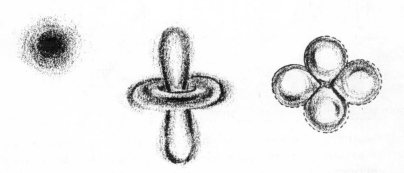

figure 6-5. Some electron cloud patterns: Hydrogen atom in lowest energy or ground state, hydrogen atom in an excited state, and carbon atom in ground state.

probability cloud pattern to another one of lower energy, a photon of a particular energy and wavelength is emitted from the atom. Thus the pattern of lines in the emission spectra of gases led ultimately to an understanding of a marvelously complex set of patterns of electron probability clouds in atoms. It was further found that in the heavier elements with more electrons in their atoms, the electrons are arranged in groups called shells at different energy levels.

It was soon realized that the chemical and physical properties of the elements are determined by the electron cloud patterns and electron shells. Years before, around 1870, a Russian chemist, Mendelyeev, had discovered a pattern of chemical properties for the different elements. He found that if the elements were arranged in order of increasing atomic weight, they fell into groups or periods with repeating patterns of chemical properties. This is demonstrated in the Periodic Table of the Elements shown partially in Table 4. Now it was possible to relate the pattern of chemical properties to the theoretical patterns of electron clouds calculated by the mathematical equations of quantum mechanics.

The structures of hundreds of thousands of chemical compounds, of crystalline substances such as minerals, and the types of reactions which occur in chemical laboratories and in the cells of living things can all be related to the pattern of the Periodic Table, to the patterns of the electron clouds of atoms, and to the patterns of spectral lines in the emission spectra of excited gases. And these interrelated patterns are connected by the fundamental laws of physics.

These remarkable conquests of modern science have led many to say, "Science is explaining everything on the basis of physical principles. There *is* nothing else." But this attitude ignores the fact that the patterns, the marvelous order, and the physical laws supply powerful evidence in support of the biblical revelation concerning God, the supreme Designer and Pattern Maker. And it should also be recognized that theoretical physicists are themselves not in complete agreement as to the physical significance of the mathematical equations which they use to describe atomic structure. Theoretical physicist Louis DeBroglie has said, "Recent theoretical views suggest that a mechanistic view of nature cannot be pushed beyond a certain point, and that the fundamental laws can only be expressed in abstract terms, defying all attempts at an intelligible description."[2]

The Nucleus of the Atom[3]

The nucleus of the atom is roughly only 1/50,000 the size of the whole

table 4. Periodic Table of the Elements (partial)

Group 1	Group 2		Group 13	Group 14	Group 15	Group 16	Group 17	Group 18
H 1 Hydrogen Reactive Gas HF								He 2 Helium Non-reactive Gas He
Li 3 Lithium Reactive Metal LiF	Be 4 Beryllium Moderately reactive Metal BeF_2		B 5 Boron Slightly reactive Non-metal BF_3	C 6 Carbon Slightly reactive Non-metal CH_4	N 7 Nitrogen Very slightly reactive Gas NH_3	O 8 Oxygen Reactive Gas H_2O, Li_2O	F 9 Fluorine Most reactive Gas HF, LiF	NE 10 Neon Non-reactive Gas Ne
Na 11 Sodium Very reactive Metal NaF	Mg 12 Magnesium Moderately reactive Metal MgF_2		Al 13 Aluminum Slightly reactive Metal AlF_3	Si 14 Silicon Very slightly reactive Metalloid SiH_4	P 15 Phosphorus Reactive Non-metal PH_3	S 16 Sulfur Moderately reactive Non-metal H_2S	Cl 17 Chlorine Very reactive Gas HCl, LiCl	Ar 18 Argon Non-reactive Gas Ar

1 ← Atomic number

Symbol →	H
Name →	Hydrogen
Reactivity →	Reactive
Character →	Gas
A stable →	HF
compound	

Only the upper part of the table containing the first eighteen elements is included for simplicity. Note the following regularities or patterns in the table: 1. The metals are grouped on the left, lower part. 2. The non-metals are grouped on the right, upper part. 3. The right-hand column is all non-reactive or noble elements. 4. The metals form stable compounds with the non-metal fluorine. 5. The non-metals on the far right form stable compounds with the metal lithium and with hydrogen. 6. The non-metals near the middle of the table form stable compounds with hydrogen but not with lithium. 7. The reactivity of the metals increases toward the bottom of the table. 8. The reactivity of the non-metals increases toward the top. All of these regularities and trends, plus many more observed properties of the chemical elements, are entirely explainable in terms of the electronic pattern or design of the respective atoms.

atom, yet it contains a number of protons equal to the number of electrons which are spread out in the outer electron cloud portion of the atom, plus a roughly equal or greater number of neutrons. These particles are packed into the nucleus with an astounding density of around 2.9 billion tons per cubic inch! Surely there must be a pattern for the arrangement and energies of these particles in the nucleus, and such is indeed the case.

The matter is too intricate to discuss here, but briefly stated, the neutrons and protons are arranged in the nucleus and move in energy levels or "shells" in a manner analogous to the electrons in the outer electron shells of the atom. The complex mathematical description of the structure of the nucleus of the atom has achieved striking success in relating the design of different atomic nuclei to their actual physical properties. Thus the wisdom and plan of the Creator is discovered in the tiny nucleus at the center of the submicroscopic atom.

Yet there is more! In the process of blasting apart atomic nuclei to learn their secrets, scientists have discovered many different types of tiny particles and various energy states of these particles which are apparently involved in holding the nucleus together by mediating the interactions between protons, neutrons, and electrons. The dozens of particles and particle energy states exhibit a bewildering variety of different properties. Once again physicists have tried to discover a pattern which relates all of these observations into a rational system. Several schemes have been proposed. One of these systems of classification is called "the eight-fold-way," a phrase which suggests the great complexity of the situation. For example, at least eight different kinds of the particles called mesons have been discovered.

Although none of the proposed systems of classification for the elementary particles has entirely succeeded in relating them all in a rational fashion, physicists believe that there is a complete pattern to be discovered which underlies all of physical reality. Christians are not surprised, for they believe in the Creator-God of the Bible, who is the originator of all of the marvelous and beautiful patterns of the universe.

In Chapter 2 we were introduced to four kinds of interaction or forces between units of matter: Gravitational, electromagnetic, strong nuclear, and weak nuclear. Table 5 compares these forces, giving their relative effect in the nucleus.

These four kinds of force are the means by which all of the design and patterns in the universe are maintained. What is the source of these organizing influences without which the physical universe would be only formless chaos? The nuclear scientist and the astronomer can describe

table 5. The Four Forces (Interactions) in a Nucleus

force	nature in nucleus	average relative strength in nucleus
Nuclear strong	Attractive	10^{39} (i.e., 1 followed by 39 zeros)
Electromagnetic	Repulsive	10^{36}
Nuclear weak	Repulsive (probably)	10^{25}
Gravitational	Attractive	1

the effects of these forces but cannot discover their source by scientific methods of inquiry. The source is revealed to us in the Bible by God the Father. The Source of all the organizing force in the universe is His Son Jesus Christ, "In whom we have redemption through his blood, even the forgiveness of sins . . . For by him were all things created . . . all things were created by him, and for him: And he is before all things, and by him all things consist (hold together)" (Colossians 1:14, 16, 17).

Thus when nuclear physicists search out the patterns in the nucleus of the atom, they are viewing at the most basic level the evidence that all things in the physical universe are the product of intelligent, purposeful design. "The works of the LORD are great, sought out of all them that have pleasure therein" (Psalm 111:2).

The Solar System—Designed or Evolved?[4]

The solar system, of which our earth is a part, has as its center the sun around which the nine planets revolve in roughly circular orbits which lie fairly close to the same plane. Associated with the planets are a total of thirty-two satellites or moons revolving around their parent bodies in elliptical, nearly circular orbits. In the region between the planets Mars and Jupiter, there is a belt of debris called asteroids orbiting the sun, composed of chunks of rock and metal ranging in size from tiny particles up to large bodies a few hundred miles across. Two smaller orbiting belts of debris actually intersect the earth's orbit and give rise to the Perseid and Geminid meteor showers around August 12 and December 13 each year. The last component of the solar system comprises the comets, loose agglomerations of solid particles and frozen gases whose orbits around the sun reach very far out into space, some beyond the planets.

The question of how the solar system originated actually lies outside the competence of scientific investigation, since science should deal with processes which can be controlled and repeated. Nevertheless, for several centuries scientists and philosophers have been spinning speculative theories to explain the origin of the system entirely on the basis of chance physical events. The most prominent of these theories proposes that the sun and planets were formed by the gravitational collapse and condensation of a great, slowly rotating cloud of gas and dust probably formed as a random eddy in a much larger gas cloud which was collapsing to form the galaxy. As the smaller cloud collapsed, the gravitational energy was transformed into heat, and the central portion formed the sun, which finally became hot enough to start the nuclear reactions which are presently believed to provide the sun's energy. The outer portions of the cloud, much cooler, condensed to form the planets and their satellites.

Can this theory, called the Nebular Hypothesis, be successfully correlated with the observed facts of the solar system? A great deal of effort has been generated along this line, but many difficulties still remain.

1. The sun accounts for almost 99.9 percent of the mass of the solar system, yet almost 99.5 percent of the rotational momentum of the system is in the planets.[5] There is no known mechanical process which could accomplish this transfer of momentum from the sun to the planets. Therefore, astronomers have developed a scheme in which magnetic lines of force attached to the rotating sun dragged the condensing clouds of dust and gas around and transferred angular momentum to them from the sun. Some astronomers feel satisfied with this theory, while others consider it to be impossible.

An exceedingly delicate balance of conditions must be assumed to make the scheme seem plausible even in theory. The assumed temperature of the gas cloud must be sufficiently high to ionize the gas partly and thus provide for interaction between the matter and the magnetic lines of force. On the other hand the temperature must be sufficiently low to permit condensation of the material to form planets. These requirements are apparently contradictory.

A review of the results of the April 1972 Nice Symposium on the Origin of the Solar System concluded: "The Symposium has also served in delineating the areas of our ignorance, in particular in relation with the hydrodynamics of the nebula and with physico-chemistry of the 'sticking process.' "[6] The "hydrodynamics of the nebula" involves the angular momentum problem which we have been discussing. Thus, though secular scientists believe a gas-dust cloud collapsed in the distant past to form the solar system, they cannot bring together adequate theoretical explanations of how the process could have occurred. Needless to say, the hypothetical process cannot be demonstrated experimentally.

2. There is no known mechanism by which small particles of dust could stick together to build up chunks big enough which finally would attract each other gravitationally, and form planets. This is the "sticking process" referred to in the previous quotation from the Nice Symposium review. Try as they will, cosmologists cannot discover physical principles capable of explaining planet formation. Yet they believe that such a process has occurred billions of times in the history of the universe.

3. No theory of the formation of the earth-moon system has yet succeeded in correlating the observed facts with the requirements of the laws of physics. The Apollo Moon explorations have revealed such differences in composition between the earth and moon that it is not possible that the moon could have originated from the earth or that the two bodies could have accumulated from the same dust cloud.

4. Although the nine planets and most of the satellites orbit around their parent bodies in the counterclockwise direction (viewed from the north polar direction), nevertheless eleven of the thirty-two satellites revolve in the opposite direction. All theories designed to explain these irregularities and the formation or capture of satellites have failed.

5. Although six of the planets rotate on their axes in the counterclockwise direction, three of the nine—Mercury, Venus, and Uranus—rotate in the other direction. Furthermore, the axis of rotation of the planet Uranus lies almost in the plane of its orbit rather than roughly at right angles, as in the cases of the other planets. Theorists are hard put to explain these deviations from the pattern by means of any evolutionary scheme.

6. The idea that the sun could be formed by the gravitational collapse of a cloud of gas involves many theoretical difficulties. A gas cloud of the type presently observed out in space, unless it were a number of times greater in mass than the sun, would tend to expand rather than contract. Just how massive it would have to be is a matter currently being debated by cosmologists.[7] Furthermore, the cloud could not contract unless there were some way in which much of the resulting heat could be radiated out of the cloud. It is not yet firmly established that a process exists that could get this heat out of the cloud.

A recently discovered mystery for astrophysicists arises from the fact that painstaking measurements have failed to detect the predicted flow of neutrinos from the core of the sun. In fact, *no* detectable neutrinos may be emanating from the sun. But the nuclear process thought to be the source of solar energy produces neutrinos.

This means either that nuclear reactions do not power the sun, or that *periodic* surges of nuclear activity provide the energy. Current speculations propose that such surges occur at periods of millions of years, accompanied by corresponding surges of neutrinos, and followed by millions of years of gradual diffusion of the resulting energy to the sun's surface. While this theory conceivably may be developed to a point that it becomes plausible, the observational evidence (a surge of solar neutrinos) for the last energy surge is long gone and the next is not expected for millions of years. Scientists can never be entirely happy with a theory when its supporting evidence is forever beyond their grasp. Other theoretical efforts to explain the absence of solar neutrinos are also unsatisfactory.[8]

7. Another review of the Nice Symposium referred to earlier says: "Yet to be discussed adequately is the detailed fragmentation of the massive cloud in which protostars are born. Also in question are the hydrodynamics and the stability considerations of the protosun nebula. Most important, there remain to be specified (and carried out!) the crucial experimental tests that can distinguish between the available viable theories. It is particularly disappointing that we have almost no useful information on the specific solid state processes at work in the accretion phase."[9] The reviewer goes on to quote seven fundamental questions posed by H. Reeves, the editor of the Symposium report:

Do the sun and planets originate in the same interstellar cloud?
If so, how was the planetary matter separated from the solar gas?
How massive was the nebula?
How did the collapsing cloud cross the thermal, magnetic, and angular momentum barriers?
What were the physical conditions in the nebula?
What was the mechanism of condensation and accretion?
How did the planets, with their present properties and solar distances, form?

It is clear that materialistic scientists are acting on faith when they insist that the solar system evolved from a nebular cloud.

8. The earth-sun system, which is to man the most important segment of the solar system, is beautifully and delicately balanced to provide an environment on the earth's surface suitable for habitation by man. A number of the provisions for man's welfare on earth are detailed in Chapter 1. The probability that all of these factors should be found conjoined on the same planet is astronomically small. Our conclusion is that Earth was surely designed by a Master Planner. " . . . the earth hath he given to the children of men" (Psalm 115:16).

The Age of the Solar System

Scientists who believe that the solar system evolved from a gas cloud need much time for their scenario to unfold. Therefore, they are always seeking indicators of great age. Most of the dating methods depend upon the decay of radioactive elements contained in rocks. Such radiometric dating procedures and the associated difficulties are considered in Chapter 8. We will now consider some of the indications that the solar system is not billions of years old.

1. Comets, one of the components of the solar system, are loose clumps of rock, ice, and frozen gases which orbit the sun in elliptical trajectories. Some of the orbits of comets are highly elliptical and carry them far out, even beyond the farthest planet, requiring hundreds of years for one cycle. Short-term comets are those having periods of 150 to 200 years of less. Each time a comet approaches the sun on the near part of its orbit, the sun's radiation warms and drives away part of the gases, dust, and frozen water it contains. Moreover, the strong gravitational force near the sun partially disrupts the solid chunks making up the core of the comet. Ultimately, these effects of the sun cause the comet to disintegrate and disappear, and this has actually been observed to happen.

Careful studies of comets by British astronomer R. A. Lyttleton and others have led to the conclusion that all of the short-term comets should have disappeared in about 10,000 years. Yet many comets still remain. The reasonable conclusion is that the solar system is about 10,000 years old.[10]

This problem of mortality among comets has led astronomers to construct many hypotheses designed to make available a continuous supply of new comets. Jan Oort proposed that the source is a distant cloud of comets surrounding the solar system, from which comets are occasionally perturbed and drawn into closer orbits by the influences of passing stars and of the larger planets. Recent analysis of this theory shows that it predicts 40,000 fewer comets than actually are observed.[11] The other major contending theory, due to Lyttleton, suggests that interstellar material picked up by the sun continually agglomerates to form new comets.[12] However, this theory would require that a preponderance of comets be observed approaching from the direction of the constellation Hercules, and that some of them have hyperbolic orbits. These requirements of the theory are not supported by observation.

Thus the two major theories of cometary supply are negated by the observational evidence as are, in fact, all of the other theories thus far proposed. Comets remain a powerful argument in favor of a young solar system and a young earth only thousands of years old rather than billions.

2. Studies of the planet Venus have revealed that temperatures on the surface reach 900°F. Emmanuel Velikovsky predicted such a finding and postulated that this observation would be strong evidence that Venus is a young object. If the planet originated in a violent event only a few thousand years ago, the present high temperature is explained, for Venus would not have had time to cool down. In any event the high surface temperatures of Venus plus other unusual features are hard to explain if the planet is really billions of years old.

Recent radar studies of the surface reveal many large craters up to 100 miles in diameter. Shocked scientists cannot explain how meteors were able to get through the dense carbon dioxide atmosphere. They also are amazed that erosion by this atmosphere has not worn away the craters long ago. Perhaps Venus is not four billion years old after all.

3. The Mariner satellites orbiting the planet Mars have returned detailed photographs of the surface. Many craters and volcanoes pock the surface, and a dust storm lasting months was observed. A significant feature of many of the craters is the sharpness of their edges. More than a few thousand years of the kind of weather activity now observed in the Martian atmosphere should have eroded the sharp edges a great deal more than is actually the case. Long-term erosion should also largely have wiped out the strong differences in color still visible on the surface of Mars.

In addition, the small amount of water on Mars should long ago have been dissociated by the powerful ultraviolet radiation from the sun, leaving considerable oxygen gas in the atmosphere after the hydrogen from the split water molecules had escaped from the planet. But though considerable hydrogen is now observed to be escaping from the planet, there is very little oxygen there. All of these facts lead to the conclusion that Mars is only a few thousand years old.[13]

4. Rocks brought by Apollo teams from the moon have been dated by various radiometric methods which give conflicting results when all of the reports are considered. Moreover, it is of interest to note that the content of radioactive elements in the moon rocks is so high that if the moon were actually millions of years old, the heat produced by radioactive decomposition would have melted the moon.[14]

5. The Poynting-Robertson effect upon particles orbiting the sun results from a particle's absorption of energy from the sun and the re-radiation of this energy in all directions. The effect is to slow down the particle in its orbit and cause it to fall into the sun. Calculations indicate that in two billion years this process should have swept all particles less than three inches in diameter from the space extending as far out as the

planet Jupiter. Yet large quantities of such materials still remain in orbit. The conclusion is that the solar system is not so old after all.[15]

6. Before the Apollo landings on the moon, astronomers speculated that there was a thick layer of meteoritic dust on the moon resulting from billions of years of bombardment by meteorites of all sizes. To their dismay, only inches to several feet of such material were found. There is a noticeable silence on this matter in current discussions of moon data.

When these and other problems stemming from the long-time scales (required to make evolutionary schemes for the solar system look feasible) are added to the manifold evidences of intelligent design, it would appear that the weight of evidence lies with creation as recorded in the opening chapters of the Bible.

Stars—Evolved or Created?[16]

The two principal instruments for viewing the stars are the reflector telescope and the spectroscope. A reflector telescope uses a large parabolic, aluminized objective mirror to collect and focus the dim light of a star so that it can be magnified by the eyepiece lens to form an image which can be observed visually or recorded on film. The spectroscope, as explained earlier in this chapter, passes the light from the star through a fine slit and then through a glass prism, or allows it to be reflected from a fine diffraction grating. The prism or the grating bends the different wavelengths of light through varying angles. The result is that the fine strip of light coming through the slit is spread out into a wide ribbon of light called a spectrum. When this ribbon of light is projected on a white surface or on a photographic film, the red light falls at one end, then the yellow, orange, green, and blue light, with the violet light at the other end.

If the light passing through a spectroscope comes from a hot gas, the spectrum may contain bright lines at particular wavelengths, corresponding to particular elements contained in the gas. Or if the light has passed through cooler gas in the outer envelope of the star, particular atoms in the cool gas may absorb their own characteristic wavelengths, producing dark lines in the spectrum. Each kind of atom produces spectral lines which can be used to identify it. Thus the spectroscope may be used to tell what elements exist in the light-radiating and in the cooler, outer gas layers of a distant star.

For thousands of years astronomers have studied the stars, noting their relative positions and their apparent daily revolution around the earth. It was only with the advent of modern astronomical instruments that more particular information about individual stars could be obtained—for example, their temperature, composition, distance, and size. The spectroscope reveals not only some of the elements composing the outer gas layers of a star, but also the temperature, for the light from a hot object becomes less red and more blue as the temperature increases.

The distances to the nearer stars can be obtained by a process called triangulation. As the earth moves in its orbit around the sun during the year, the nearer stars appear to move against the background of very distant stars. This apparent movement, called parallax, is what you observe from a moving automobile when the objects at the side of the road appear to be changing position more rapidly than, say, a distant mountain. Thus, from the angular movement of a near star as the earth moves in six months from one side to the other of its orbit, the distance of the star can be calculated, based upon our knowledge of the distance across the earth's orbit, some 186 million miles. The distance to the nearest star to our solar system, α-Centauri, is about 4.3 light years, a light year being the distance light can travel in a year at 186,000 miles per second, or about 5.88 trillion miles (5.88 x 10^{12} miles). This method is only reliable for stars up to 300 light years away, but it tells us that the universe which we view as the starry heavens is surely very large, for the general background of stars shows no parallax movement at all and must, therefore, be far more distant.

From the temperature of a star determined from the color of its light, it is possible to estimate the brightness of its surface. Then, by combining this information with its distance and a measurement of its apparent brightness viewed from the earth, astronomers can calculate the size of the star, even though all stars, due to their great distance, appear only as points of light in the telescope. Such measurements for many stars reveal that our sun is, roughly speaking, an average star in diameter (865,000 miles), mass (2 x 10^{27} tons), and temperature (about 10,000°F.). There are actually only a relatively limited number of stars which are close enough for the very difficult parallax distance measurements to be made. Therefore, indirect methods based upon assumption and theory are required for the vast majority of stars.

Nevertheless, a great deal has been learned about the stars, and many different kinds of stars have been discovered. There are white dwarfs, hotter and smaller than our sun; the "main sequence" stars, a large group of stars with a wide range of temperatures and masses which includes the sun; and the giants and the super giants, both of which tend to be cooler than the sun. Then there are the pulsating stars, which vary in brightness and are divided into many different types, among which are the Cepheid variables, the RR Lyrae variables, and the semiregular and irregular variables. Each of these kinds of stars contains subclassifications meaningful to astronomers, and there are almost endless variations based upon composition and special features of structure or activity, such as the shell stars, Wolf-Rayet stars, X-ray stars, planetary nebula stars, flare stars, pulsars, and novae and supernovae.

Most astronomers believe that stars evolve from vast clouds of gas and dust through various stages of youth, maturity, and old age, finally to become dark celestial cinders.[17] Very complex mathematical models have been devised to explain star evolution, but many theoretical difficulties remain unsolved. In the first place, it is difficult to explain why a cloud of gas should collapse. One astronomer suggested that if we did not observe that stars actually exist, theoretical considerations would lead to the conclusion that they could not evolve. But, so the argument goes, since they exist, they did evolve.

Another difficulty is that if a gas cloud collapses as the theories propose, the entropy of the system would have to decrease, thus violating the second law of thermodynamics—unless large quantities of gravitational heat energy can be radiated out of the cloud. Until recently no mechanism was known which could accomplish this energy escape. Now it is proposed that OH molecules which exist in some interstellar clouds can radiate the heat energy from the cloud. However, it has yet to be observed that gas clouds are actually condensing by such a process to form new stars. An additional difficulty is posed by the fact, established in recent investigations, that the mass of neutral hydrogen in our galaxy is apparently only about 0.1 percent of the total galactic mass. Thus there does not seem to be enough hydrogen available to sustain the continual birth of new stars that current theory calls for.

There is really no compelling reason for calling some stars "young" and others "old," except that most astronomers desire to have an evolving universe which was not designed and created by a sovereign God. While it is true that some astronomers who believe in God also believe in some type of evolution of the universe, it is also true that many objections can be raised to the theory of star evolution. For example, a large percentage of stars are members of small groups which are held together by mutual gravitational attraction. Often a binary star consists of one "old" and one "new" star which supposedly evolved together and so are of the same age. This discrepancy is explained by supposing that the "old" star for some reason aged more rapidly. Such adjustments are typical of all evolutionary theories, including Darwin's. It is always possible to imagine an explanation for any discrepancy because a star or fossil cannot be experimented with to demonstrate that the imagined process could or could not, did or did not actually happen.

Nevertheless, a complete evolutionary theory has been devised for stars. The stars have been classified according to temperature and size, the different classifications being denoted by the letters OBAFGK-MQRNS. This series progresses from the very large, very hot O and B stars to the very small and relative cool N and S stars. These various types of stars are supposedly at different stages of their evolutionary history and therefore must be of greatly differing ages. Thus the O and B stars which are radiating energy and losing mass at prodigious rates are supposedly very young, whereas the G stars (the class of our sun) are supposedly very old.

Numerous difficulties plague the evolutionary star scenario. The O and B stars are burning out at such fantastic rates that extrapolation of this process just a few thousand years into the past leads to infinite masses. Yet they are supposedly much older than this, an obvious absurdity. The chemical composition of a star should change as it evolves, yet the stars in the different classifications, that is, the stars of different ages and stages of evolution, show no consistent evidence of a progressive change in composition. Furthermore, no real difference is observed between the composition of the stars and that of the interstellar material found in the space between the stars. Such evidence does not fit the evolutionary theory but, rather, suggests that all stars were created at the same time a few thousand years ago so that there has not been time for differences in chemical composition to develop. (See Footnote 16.)

The larger groups of stars called star clusters also pose some problems for the great age chronologies. Most clusters contain hundreds of thousands of stars, all moving like a swarm of bees, but held together by gravitational attraction. However, in some of these clusters many of the stars are moving at such high velocities that the cluster simply could not have held together over millions of years. Yet they are still together, indicating a much younger age.

In I Corinthians 15:41 the Apostle Paul tells us, "There is one glory of the sun, and another glory of the moon, and another glory of the stars: for one star differeth from another star in glory." Surely, "the heavens declare the glory of God," for only the God revealed in the Bible, whose glory is His absolute divine perfection, could be responsible for such a vast and marvelous creation. Yet there is more to be discovered as we move out from our solar system to examine the structure of the visible universe.

The Galaxies

As one views the heavens on a clear night, the band of light encircling the sky, known as the Milky Way, is strikingly prominent. The telescope resolves some of this cloud of light into individual stars, which suggests that they must be very far away—but how far? And just what is the Milky Way? Three much smaller patches of hazy light are visible to the naked eye. Powerful telescopes have also resolved many stars in these objects, so that they, too, would seem to be vast clouds of very distant stars. They have been named the Large and Small Magellanic Clouds and the Andromeda Galaxy.

Such distant objects are much too far away to have measurable parallaxes, so an indirect method was developed for estimating their distances. The original method used was based upon the properties of the Cepheid variable stars mentioned earlier. Studies of the Cepheid variables in certain star clusters revealed a regular relationship between their periods of variation (one to 100 days) and their relative apparent brightness in any particular cluster. Astronomers then reasoned that if the correct distances to some closer Cepheids could be measured, and if it could be assumed that the period-brightness relationship was universal for Cepheids wherever found, the result would be a known relationship between the period and the absolute brightness. Thus the distance to any Cepheid could be determined by measuring its period of variation and its apparent brightness, then performing a simple calculation.

Unfortunately, no Cepheids are close enough to have measurable parallaxes, so astronomers made statistical studies of the apparent relative motions of the nearer ones. All stars are moving in random directions and speeds, and the apparent motion of any star in one year as viewed from the earth is called the "proper motion" of that star. By measuring the proper motions and radial velocities over a period of years of some Cepheid variable stars and analyzing this information statistically, scientists determined the relationship between the period and the absolute brightness of the Cepheids, so that they could be used as astronomical distance markers.

The initial studies were made with the assumption that all of the Cepheids had the same intrinsic brightness versus period relation, which is not really the case. In addition, the absorption of their light by intervening dust in our galaxy was not correctly estimated. As a result it is believed that a major error was made. It was not until the early 1950's that it was decided that the Cepheids are actually four times brighter than originally thought. This meant that they were twice as far away as originally calculated. Consequently the accepted size of the universe suddenly doubled, a fact which made newspaper headlines.

The presently-accepted scale of the universe is based on a system of

measurement which has been built up of successive links of logical interpretation of astronomical data. The links are as follows:

Average earth-sun distance (1 astronomical unit = 92,960,000 miles,
↓ measured by triangulation within the solar system)

Stellar Parallax method (Distance estimated from apparent motion of star
↓ caused by earth's orbital motion)

Calibrate the Main Sequence method (Based on the Hertzprung-Russell
↓ diagram relating absolute brightness to temperature of normal stars)

Calibrate Cepheid method (Absolute brightness inferred from period)
↓

Calibrate Brightest Star method (Brightest stars assumed to have same
↓ absolute brightness in all galaxies)

Calibrate Galactic Red Shift method (Red shift of light from galaxies
assumed to be caused by recession of galaxies in an expanding
universe–to be considered below)

In spite of the problems and uncertainties in the use of Cepheid
variable star and other methods of measuring distances, it would appear
their use has provided a roughly valid measuring stick for the nearer parts
of the universe. What are the apparent distances to the nearby galaxies?
The two Magellanic clouds are considered to lie about 150,000 to 200,000
light years from the sun, the Andromeda Galaxy almost two million light
years. Astronomers believe that there are 20 galaxies within two and a half
million light years and many thousands within 50 million light years;
there may be a billion galaxies within photographic range of the 200-inch
Mount Palomar telescope.

The galaxies appear, then, to be vast assemblages of as many as 100
billion or more stars averaging about the same mass as the sun. Those
called spiral galaxies, disk-shaped with spiral arms composed of stars and
gas, are observed to be rotating around the center of galactic mass. The
nearby Andromeda is an example of a spiral galaxy. The Milky Way is
thought to be a spiral galaxy of which the solar system is a member. Since
the solar system is supposedly located in the disk, along the direction of
the disk in our sky the density of stars appears much higher, with the
result that we have a band high in star density in our sky. The diameter
of the Milky Way galaxy is of the order of 100,000 light years according
to present estimates.

Did Galaxies Evolve?

Galaxies are classified roughly into three categories: Spirals and ellipti-
cals, making up the majority, and irregulars, which comprise a small

minority. But there are about a dozen intermediate classifications, used by astronomers to describe the observed objects. Numerous attempts have been made in the past to develop an evolutionary theory for galaxies, but none has proved successful.

Supposedly a huge rotating gas cloud underwent gravitational collapse to form an elliptical galaxy, spread out into a rotating disk, and developed spiral arms which slowly wound up as the galaxy continued to turn. On the other hand, some theories postulated the reverse evolutionary course from spiral to elliptical irregular.

The current view is that galaxies do not evolve from one kind to another, but that each one as it originates takes on a type of structure determined primarily by the speed of its rotation. One difficulty with all such theories is that continued rotation would wipe out the spiral arms and produce a circular ring structure which is not observed. The fairly common "barred spirals" are particularly difficult to explain, for there is no known force that would preserve the bars.

Astronomer George Abell has stated, "There is much doubt, however, that galaxies evolve from one type to another at all."[18] The creation scientist, considering all of the evidence, concludes that creation by God is an explanation of the origin of galaxies as good as or better than the evolutionary theory.

Is the Universe Expanding?[19]

As more powerful telescopes were trained on ever more distant galaxies four decades ago, a curious fact was discovered by spectroscopic analysis of their light. It was observed that the characteristic spectral lines of the elements were often shifted from their normal wavelengths. In particular the spectra of the galaxies believed to be more distant were shifted toward the red or long-wavelength end of the spectrum. The amount of shift appeared to increase with the distance. This so-called "red shift" has been interpreted to mean that the distant galaxies are moving away from the sun with velocities which are appreciable fractions of the speed of light. This is called the Doppler effect.

Everyone has noticed the Doppler effect on the pitch of the sound of a whistle or horn on a moving train or automobile. The pitch is raised as the vehicle approaches and lowered as it recedes. In the case of light from stars, a simple formula translates the red shift into a velocity of approach or recession. Some of the more distant galaxies appeared to be moving away from the solar system with velocities approaching half the speed of light. The natural logical step was to correlate the observed red shift of the

nearer galaxies, whose distances had been estimated by the methods outlined on page 151. This correlation then led to a correlation between red
shift and distance.

Thus the red shift provides astronomers with what they consider to be
a yardstick for measuring distances to the farthest observable regions of
the universe. They believe that the galaxies which have been observed
with red shifts equivalent to velocities of recession greater than half the
speed of light are more than five billion light years away. Moreover, if
the red shift is indeed a Doppler effect resulting from rapid recession of
the galaxies from the earth, the universe must be expanding. Practically
all astronomers believe this to be the case.

But is the red shift of galaxies actually a Doppler effect indicating an
expanding universe, and is the universe as large as astronomers believe?
It has been suggested that some physical effect acting over large distances
depletes the energy of photons and thus produces the observed red shift.
A recent theory proposes that collisions between photons may be responsible for some of the red shift, and some recent observations offer
support for this theory. Another very serious question as to the validity
of the red shift as a yardstick arises from the discovery of the quasars,
which possess very large red shifts.[20] Quasars are faint objects with quite
large red shifts, suggesting that their distances from the earth are very
great.

Three additional observations relative to quasars are important.
Changes in brightness have been observed to occur in quasars in the space
of one day, which means that they must not be larger than roughly one
light day across. Yet if they are as distant as their red shifts indicate, it
would be impossible for an object of the corresponding size to radiate
energy at the observed rate.

Some astronomers, therefore, have concluded that the quasars are
much closer than their red shifts indicate. This would mean that the red
shift is not a reliable indicator of distance. A further difficulty stems
from the fact that some quasars have been observed with as many as five
greatly differing red shifts. Finally, radio telescope observations of some
quasars indicate expansion rates of two or three times the speed of light
if the quasars are actually as distant as their red shifts have been interpreted to mean. But according to relativity theory, nothing can exceed
the speed of light.

Thus it can be seen that the currently adopted astronomical scale of
distances for the universe is subject to serious questions as a result of recently acquired observational data. And it should be remembered that the
red shift distance scale was originally developed upon the foundation of

the Cepheid variable star distance scale, which itself has a considerable degree of possible error. But is it a problem for biblical creationists if the universe is in fact billions of light years across and expanding? The obvious problem is that it would presumably take light ten billion years to travel ten billion light years. This is not easily reconciled with the six to ten thousand years since creation indicated in the biblical record.

Several possible solutions to this problem have been suggested:

1. The red shift and Cepheid distance scales may prove to be erroneous, resulting in a distance scale collapsed to around ten thousand light years for the radius of the universe. It is easy to imagine that the accepted scale of the universe might indeed be reduced in the future. But one finds it difficult to conceive that the current view of the size of the universe is in error by a factor of one million. Thus this solution involves some difficulties.

2. The time of light transit across great distances may prove to be much less than has been supposed on the basis of the assumed constancy of the speed of light. Einstein's theory of relativity, based upon the assumption that the speed of light is constant for all observers, has come under strong criticism in recent years.[21] The speed of light may depend upon the velocity of the source after all. If this be the case, the theory advanced by MIT professors Moon and Spencer in 1953 may prove to be correct.[22]

They proposed that light travels in curved space. From a study of binary stars they adduced evidence that the radius of curvature of space is five light years. They calculated that as a consequence of this, the light transit time from the farthest reaches of the universe would never exceed 15.71 years. This view remains highly speculative and requires more supporting data from observation and experiment.

3. Light from the stars may have been created instantaneously in rays throughout space at the same time the stars were created. The simple form of this model involves some difficulty. Light now arriving upon earth from stars supposedly many tens of thousands to millions of light years distant indicates the occurrence of such past historical events as pulsating light intensities and supernovae. But if the light was created in transit less than ten thousand years ago, the light rays must have been created so as to give evidence of historical events which actually never occurred. This seems to be logically unacceptable.

4. A modification of the previous view is suggested by the language of the Scriptures. Thirteen times in the Old Testament, as in Job 9:8, Psalm 104:2, Isaiah 40:22, Jeremiah 10:12, and Zechariah 12:1, God is pictured as the One who "stretchest out the heavens." This interesting expression,

obviously beyond the full comprehension of man, may suggest a process by which space, stars, and interconnecting star light were created by God by a rapid expansion or stretching process out of nothing without time being required for the light to travel vast distances across the universe to earth. Further study of the Scriptures and advancing knowledge of the universe may lead to more definite answers to these questions.

The Origin of the Universe

Astronomers who do not accept the Bible are as prone to evolutionary thinking as are their unbelieving counterparts in the biological sciences. The most widely held view of the origin of the universe, based upon the evidence for an expanding universe, is that the universe originated in the explosion of a primordial concentration of matter-energy. Where this original nucleus came from they do not attempt to explain, other than to suggest that it may have come from the collapse of a previously existing universe. In their view, the original explosion produced the expanding universe, at first in the form of an expanding cloud composed mostly of hydrogen gas. Supposedly portions of this cloud contracted under the influence of gravity to form galaxies, and stars formed with the galaxies as discussed previously in this chapter.

There are many difficulties with all such "big bang" theories of the origin of the universe.[23] In the first place, analysis of the various proposed models for the original matter-energy fireball by the principles of classical physics (non-relativistic physics) reveals that the ball would collapse rather than expand. This is because the force of gravity around such a super-condensed mass (10^{14} to 10^{25} g/cm^3) would be so great that even photons of light could not escape. The prediction is that the ball containing all of the matter-energy of the present universe would collapse eternally into a so-called black hole.[24]

In the second place, it cannot be demonstrated that, if the fireball did succeed in exploding, the resulting homogeneous cloud of expanding gas would condense into galaxies. The laws of physics point merely to a continuing expansion of the hypothetical gas cloud. To get around this problem, Prof. James Gunn of the California Institute of Technology in Pasadena proposed in a public lecture in 1972 that the original nucleus of matter-energy had to have "lumps." That is, it had to contain an original design, at least a simple one to get the evolutionary scenario moving.

A third and related difficulty with the big bang theories arises from the fact that the original cloud was surely much simpler in structure than is the present universe. An exact description of that early state of the uni-

verse would require vastly less information than would such a description of today's universe. But the Second Law of Thermodynamics discussed in Chapter 2 requires that natural, random processes cannot produce an increase of order and information content. This problem is at the
root of current controversy among cosmologists.

Creationist scientists, on the other hand, believe the biblical record of
creation: "In the beginning God created the heaven and the earth." They
observe marvelous evidences of intelligent, purposeful design wherever
they search, from the heart of the atom out to the farthest galaxy. Every
living thing—single cell, complex plant or animal, or ecological community— is so replete with special design and order as to be inexplicable
in any scientifically satisfactory sense by natural, chance chemical processes from non-living matter. To believe in such an origin of either the
physical universe or the world of living creatures requires implicit faith
in assumed processes and alleged events which cannot be duplicated or
demonstrated in any laboratory.

In the evolutionary view the origin of life stems from the same physical
laws which supposedly brought into being the universe of time, space,
and matter by a primeval explosion. But the origin of the fantastically
complex system represented by those physical laws is taken for granted.
Even granting the evolutionary development theories, the question of
ultimate origins is ignored and left unanswered, a nagging thorn in the
side of all evolutionary theorists.

How much more rational and in accord with the body of scientific data
is the biblical record of creation by the infinite-personal Spirit, by Whom
and for Whom are all things. "Of old hast thou laid the foundation of
the earth: and the heavens are the work of thy hands" (Psalm 102:25).
"Thou hast created all things, and for thy pleasure they are and were
created" (Rev. 4:11b). He stretched out the heavens, flinging billions of
galaxies and trillions of stars into their places, binding them all into a universe by the system of physical law of which He is the architect and ener-
gizer. At the center of this universe—the center of divine concern if not
the physical center—He placed a very specially designed grain of sand
called the earth and put upon it man, created in His own image. And the
grand purpose of all the rest of the creation is to show forth His glory and
to inspire man to glorify the Creator in his divinely appointed dominion
over the earth.

And perhaps one of the most astounding and precious truths of the
biblical revelation of God and creation is the fact that the infinite, holy,
omnipotent Creator of the vast universe is personally and lovingly concerned with sinful men upon the earth. We marvel and rejoice with the

Psalmist, "When I consider thy heavens, the work of thy fingers, the moon and the stars, which thou hast ordained; What is man, that thou art mindful of him? and the son of man that thou visitest him?" (Psalm 8:3, 4).

7

Beliefs &
Interpretations
of Evidence

Philosophies of Beginnings

The opening sentence of the Bible answers the most fundamental question of philosophy and establishes the ground of reality for the rest of the biblical revelation of origins, of human history, and of the future consummation of the ages. The question is, "What is eternal and therefore the source of all else that is real?" The Bible answers, "In the beginning God created the heaven and the earth." Thus the Bible makes it clear that infinite, personal Spirit only is eternal; everything else—every spiritual being and material thing—had a beginning, was created by God the infinite Spirit, and is completely dependent upon Him for continued existence.

The biblical conception of reality grounded wholly in eternal, personal Spirit is unique among the philosophies espoused by men. It is eminently reasonable and leads to a consistent and satisfying understanding of the world and of man's place in it. Broadly speaking, there are two other philosophical viewpoints: The material cosmos is the eternal reality and there is no spirit. Or, both spirit and the material cosmos are eternal. Out of these philosophies has come the evolutionary conception of the origin of the world and man as they are today and the effort to uncover and understand the processes of origins by scientific examination of nature. This book has been designed to explain how the facts observed in nature best agree with the biblical record of the origin of all things by divine special creation.

In earlier chapters it has been shown that the study of origins lies outside the province of the experimental scientific enterprise, strictly defined. Nevertheless, modern scientists continue to seek scientific explanations for the beginning of the world. Many ancient peoples who had either lost or rejected the divine revelation of beginnings satisfied man's innate curiosity about his origin and his destiny by means of mythology.

The best known of the ancient creation myths is the Babylonian epic poem known as *Enuma Elish* ("When above"), the title derived from the two opening words. Archaeologist Allan A. MacRae has given a condensed analysis of the contents of this ancient creation account which, he says, is very different from that contained in Genesis 1. It tells of the coming into being of two parties of deities who engage in bitter conflict. The winning party is led by the chief deity of Babylon, who therefore receives the outstanding place of authority in the cosmos. Somewhat as a by-product of the warfare of the gods, he sets the sky in place, founds the earth, and puts the moon and stars in motion, creating men to serve the gods. It is notable that *Enuma Elish* does not speak of the creation of the sun, no doubt because the sun-god is designated as the principal deity.[1]

The following quotations from *Enuma Elish* and discussion by Merrill F. Unger will enable the reader better to evaluate and contrast the mythological and biblical accounts of origins.

In the opening tablet, only Apsu (male) and Taimat (female) exist. These two become the parents of the gods.
When above the heavens had not [yet] been named,
[And] below the earth had not [yet] existed as such,
[When] only Apsu primeval, their begetter, [existed]
[And] mother [mummu] Tiamat, who gave birth to them all;
[When] their waters [yet] intermingled,
[And] no dry land had been formed [and] not
[Even] a marsh could be seen;
When none of the gods had been brought forth,
Then were the gods created in the midst of them [Apsu and Tiamat].
Lahmu and Lahamu [deities] they [Apsu and Tiamat] begat.

The newly created gods become so annoying in their conduct that Apsu decides to do away with them. The great god Ea, however, discovers the plan and slays Apsu. Ea then begets Marduk, the city god of Babylon. Tiamat, in the meantime, prepared to avenge the death of her husband, Apsu. She creates monsters and sets Kingu, one of her children, at the head of her army.

In the next three tablets it is told how Marduk is chosen by Ea to battle Tiamat's army. He is elevated to supremacy among the gods. In the battle, Tiamat is slain. This supposedly represents the victory of order over chaos. Finally, Marduk creates the cosmos out of the corpse of Tiamat.

Tablet five discusses the creation of the stars and of time. The sixth tablet is important in that it gives the creation of man. Marduk states:
Blood I will form and cause bone to be:
Then I will set up lullu, *"Man" shall be his name.*
Yes, I will create lullu: *Man!*
[Upon him] shall the service of the gods be imposed that they may rest. . . .

Tablet seven finishes the epic by describing the elevation of Marduk to supremacy among the pantheon in a great festive banquet.[2]

It is hardly necessary to comment on the total contrast between the majestic Genesis account of creation and the Babylonian tale of squabbling gods. The difference in every respect between the eternal, omnipotent, omniscient, omnipresent Creator and Lord of the Bible and the fantastic mythological deities of *Enuma Elish* is striking. Similar contrasts exist between the Bible and all other ancient accounts of beginnings.

While the modern materialistic conception of cosmic and biological evolution excludes explicit mythology, it nevertheless shares certain fundamental ideas with some of the ancient philosophies. One of these is that the cosmos is somehow eternal and exists independently of the power of any God. Consequently there never was a supernatural creation of the natural order which materialistic science investigates. Implicit in this view is the idea that time never had a beginning, whereas the Bible teaches that time itself had a beginning. Chapter 8 will cover the subject of time in considerable detail.

The materialistic, evolutionary philosophy, progressively gaining dominance in the various fields of scientific enterprise, gradually bent scientific research almost entirely into programs which would produce evidence that could be inserted into a logical structure supporting evolutionary theory. Several of the kinds of evidence adduced in support of the theory have been discussed in earlier chapters. The remainder of this chapter will consider additional important classes of evidence and suggest interpretations which are in accord with the biblical record of creation.

Comparative Anatomy and Taxonomy

Do similarities between different creatures qualify as evidence for genetic relationship? For example, do the many physical similarities between the chimpanzee and man validate the idea that man and chimp are descendants of a common ancestor? And is degree of similarity related to closeness of relationship among living things? For example, is the similarity series fish-lizard-ape-man the consequence of a real historical process of evolution from fish to man?

figure 7-1. Photomicrograph of bird's flight feather at about 400X magnification. From both sides of the main shaft (rachis) the parallel barbs extend at an angle. The much smaller barbules extend at an angle from both sides of the barbs. The tiny hooks (hamuli) which are arranged on the barbules catch in the adjacent barbules, linking the whole feather together with a zipper-like action. If the feather is pulled apart, the bird can reset the zippers by pulling the feather through its beak. Could feathers have evolved from reptile scales as some evolutionists have suggested?

The answers to these two questions must both be negative for two basic reasons. First, as explained in Chapter 5, the process by which living things originated was a historical process requiring historical evidence (i.e., human testimony) for its study. But historical evidence is lacking and the process is not reproducible, so neither secular history nor experimental science can supply the required evidence. The available evidence, therefore, is circumstantial in nature, necessitating interpretation, the conclusions of which are strongly influenced by the *a priori* assumptions of the interpreter.

Second, the idea that a similarity sequence indicates genetic relationship leads to absurd conclusions. For an illustration of this, one need only consider the eye of the octopus, which is structurally quite similar to the human eye in most respects. Can this reasonably be interpreted as evidence for close evolutionary relationship between the octopus and man? Obviously not. Defenders of evolution consider similarities in widely divergent animal groups to be the result of convergent evolution. Nevertheless, there are so many seemingly fantastic examples of supposed convergent evolution that the similarity argument becomes rather suspect, if not actually invalid.

How, then, are similarities between different kinds of living creatures to be interpreted? To answer this, consider the following question: Why do practically all automobiles have four wheels rather than three or five? Quite simply, experience has shown that four wheels afford the most practical arrangement for an automobile. Therefore, automobiles, while differing in many other respects, are all designed by practical-minded engineers around the basic four-wheel scheme.

Thus it is only reasonable and to be expected that the God of creation would use a practical basic design framework for, let us say, the design of all vertebrates. Except for snakes they are virtually all quadrupeds, for the basic framework of backbone and four limbs is eminently practical and adaptable to many specific variations. This is what we actually observe in nature, one aspect of an orderly universe which is the result of a systematic plan and design framed by the omniscient Creator.

Taxonomy is the systematic classification of living creatures according to form. The founder of this science, Linnaeus, believed that he was merely systematizing the knowledge of the Creator's handiwork. Later, with the advent of Darwinism, the fact that plants and animals could be classified was taken as evidence for evolutionary relationship. A "natural" taxonomy became the goal, one in which the system of classification paralleled the supposed course of evolutionary development.

Taxonomy attempts to classify plants and animals into groups of increasing size: species, genera, families, orders, classes, phyla, and kingdoms. The species concept is not easy to define precisely. The current definition is: Species are groups of interbreeding natural populations that are reproductively isolated from other such groups.[3] Thus a species is considered as a gene pool, each individual in the population holding temporarily a small portion of the genes in that pool. The members of the population interbreed and are normally prevented from breeding with the members of other species by numerous protective devices. In general, the combinations formed from the species' gene pool are harmonious, and occasional combinations produced by mixture with genes from other species' gene pools are normally inharmonious and soon excluded by natural selection.

The above species definition, while usually applied without difficulty, is still in numerous cases subject to problems leading to the necessity for arbitrary decisions by taxonomists. Reproductive isolation between two populations (meaning they do not interbreed) can break down in changing environments, or it may never have been completely established. So-called sibling species are exceedingly difficult at times to distinguish, and this sometimes can only be done on the basis of subtle internal differences. In the case of the higher categories, however, there is generally no particular difficulty in assigning a species to its respective genus, family, etc.

How does taxonomy fit into the biblical creationist interpretation of biology? The fundamental scriptural teaching on this subject is the ten times repeated statement in Genesis 1 that God created each "kind" of plant and animal to reproduce "after its kind." The term translated "kind" is not precisely defined by its usage in the Bible. Therefore the Christian can draw conclusions from his observation of the biological world.

In view of the fact that variation of species within limits has been observed and that the definition of species still leaves some arbitrary character in the system of classification, we can conclude that the creation kinds were in general probably higher than the species category, perhaps at roughly the genus level, or even in some cases that of the family. This is a good area for Christians in the biological sciences to carry on biblically-oriented research. It surely should be clear, however, that the charge that biblical creationists insist on absolute fixity of all species is false, especially when the species definition allows some arbitrary species designations.

The second conclusion from taxonomy is that the generally unambiguous classification of all living things into the higher categories and the demonstrated impossibility of transition from one to another agree with the biblical teaching that the Creator formed kinds which are forever separate. The fact that within the categories exist similarities of structure and form agrees with our earlier conclusion that a rational Creator would employ basic plans with modifications for the creation of the different subdivisions within each category.

If one keeps in mind the fact stated earlier that similarity does not verify the hypothesis of genetic relationship, it will be clear that taxonomy cannot be considered as scientific support for the thesis of evolutionary relationship. It is important also to realize that although a large amount of evidence has been gathered which demonstrates genetic variation among populations of many sorts of plants and animals, the observed changes have been trivial when compared to the changes required by the evolutionary theory. In other words, the actual experimental data of the biological sciences supports the biblical principle that various kinds of life were created with impassable genetic barriers separating them. The variability observed in plants and animals is part of the Creator's provision which makes each kind capable of adaptation to a changing environment.

Comparative Protein Structure

Perhaps the most recently developed type of evidence adduced in support of the evolutionary hypothesis comes from the study of amino acid sequences of proteins from different plants and animals. It will be remembered from the discussion in Chapter 4 that proteins are long chains of the twenty commonly occurring amino acids arranged in specific sequences which determine the properties of the specific proteins. The fundamental structure of any protein is described by listing the order of the different amino acids in the long molecule. Many of the proteins produced in living cells serve as enzymes (catalysts or promoters) for reactions which the cell must carry out in the course of the many metabolic processes which make life possible.

In general, each enzyme protein catalyzes a specific reaction in a chain of successive reactions which comprise what is termed a metabolic pathway. One such pathway found in plants and animals is that by which the sugar glucose is oxidized to provide energy for the cell. The sequence of reactions is quite complicated, and each step requires a specific enzyme. One of these enzymes, cytochrome c, has been extracted from many different organisms, and the sequence of amino acids in the enzyme molecule has been determined for each organism. It has been found that the cytochrome c molecule is quite similar for all of the organisms. In particular, there are regions in the protein amino acid chain in which the sequence of amino acids is identical in every cytochrome c. These are apparently parts of the molecule which are essential for its enzyme activity.

In the other less functional regions of the cytochrome c molecules, some of the amino acid units vary from organism to organism. Dr. Richard Dickerson of the California Institute of Technology analyzed these variations in terms of the average numbers of changes between groups of animals and plants. These numbers were then plotted against the assumed number of years back to the supposed time of evolutionary divergence from common ancestors which led to the groups. A fair straight-line relationship was demonstrated, which is interpreted as evidence for a constant rate of mutational change in cytochrome *c* with time, and also as evidence that the evolutionary development actually occurred in accordance with Darwinian theory.[4]

The following critical comments may be made relative to variable amino acid sequences in cytochrome *c* from different organisms:

1. Is this in principle any different from the arrangement of organisms in a similarity series according to bodily form and structure? The cytochrome *c* molecules are arranged in a series according to certain variations in amino acid sequence. This is actually a series based upon molecular morphology (shape) which does not verify an evolutionary history any more than does a similarity series of outward forms and structure. It is only circumstantial evidence for evolution.

2. The invariance of all of the cytochrome *c*'s in their critical parts is evidence for intelligent, purposeful design. A certain basic design is essential for the functioning of this vital enzyme in all living things.

3. The data of cytochrome *c* amino acid sequences yields no evidence for the evolutionary origin of this basic design for the enzyme.

4. Although, as was explained earlier, the amino acid changes between groups of organisms can be interpreted in a manner which supports the evolutionary theory, this evidence is, nevertheless, circumstantial. Closer analysis of the data reveals inconsistencies relative to the supposed history of evolution. Table 1 shows the number of amino acid changes between pairs of animals in the vertebrate group. When these numbers are divided into the assumed time in millions of years back to the supposed divergence of the ancestors of the members of a pair from some assumed or imagined common ancestor, the result is roughly the time in millions of years required for a change of one percent in the 104-unit amino acid chain.

As reported in Dr. Dickerson's article, this time is about 20 million years between groups. The fact that this value is fairly constant between the different groups and over varying time periods is adduced as support for the evolutionary assumptions. But observe in Table 2 that such values within the vertebrate group vary all the way from seven million years to 50 million years for this selected set of pairs. The average value is about 25 million years, but the spread of values is so wide that it can hardly be said that the data offers good support for the theory that the vertebrates are related by evolution and that the rate of change of the cytochrome *c* molecule was constant with time within the vertebrate group. Perhaps the

table 6. Cytochrome c Amino Acid Sequences[4] for positions 62 to 84 in the peptide chains from 38 different species. The segment from position 70 to 80 is invariant, for it is the heart of the active center of the enzyme molecule. In addition 24 other sites are also invariant. Another 23 sites are occupied only by one or the other of a pair of very similar amino acids. There is no evidence for the evolutionary development of the overall structure of the enzyme nor of the active center and its function of catalyzing vital oxidation reactions in living cells. Thus the evidence supports the view that cytochrome *c* was designed, not evolved.

Symbols for the amino acids, classified by character of side-chains:

   F(phenylalanine), Y(tyrosine)—hydrophobic with a benzene-type ring.
   I(isoleucine), L(leucine), M(methionine), V(valine)—hydrophobic, without benzene ring.
   K(lysine), R(arginine), X(methylated lysine)—hydrophilic basic.
   D(aspartic acid), E(glutamic acid)—hydrophilic, acidic.
   A(alanine), N(asparagine), P(proline), S(serine), T(threonine)—hydrophilic but small, or polar but uncharged.
   G(glycine)—no side-chain.

	62	65	70	75	80
Man, chimpanzee	—D—T—L—M—E—Y—L—E—N—P—K—K—Y—I—P—G—T—K—M—I—F—V—G—
Rhesus monkey	—D—T—L—M—E—Y—L—E—N—P—K—K—Y—I—P—G—T—K—M—I—F—V—G—
Horse	—E—T—L—M—E—Y—L—E—N—P—K—K—Y—I—P—G—T—K—M—I—F—A—G—
Donkey	—E—T—L—M—E—Y—L—E—N—P—K—K—Y—I—P—G—T—K—M—I—F—A—G—
Cow, pig, sheep	—E—T—L—M—E—Y—L—E—N—P—K—K—Y—I—P—G—T—K—M—I—F—A—G—
Dog	—E—T—L—M—E—Y—L—E—N—P—K—K—Y—I—P—G—T—K—M—I—F—A—G—
Rabbit	—D—T—L—M—E—Y—L—E—N—P—K—K—Y—I—P—G—T—K—M—I—F—A—G—
Calif. gray whale	—E—T—L—M—E—Y—L—E—N—P—K—K—Y—I—P—G—T—K—M—I—F—A—G—
Great gray kangaroo	—D—T—L—M—E—Y—L—E—N—P—K—K—Y—I—P—G—T—K—M—I—F—A—G—
Chicken, turkey	—D—T—L—M—E—Y—L—E—N—P—K—K—Y—I—P—G—T—K—M—I—F—A—G—
Pigeon	—D—T—L—M—E—Y—L—E—N—P—K—K—Y—I—P—G—T—K—M—I—F—A—G—
Pekin duck	—D—T—L—M—E—Y—L—E—N—P—K—K—Y—I—P—G—T—K—M—I—F—A—G—
Snapping turtle	—E—T—L—M—E—Y—L—E—N—P—K—K—Y—I—P—G—T—K—M—I—F—A—G—
Rattlesnake	—D—T—L—M—E—Y—L—E—N—P—K—K—Y—I—P—G—T—K—M—V—F—T—G—
Bullfrog	—D—T—L—M—E—Y—L—E—N—P—K—K—Y—I—P—G—T—K—M—I—F—A—G—
Tuna	—D—T—L—M—E—Y—L—E—N—P—K—K—Y—I—P—G—T—K—M—I—F—A—G—
Dogfish	—E—T—L—R— I —I—Y—L—E—N—P—K—K—Y—I—P—G—T—K—M—I—F—A—G—
Samia cynthia (moth)	—D—T—L—F— E—Y—L—E—N—P—K—K—Y—I—P—G—T—K—M—V—F—A—G—
Tobacco hornworm moth	—D—T—L—F— E—Y—L—E—N—P—K—K—Y—I—P—G—T—K—M—V—F—A—G—
Screwworm fly	—D—T—L—F— E—Y—L—E—N—P—K—K—Y—I—P—G—T—K—M—I—F—A—G—
Drosophila (fruit fly)	—D—T—L—F— E—Y—L—E—N—P—K—K—Y—I—P—G—T—K—M—I—F—A—G—
Baker's yeast	—N—N—M—S— E—Y—L—T—N—P—X—K—Y—I—P—G—T—K—M—A—F—G—G—
Candida krusei (yeast)	—P—T—M—S— D—Y—L—E—N—P—X—K—Y—I—P—G—T—K—M—A—F—G—G—
Neurospora crassa (mold)	—N—T—L—F— E—Y—L—E—N—P—X—K—Y—I—P—G—T—K—M—A—F—G—G—
Wheat germ	—N—T—L—Y— D—Y—L—L—N—P—X—K—Y—I—P—G—T—K—M—V—F—P—G—
Buckwheat seed	—D—T—L—Y— E—Y—L—L—N—P—X—K—Y—I—P—G—T—K—M—V—F—P—G—
Sunflower seed	—N—T—L—Y— D—Y—L—E—N—P—X—K—Y—I—P—G—T—K—M—V—F—P—G—
Mung bean	—K—T—L—Y— D—Y—L—E—N—P—X—K—Y—I—P—G—T—K—M—V—F—P—G—
Cauliflower	—K—T—L—Y— D—Y—L—E—N—P—X—K—Y—I—P—G—T—K—M—V—F—P—G—
Pumpkin	—K—T—L—Y— D—Y—L—E—N—P—X—K—Y—I—P—G—T—K—M—V—F—P—G—
Sesame seed	—N—T—L—Y— D—Y—L—E—N—P—X—K—Y—I—P—G—T—K—M—V—F—P—G—
Castor bean	—N—T—L—Y— A—Y—L—E—N—P—X—K—Y—I—P—G—T—K—M—V—F—P—G—
Cottonseed	—N—T—L—Y— D—Y—L—E—N—P—X—K—Y—I—P—G—T—K—M—V—F—P—G—
Abutilon seed	—N—T—L—Y— D—Y—L—E—N—P—X—K—Y—I—P—G—T—K—M—V—F—P—G—

great time assumed never existed after all.

5. The metabolic pathway involving cytochrome *c* is only one of many which are found widely distributed throughout all living things. This almost universal distribution of identical or very similar chemical systems in plants and animals is taken to be evidence for genetic relationship and therefore as evidence for evolution of all life from common ancestors. The biblical creationist, on the other hand, takes this as evidence for a common Creator of all life Who used a common set of basic metabolic patterns with adaptations to meet the needs of each creature.

6. The differences found in the less critical portions of the enzyme molecules from different creatures may be explained in several ways. They may be the result either of initially created differences or of random, neutral mutations, or of both.

table 7. Differences in Vertebrate Cytochrome c

Animal pair		No. different amino acids[4]	Alleged time since common ancestor (million years)[5]	Millions of years for 1% change
Dogfish-	Tuna	19	420	22
	Turtle	18	420	23
	Donkey	16	420	26
	Rattlesnake	13	420	32
	Man	21	420	50
	Kangaroo	19	420	22
Tuna-	Turtle	17	370	22
	Donkey	15	370	25
	Rattlesnake	25	370	15
	Man	20	370	19
Turtle-	Donkey	10	300	30
	Rattlesnake	20	300	15
	Man	12	300	25
Donkey-	Rattlesnake	19	300	16
	Man	11	80	7
Man-	Rattlesnake	11	300	27
	Pigeon	10	300	30
	Dog	11	80	7
Rabbit-	Man	9	80	9
	Donkey	5	80	16
	Duck	6	300	50
	Pigeon	7	300	43
Duck-	Kangaroo	10	300	30
	Tuna	15	370	25
	Dogfish	15	420	28
Dog-	Tuna	17	370	22
	Pigeon	8	300	38

7. Actually, however, the overall picture is complicated by the discovery in recent years of various alternate metabolic pathways to some of the common enzyme systems. These and other surprising variations in internal chemistry of many organisms are often difficult to explain from the evolutionary point of view. They provide no difficulty, however, for the biblical creation model of origins. Such variations illustrate the infinite wisdom and power of the Creator in His capacity to design and create a seemingly unlimited number of working life systems and to fit them to participate successfully in a complex biosphere which man is really only beginning to understand.

The Development of the Embryo[6]

Almost all life is cellular, and each type of organism has a stage in which it exists as a single cell. In the vertebrates the fertilized egg cell develops through a succession of stages to the many-celled adult form. This succession of stages, the process of embryonic development, is sometimes called ontogeny. In the early part of the nineteenth century proposals were made which led German embryologist Ernst Haeckel in 1866 to announce his "fundamental biogenetic law." His idea was that a higher creature in the course of its embryonic development from the single cell stage successively passes through stages similar to the adult forms of the successive evolutionary ancestors which supposedly preceded it during millions of years of evolution from single-celled life to the complex many-celled creature. Since a term for this alleged evolutionary process is "phylogeny," a slogan became popular in some circles: "Ontogeny recapitulates phylogeny." While such an expression may sound erudite and stick in the minds of college students, it does not necessarily correspond to the scientific evidence.

The theory of embryonic recapitulation and the corresponding slogan were widely accepted for many years, in spite of the fact that from the beginning many scientists rejected it because of the large amount of evidence from embryology which contradicts it. The most famous evidence offered in the support of the theory was the presence of the so-called "gill pouches" in the embryos of fish, mammals, and human beings at a certain stage of development. In the fish this structure of blood vessels and supporting membranes becomes perforated to form gill slits by which the fish ultimately breathes. The human and other embryos, in contrast, carry out respiration through the placenta and transform the pouches into other organs having no connection with respiration. The idea that the human embryo has "gill slits" is a misrepresentation of facts based upon superficial knowledge, a typical cause of error.

A few of the numerous facts of embryonic development which contradict the theory of embryonic recapitulation are the following: 1. Children develop tongues before teeth, the reverse of evolutionary theory. 2. Vertebrate embryos form the heart before the rest of the circulatory system, the reverse of theory. 3. Some creatures are very similar in the adult stage but quite different in the egg or larval stages, the reverse of theory. 4. Moths, butterflies, and some other insects go through a pupal stage in which all internal structure dissolves into formless jelly, for which there could be no corresponding evolutionary ancestor. 5. In some cases, the early stages resemble their own adult form more than they do the adult forms of supposed ancestors, contrary to the theory. 6. The respiratory surface of the lung is the last to appear in the embryo, whereas it must have been present throughout the alleged evolutionary history. 7. Some parts of an embryo may have stages which seem to exhibit recapitulation, whereas other parts show no correlation with the recapitulation theory whatsoever.

But since some similarities to supposed evolutionary ancestors exist in the series of stages in the embryonic development of various animals, how

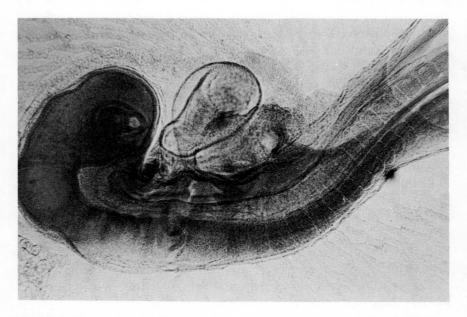

figure 7-2. Photomicrograph at 40x of chick embryo 43 hours old. Does this embryo portray millions of years of evolutionary history? Or is it developing according to an efficient plan conceived by a wise Bio-Engineer?

does this fact fit with biblical creation? The obvious explanation is that each embryo develops its organs through those stages and in the order which meet its needs at each level of its developmental process. For instance, since the nervous system is the most complex structure, its formation begins very early in the vertebrate embryos.

Therefore the early stages of vertebrate embryos all have a worm-like appearance because of the prominent bulge of the developing brain attached to the long embryonic spinal cord. Embryonic development points not to unplanned evolution, but to the intelligent programming of a complex building operation.

Vestigial, Rudimentary, and Atavistic Structures

Vestigial organs are structures now supposedly useless or unnecessary which were functional in evolutionary ancestors. A century ago the German anatomist, Wiedersheim, claimed there were 180 such structures in the human body. Since that time, all but about six of these structures have been proved to be functional. The classic example is the human appendix, which allegedly has degenerated from an important organ in our hypothetical plant-eating ancestors to become a non-functional relic in humans. In recent years, however, it has been concluded that the appendix, rich in lymphoid tissue, serves to guard the body against infection, particularly in early years, being in this respect comparable to the tonsils and adenoids.

An example of rudimentary organs would be the rudimentary mammary glands in the human male. One theory proposes that the males among our ancestors were able to nurse their young, but the notion is difficult to defend and absolutely no supporting evidence exists. A very reasonable explanation is that though the male possesses in his chromosomal complement the genes for the female physiological structures, the development of the male individual is controlled by the "X" sex chromosome to produce the normal male characters which include the non-functional rudimentary mammary glands. There is no difficulty whatever here for the biblical creation viewpoint.

Atavistic structures supposedly are freak throwbacks to anatomical features possessed by hypothetical evolutionary ancestors. Occasionally a human baby is born with a tail-like appendage and this is said to be evidence that our ancestors had tails. Actually, such rare congenital deformities are usually a type of fatty tumor having no relationship to the tail of a monkey. Furthermore, the human coccyx or tail bone provide essential anchorage points for important muscles. Sadly, superficial knowledge has led to erroneous interpretation and even misrepresentation of the facts.

Animal and Plant Distribution

Particular kinds of plants and animals are not found evenly distributed over the surface of the earth. Rather, each type is generally found to inhabit a certain range or area, or perhaps several separate areas. The science of zoogeography involves the study of the facts of animal distribution and an effort to explain or relate the observed data. The theories of animal distribution advanced by zoogeographers are usually based upon evolutionary presuppositions. Such theories, however, afford many difficulties, for the evidence defies any simple or completely systematic analysis.

The basic assumption is that each animal originated at some point on the earth's surface and radiated from that point while undergoing continuing evolutionary adaptation. To correlate this idea with the facts of animal distribution requires many assumptions. It is sometimes necessary to postulate former "land bridges" and island chains connecting now separate land masses when there is no geological evidence for such connections.

One example of a fact difficult to explain on an evolutionary basis is the existence of tapirs both in Latin America and in Maylasia on the opposite sides of the world, with no populations occupying intermediate locations. A similar surprise is afforded by the distribution of the true alligator, which is found only in the southeastern United States and in India and China.

One of the assumptions is that great periods of time were required for the present distribution of animals to occur. It has been demonstrated, however, that animals can emigrate large distances in only a few years or decades by many means. The dispersal of insects and land animals, especially the smaller ones, can occur by wind, water currents, floating rafts of vegetation, and on the feet and plumage of flying birds. The rapidity with which immigrating plants and animals have become established on the volcanically decimated Krakatao Island since 1883 and on the new island of Surtsey off the coast of Iceland show that vast periods of time are not required for the development of soil, flora, and fauna on virgin land.

The present distribution of some plants and animals is entirely different from that of the past suggested by the fossil record. One example is provided by the group of trees which includes the Norfolk Pine, the

Star Pine, and the Monkey Puzzle tree. These trees are now native to South America, but fossils of this group are found in North America, for example, in the petrified forest of Arizona. The Dawn Redwood was found still living in China, but its fossils are found in North America. The Gingko tree is another tree native to China, fossils of which are found in the United States. A similar situation is found in the case of the fossil insects found in the Baltic amber, species of which are presently native to areas of the world far distant from the Baltic Sea.

The biblical record requires that the present pattern of mammal distribution has resulted by dispersal from the resting place of the ark in the Middle East. There has been adequate time since the Flood, and there are ample means for such a distribution to take place. Furthermore, the animals were directed to the ark supernaturally, and the Scriptures suggest that the replenishing of the earth's surface was providentially directed. Therefore, it seems likely that more than natural causes were involved. Those who base their interpretations of the evidence on purely natural causes have great difficulty in explaining the observed data, but they continue to seek evidence from the fossil record and other sources which will fit an evolutionary framework. Those who accept the biblical record do not believe that scientific research will succeed in elucidating such an exceedingly complex phenomenon which involved both natural and supernatural events.

Mutations

The observed occurrence of mutations spontaneously in nature is used as evidence for the theory of evolution. Since 1928 the process of mutation has been investigated through the use of radiation. Dr. H. J. Muller first made the discovery of this possibility through his work with the fruit fly. However, the realization that most mutations were harmful to the species made scientists cautious, unwilling for the most part to make great claims for the advantages of mutations as an evolutionary mechanism.

It was shown, for example, that a one-percent advantage of a mutant over a normal member of a species would eventually allow the mutation to dominate the species. What is not generally publicized is the amount of time required for this dominance to take place.

Analysis of a hypothetical mathematical model of a large population containing 0.01 percent of individuals possessing a particular mutation conferring a one-percent breeding advantage showed that the mutation would increase from 0.01 percent to 0.1 percent frequency among the population only after 900,230 generations. Thus, achieving the evolution of the smallest significant change would still require more time than the evolutionary theorist has at his disposal, even if we grant him the billions of years he claims. This, together with the fact that no mutation with a one-percent advantage is yet known, makes it seem highly unlikely that mutation has played a significant role in the development of life on earth.

Paralleling the fruit fly work is the investigation of the effects of neutron irradiation of roses. Dr. Walter E. Lammerts, while Director of Research for the Germain's Horticultural Research Division, carried out extensive research in this area. He states, "More mutations were obtained by the irradiation of 50 rose 'budding eyes' than one could find in a field of a million rose plants in a whole lifetime of patient searching. . . ."[7]

Even though some of the mutations were useful from a horticultural standpoint in that they possessed additional petals of a unique color, every single mutation was found to be weaker than the variety originally irradiated. Similar results have been obtained by other researchers in this field.

Geneticists agree that mutations are generally harmful:

Mutations and mutation rates have been studied in a wide variety of experimental animals and plants, and in man. There is one general result that clearly emerges: almost all mutations are harmful. The degree of harm ranges from mutant genes that kill their carrier, to those that cause only minor impairment. Even if we did not have a great deal of data on this point, we could still be quite sure on theoretical grounds that mutants would usually be detrimental. For a mutation is a random change in a highly organized, reasonably smoothly functioning living body. A random change in the highly integrated system of chemical processes which constitute life is almost certain to impair it—just as a random interchange of connections in a television set is not likely to improve the picture.[8]

In spite of the shortcomings of mutations as a mechanism for evolutionary change, they remain today the backbone of evolutionary theory. After over a half century of experimentation with mutations, no one has yet produced a new species by either macromutation or selection of micromutations. Nevertheless, the general public is led to believe that mutations have been demonstrated scientifically to be the means of evolutionary change.

The mutation which has been most publicized is the one connected with light and dark moths in England. This mutation affects the ratio of light phase to dark phase moths in the population of the peppered moth (*Biston betularia*). This is not unusual, for there are many species of moths and butterflies which have different color phases in the same species. In these moths, the dark phase is somewhat more vigorous than the light phase, but this is normally not the most important factor in their survival, because they sit on trunks of trees in the daytime and birds eat them, selecting first the ones that contrast most with the background. On light trees the birds can see the dark moths better, and on dark trees the birds can see the light moths better.

Where these moths lived in England before the Industrial Revolution, most of the trees were light in color, so the birds ate the dark moths more readily, because they could see them better against the light background. Therefore, the dark moths were rare. They did not disappear completely, for mutations produced more from time to time. When the Industrial Revolution came along, air pollution killed lichens on the bark of trees and otherwise darkened the surface, and so the situation changed.

Now the light moths became more conspicuous against a dark background. The birds could see the light moths better and ate more of them. This gave the dark moths the advantage. They tended to live longer and reproduce more. So the population changed and the dark moths became more numerous. Now people are becoming "ecology conscious," and industries are being more careful about disposing of their wastes. As a result, the trees are becoming lighter again. So the dark moths are becoming more conspicuous, and the proportion of light moths again is increasing in these areas.

There is nothing mysterious about the case of the dark and light moths. One mutation makes the difference between them, and the birds eat more of the moths which contrast with the background. This is an illustration of "natural selection" in the sense that in nature the birds select the moths they are better able to see. But it really is not *evolution*. The moths are just the same as they were before the Industrial Revolution, and they are not becoming anything different.

Nevertheless, many evolutionists cite this as an outstanding case of evolution. The man who proved that the birds really do eat more of the moths of the phase that contrasts with the background said that if Darwin had lived to see this, he "would have witnessed the fulfillment of his life's work." This is an exaggeration, to say the least, since Darwin devoted his life in attempting to make it seem reasonable that all forms of life on earth evolved from one or a few simple forms; this is a very different matter from birds selecting dark or light moths according to the type they can see more readily on a certain background.

The Fossil Horses

The most famous fossils which supposedly illustrate an evolving series are the horses. They start with the little "dawn horse," which had three toes on its back feet and four in front. Formerly, some of these were called by the name *Eohippus*, but it has been decided that they are the same as the European form called *Hyracotherium*, and since the ones in Europe were named first, their name has priority.

The first fossil found was a single tooth, and it was first identified as belonging to a monkey. When more teeth were found, attached to some bone, it was seen that the first identification was in error, and it was said to be something like a coney or hyrax, and hence the name *Hyracotherium*, or hyrax-like beast. Later it was said to be a horse. Other fossil forms were found in Europe and America and were put together in a branching series to represent the horse family. But as more was learned about them, they did not fit so well in such a series; and, as in the case of the fossil elephants, it seemed that the various forms were not connected after all. It is to be remembered that they were not found as a series, one in a layer above the next, as represented in diagrams. Also, as Professor Kerkut has pointed out, in many cases there is no way of knowing how much was found, and it makes a great difference whether a reconstruction is from a complete skeleton or from a single tooth or bone fragment.

More than a dozen different evolutionary pedigrees have been proposed for the horse, a fact which illustrates the degree of disagreement among paleontologists. However, a general sequence of limited evolutionary development has been suggested: 1. An increase in size, from that of a cat to that larger than some existing horses; 2. enlargement and lengthening of the head anterior to the eyes; 3. increased length and mobility of the neck; 4. changes of the pre-molar and molar teeth from types suited to browsing to types suited for grazing; 5. elongation of the limbs for speedy running; 6. reduction of the number of toes to one long toe.[9]

All of the proposed horse series are laden with difficulties. One displayed some years ago in the American Museum of Natural History has the number of pairs of ribs evolving in order from eighteen (*Eohippus*) to fifteen (*Orohippus*) to nineteen (*Pliohippus*) to eighteen again (*Equus Scotti*). Similarly, the number of lumbar vertebrae in these fossils moves from six or seven (*Eophippus*) to eight (*Orohippus*) and back to six (*Equus Scotti*). The last of the supposed horse series makes its first appearance in India, whereas all of its alleged ancestors were uncovered in the United States. Of course, such anomalies as these are not mentioned when neat diagrams of the supposed horse family tree are reproduced in science textbooks or popular periodicals. The student reader is led to believe that horse evolution is a firmly established fact.

When we consider the difficulty of relating supposedly "late" types to "early" types, the possibility that size changes may have been due to poor feed or degree of maturity at death, the possibility that some of these fossils (especially *Eohippus*) may represent genera totally unrelated to the horse, and the possibility that at least some of the "developments" represent local mutations rather than a generalized species' mutation, it becomes apparent that the horse series is hypothetical only. No conclusive evidence is available to support this theory.

Physiology, Philosophy and Tacit Assumption

Because the philosophy of materialistic evolution has come to dominate the thinking of scientists, most of the scientific literature in the various sciences is flavored by the tacit if not explicit assumption that the facts being studied or discussed have an evolutionary explanation. The more difficult it is to imagine some plausible evolutionary origin, the less frequent and more indefinite become the allusions to evolution. The scientific discipline called physiology or biophysics is one in which allusions to evolution are relatively hard to come by, simply because it is exceedingly difficult to maintain that the magnificently engineered and efficiently operating mechanisms of living things are the products of accident. Consequently, open allusions to evolution are relatively scarce in the literature of physiology.

Dr. David A. Kaufmann found recently in a survey of seventeen basic texts on physiology that thirteen of the authors made no reference to evolution.[10] Yet even when not explicitly mentioned, the assumption of evolutionary origin seems often to be hovering in the background. An illustration may be found in an article on muscle control by P. A. Merton of the University of Cambridge published in *Scientific American*.[11] In this report of current incomplete knowledge of the complex and highly sophisticated servo-mechanisms by which our muscle contractions are automatically controlled to carry out the actions which we desire, the author makes just one brief allusion to evolution.

After noting that the liver, for instance, is not sensitive to pain, he remarks that this should not be surprising because for an animal to develop pain-sensitive nerves in its liver " . . . would give the animal a negligible evolutionary advantage . . ."[12] Apart from this brief lapse from science, the article serves as an eloquent argument for intelligent, purposeful design in human physiology. Yet the assumption of evolution is there.

Dr. Kaufmann, on the other hand, writes from the viewpoint of biblical creation, when he describes some of the biological control systems which are so essential to the life of all creatures, but especially to the higher animals and to man. He lists ten classes of control systems found in the human body:

1. Internal environment and homeostasis
2. Nervous control systems
3. Hormonal control systems
4. Contractile control systems
5. Circulatory control systems
6. Respiratory control systems
7. Electrolyte control systems
8. Digestion and absorption control systems
9. Resting and energy metabolism
10. Regeneration and reproduction systems

It would appear that all of these control systems in the human body utilize the principle of negative feedback which is the basis of numerous control systems devised by scientists and engineers and used in every part of a modern society, in our automobiles, air conditioning, communications networks, and manufacturing plants. One of the examples offered by Kaufmann is the body's temperature control system for maintaining the body core temperature relatively constant at 99.6°F:

In the hypothalamus a pre-determined ideal core body temperature for homeostasis is sent to a comparing device along with the actual core body temperature that is picked up by a temperature sensor. If there is a significant discrepancy, an error signal of too hot or too cold is relayed to an antirise center or antidrop center respectively. All these postulated structures are located in the hypothalamus, a conglomeration of nuclei in the diencephalon of the brain. If the antirise center is stimulated, it kicks on the sweating and vasodilation mechanisms, which release heat to the environment and decrease heat production in the body. If the antidrop center is stimulated, it kicks on the shivering and vasoconstriction mechanisms which preserve heat and produce heat in the body. Its arrangement and function are very similar to that of the thermostatically controlled household furnace. It is obvious that core body temperature is not the only example of a negative feedback control system that regulates an optimal life-maintaining situation in the human body. Other examples are: Blood pressure, blood sugar concentrations, oxygen and carbon dioxide levels in the blood, muscle tone, etc.[13]

Physiology reveals the excellent wisdom of the great Engineer, God the Creator. A Christian because of his faith readily recognizes the hand of his heavenly Father in all of the marvels of nature. But the one who does not believe, tacitly or explicitly assumes God out of science because of his philosophy. He usually does this by assuming the chance, evolutionary origin of even the most wonderful works of the Creator.

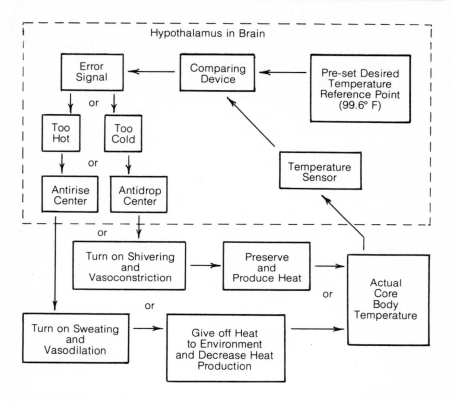

figure 7-3. Diagram of hypothalamic control of core body temperature in the human.[12]

Conclusion

In the course of this book we have attempted consistently to draw the line between reproducible science and philosophical speculation. The present chapter has been devoted to an examination of several types of evidence commonly adduced in support of evolutionary theory. The evolutionary interpretations are a consequence of the materialistic philosophy of the interpreters. The evidence can also be interpreted within the framework of the biblical philosophy and the scriptural account of creation.

Neither the evolutionary model nor the creation model of origins is scientific, in the sense that neither can be verified by the experimental methods of science. Much data can be adduced as evidence in support of evolution. On the other hand, a strong case for special creation can be developed on the basis of the fact that if evolutionary theory fails to explain the data, creation is the only alternative. In law, just one negative fact can destroy an otherwise unchallenged legal case. But mountains of facts have been marshalled from all of the sciences which refuse to fit rationally into the evolutionary scheme of things. Thus special creation remains as the only alternative, and design and purpose in the universe become powerful support for creation.

The Scriptures tell us in Romans 1:20 that men who reject the God of creation in spite of the evidence from the creation that He is, are "without excuse." Nevertheless, we must always remember that the unregenerate human heart is "at enmity against God" and "blinded" to the "light of the glorious gospel of Christ," the Creator and Redeemer. The intellect of man is corrupted by the Fall just as completely as are his affections and will. Therefore, the final choice relative to creation and evolution must be made by faith.

"Through faith we understand that the worlds were framed by the word of God, so that things which are seen were not made of things which do appear" (Hebrews 11:3).

8

The Age of the Earth

Biblical Chronologies

A literal reading of the first chapter of Genesis imparts the distinct understanding that the creation of the entire universe took place in the space
of six days. That the days of creation were indeed time periods equivalent
in length to normal solar days and that they were consecutive days is, in
our view, established by Exodus 20:11. And while the genealogies of
Genesis and I Chronicles are demonstrably incomplete at certain points,
it does not seem reasonable to believe that any unrecorded portions can
total more than several thousand years.

Therefore, the greater part of those who are actively developing the
new science-based apologetic for biblical creation agree that the age of the
earth is of the order of ten thousand to perhaps twenty thousand years.
This conclusion is admittedly dependent upon interpretation, but it is the
kind of straightforward interpretation which has been practiced by Bible-
believing Christians for thousands of years when they seek to harmonize
various parts of the Bible.

Some of the scriptural data adduced in support of the view that the
earth is young are outlined in Appendix B. In addition, two relatively

new approaches to the interpretation of the genealogies of Genesis 5 and 11 are described briefly.[1] These studies of biblical chronology are the work of men who are devoted to the Scriptures and who accept them as divine revelation. Their results differ somewhat, yet both interpretations extend the traditional chronology of Bishop Ussher a few thousand years. This is all that the text of the Bible seems to allow. The earth, we believe, is only thousands of years old, not the millions and billions of years claimed by those who accept evolutionary theories of origins.

Time and Evolution

The origin of the world and the appearance and subsequent evolutionary development of life without a Creator by entirely random chemical and physical processes is surely extremely improbable and cannot be made to seem plausible if only thousands of years are available. The significance of *time* in the study of earth and life origins, therefore, is very great.

If the earth is only thousands of years old, intelligent, purposeful creation is the only acceptable explanation. If the earth is billions of years old, on the other hand, it becomes easier to assume that the exceedingly unlikely spontaneous arrangements of the evolutionary thesis might have occurred. Time—vast ages of time—in a sense becomes the essential creative agent. In the words of biologist George Wald, "Time is the hero."

This explains why Charles Lyell's uniformitarian geology, postulating great ages for the formation of all earth features at present rates of earth activity, was so quickly espoused after 1830, and why long-term chronologies are so widely accepted in scientific and academic circles. These chronologies are part of a two-pronged attack upon the Bible, attempting to discredit its historical record and to promote the evolutionary hypothesis which effectively dispenses with God and makes autonomous man the measure of all things. This final chapter is devoted to an examination of time and its measures with their application to the age of the earth.

Time Defined and Measured

The word "time" embraces several meanings in the English language, depending upon the context in which it is used. But what is the technical definition of the word? Time may be defined as the potentiality for a succession of events in the real world. The passage of time and the measurement of time involve changes in the world in which physical objects interact and energy is either exchanged between objects or transformed from one form to another, or in which objects emit radiant energy.

In Chapter 2 it was shown that continual processes of change characterize the entire universe. It was also shown that many kinds of change are cyclic, as in the rotation of the earth on its axis and its revolution around the sun, the swinging of a pendulum, the vibration of a spring, or the oscillation of electricity in a tuned radio circuit. Quite often cyclic changes occur at regular intervals, as the five cases just mentioned illustrate.

A cyclic process of change can be used to measure time if each successive cycle takes the same length of time. A wristwatch operates on this principle, as does an atomic clock, which depends upon the frequency of light waves emitted by excited atoms. Non-cyclic processes of change may also be used to measure time if the rate of the process is constant, or if it is known how the process varies from a constant rate.

Many different processes of change may be used as clocks to measure time, but for such a clock or timer to be reliable it must meet the following requirements:

1. The time units must be meaningful and readable.

2. The timer must be sensitive enough to measure the interval in question. The same timer would not be used for a hundred yard dash and the return of Halley's comet.

3. We must know when the timer was started. True, some clocks have a calendar, but a clock does not tell how many times its hands have gone around.

4. We must not only know when the timer was started, but what the reading was on the timer scale when it started. Was the stop watch at zero when the race began? Or was it on thirty seconds?

5. The timer must run at a uniform rate; if it does not, we must know what the irregularities are in order to have a meaningful timer.

6. The timer must not have been disturbed in any way or reset since it was started.

Time can be measured for any process for which there is a timer which meets the above essential qualifications. Two general classes of timing or dating methods are used by earth scientists. One involves the measurement of the content in rocks of such radioactive elements as uranium and thorium, which gradually change to lead as they give off radiations over a long period of time. These are known as radiometric methods for geological dating.

The other class of geological dating methods is based upon more directly observable events and materials, such as the length of time it would take for the world population to develop, or the length of time necessary for certain sediments to build up on the earth's crust.

A third class of dating—by measuring chemical changes—has recently been inaugurated with the development of a new technique for dating bones by determining how much of a particular amino acid has changed from the L to the D form. This is a purely chemical method.

We will now examine some of the methods by which estimates have been made of the age of rocks in the earth's crust to see if they meet the requirements of a good timer and also to ascertain the age estimates which they provide. It will become evident that none of the methods of geological dating meets all of the requirements. In addition, while some of the methods yield very high values—billions of years—for the age of the earth, others yield values measured in thousands of years. These are called long-term and short-term earth chronologies, respectively. The short-term chronologies do not seem to fit the traditional uniformitarian view of earth history, but many fit biblical chronology.

The Age of the Oceans

The ocean's age may be calculated from data concerning the total amount of salts present in the oceans, and the rate at which the salts are accumulating in the oceans.[2] These salts are transported from the land into the oceans by the river systems of the world. Uranium salts are being carried into the oceans over 100 times as fast as they are being removed by salt spray and other means, in contrast to other salts such as those of sodium and aluminum which are now entering and leaving the ocean in more or less equal amounts.

Thus uranium content can be the basis for an estimate of the age of the oceans. The estimated total uranium content of the oceans and ocean sediments is less than 100 billion tons. The amount of uranium carried into the ocean annually is between 10,000 and one million tons. These figures yield an estimated age of the oceans of between 100,000 and ten million years, assuming that the initial uranium content was zero and that the rate of addition of uranium has remained constant. This range of values for the age of the oceans is much smaller than the four billion years usually assumed by evolutionary scientists.

It has been assumed for the above estimate that the uranium "clock" has been running at a uniform rate. The assumption that geologic processes have been operating at constant rates is the basic assumption of uniformitarian historical geology. If it is true, however, that waters covered the earth some 5,000 years ago in a great Flood, then the rate at which uranium was rinsed out of the earth and into the oceans was greater in the past than at present. This would result in a shorter time needed to reach the present uranium content.

Furthermore, we assumed that our uranium "clock" was set at zero when the oceans began. It would not be unreasonable to suppose that the oceans were created with some uranium already present. That is to say, the uranium clock was not set at zero time when the ocean was formed. It would be reasonable to conclude, then, that the age of the oceans, and of the earth, if both were formed at the same time, is 10,000 years or less.

Other short-term chronologies for the oceans are based upon the oceanic content of various chemical elements and compounds relative to the annual inflow of these substances from all known sources. One of the most thorough studies of this kind of data revealed that of fifty-one chemical elements contained in ocean water, twenty could have accumulated to their present concentrations in one thousand years or less. An additional nine of the elements would have required no more than ten thousand years, and eight other elements no more than 100,000 years.[3]

Compounds of nitrogen in the ocean, largely nitrates, also appear to be increasing in amount. The excess of input from rivers and rain is estimated to be about 77 million tons and the total oceanic content about 1,000 billion tons. Dividing the oceanic content by the annual input, we obtain 13,000 years as the apparent age of the oceans.[4]

Nitrates are quite stable in the ocean, so evolutionary scientists are concerned with discovering some way in which 77 million tons of nitrogen can be escaping annually from the oceans. The best hope is that denitrifying microorganisms can account for the release of this much free nitrogen from the ocean to the atmosphere. The rate of this process has not yet been shown to be sufficient to solve the problem.[5] Nitrogen still suggests that the ocean is only about 13,000 years old.

We would add that from the creation point of view, the oceans were surely created with an original nitrate content, for the phytoplankton (the microscopic photosynthetic plants of the sea) require nitrates for their growth. Moreover, some microorganisms, notably the blue-green algae, actively convert atmospheric nitrogen to nitrate.

The Atmospheric Helium Clock

Just as uranium content is building up in the oceans via drain-off of continental rivers, in a similar manner helium-4, the most abundant isotope of helium (atoms of the same element which differ from each other in atomic weight because of different numbers of neutrons in their nuclei are called isotopes), is flowing into the atmosphere from at least three sources:
1. From helium produced by radioactive decay of uranium and thorium

in the earth's crust and oceans; 2. from cosmic helium raining on earth, mainly from the sun's corona; and 3. from cosmic ray-caused nuclear reactions in the earth's crust.

The atmosphere now contains about 4 billion tons of He-4. If we consider the radioactive decay of uranium and thorium as the only source of helium, if we presume that the decay rate of uranium and thorium has not changed during earth history, if we speculate that the rate of release of He-4 from the earth's crust has been constant, and if we assume a zero content of He-4 in the original atmosphere, the maximum age of our atmosphere is 400,000 years. One prominent scientist has calculated the total annual rate of helium-4 flow into the atmosphere, not including cosmic helium, to be 330,000 tons per year. From this rate we find that the atmosphere has a maximum age of 12,000 years.[6]

When one assumes 1. that the atmosphere is as old as the earth, 2. that it was created with a certain initial He-4 content, 3. that the normal annual inflow of He-4 from the sun's corona has added to the helium inventory, and 4. that one or more sudden disturbances in the solar system or within the earth may have added to the atmospheric He-4 content, then an age of about 10,000 years for the atmosphere is well within reason.

However, if as many scientists claim, the earth's atmosphere is about four billion years old, the atmosphere should contain at least 30 times more He-4 than it does at present. If it is assumed that the atmosphere is four billion years old, then a great amount of He-4 must have escaped somehow, whereas Dr. Ferguson of the Environmental Science Services Administration says, "The whole problem of how helium manages to escape from the earth's atmosphere remains unsolved. All of the suggested mechanisms are still highly speculative." If all the mechanisms to accomplish this are highly speculative, it would also seem that the theory of cosmic evolution is quite speculative.

Erosion and Sedimentation Clock

In the western world, the concept of a very old earth originated only about 200 years ago, principally with the work of James Hutton (1726-1797), who announced his ideas in 1785. Around 1830 Hutton's ideas of gradualism as an alternative to catastrophism, or sudden change, began to have wide acceptance through the efforts of Sir Charles Lyell, who discussed it in the first geology textbook to be published. Different strata of the earth were supposed to represent different time periods. This method has become one of the best known "earth clocks."

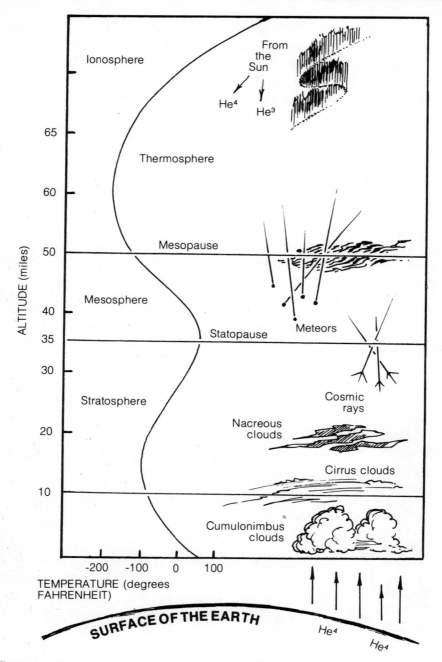

figure 8-1. Schematic diagram of the atmosphere indicating continual addition of helium from the earth's crust. It is believed that large quantities of helium are also added to the atmosphere by cosmic rays and the solar wind.

Geologists studying the rates of volcanic activity, erosion, and sedimentation have observed that these processes are now occurring at fairly uniform rates. Many geologists assume that these rates have remained the same throughout time. In his textbook on geology B. F. Howell explains how it is possible to obtain average rates of deposition for many types of sediments. By studying exposed rocks or rock strata all over the world, and assuming that the many layers were piled on top of one another, one can draw up a universal stratigraphic column or "geologic" column.

Certain adjustments must be made to this column because there are often gaps of missing sediments in different parts of the earth. When the thickness of each formation is divided by the normal or present rate of accumulation of that type of sediment, the time span represented by each type of formation can be estimated. Addition of all these times gives a figure for the approximate age of any individual rock back to the beginning of the Cambrian period. So here we see how the geologist has attempted to set up a hypothetical "sediments" clock.

Many flaws exist in the "sediments" clock, and we should point out that not all geologists are happy with this "clock." But without question the great majority of geologists and other earth scientists hold to the view that the sedimentary rocks were laid down by volcanic and sedimentary

figure 8-2. The Grand Canyon of the Colorado River, the most famous display of eroded sedimentary beds. Some of the fossils found in these rocks, notably the fossil pollen, do not fit the evolutionary interpretations. Vast spans of supposed earth history are missing from these strata at several levels, not being represented by beds containing fossils appropriate to the evolutionary theory.

processes millions of years ago, plants and animals trapped and preserved in these sediments as fossils being evidence of plants and animals which lived in the past.

It is generally assumed that plants and animals have evolved from one-celled beginnings up to the complex organisms of today. So the complexity of a fossil is considered a clue to its age and also to the age of the layer or stratum in which it is found. Certain fossils are chosen as index fossils because they are supposedly characteristic of the stage of the evolutionary process represented by a particular historic era in the past.

Some of the difficulties encountered in the uniformitarian interpretation of the fossil and sedimentary rock data were discussed in Chapter 3. These problems included missing strata, reversed strata (i.e., fossils found lying in the reverse of the assumed evolutionary order), living fossils (sometimes the fossils had been used for indexing certain strata), evidences of catastrophic global flooding and volcanic activity, polystrate fossils that could not possibly have been buried slowly, and the fact that fossils simply are not formed under the conditions assumed in uniformitarian geologic theory. Thus there is much evidence that the rock strata clock is not a reliable clock when interpreted according to uniformitarian theory.

But the sediments on the ocean floors can be used as a clock to determine a limit for the age of the earth, according to Prof. Stuart E. Nevins, an oceanographer on the faculty of Christian Heritage College in San Diego.[7] The average depth of sediments deposited on the ocean floors is estimated to be just over one-half mile. This amounts to about 8.2×10^{17} tons. The present rate at which sediments from the continents are being washed into the oceans or deposited from underground springs is about 2.75×10^{10} tons per year. The current theory of plate tectonics pictures large quantities of these ocean floor sediments being subducted or buried deep in the earth's mantle where great moving plates of the earth's crust meet. But this is estimated to be only about 2.75×10^{9} tons per year, or just one-tenth of the annual new sediments being added.

Now assuming uniformitarian conditions in the past, let us calculate the age of the earth from this data. Our formula is

$$\text{Age in years} = \frac{\text{mass of sediments on ocean floors}}{\text{mass added new each year - mass subducted each year}}$$

$$\text{Age in years} = \frac{8.2 \times 10^{17}}{2.75 \times 10^{10} - .275 \times 10^{10}} = 33 \times 10^{6} \text{ years.}$$

Thirty-three million years is less than one percent of the 4.5 billion years commonly cited for the age of the earth. Moreover, recent data from deep sea drilling in ocean sediments indicate that sedimentation rates in the recent past were perhaps ten to one hundred times as great as at present. If to this is added the vast quantities of sediments which must have been dumped rapidly on the ocean floors during the Flood of Noah, we can see that the thickness of ocean sediments is actually far more consistent with the biblical model of creation and the Flood over a time span of around 10,000 years than with the uniformitarian model. Billions of years of erosion and sedimentation should have loaded up to sixty miles of non-existent sediments on the ocean floors. Since the sediments are missing, are we not justified in concluding that the billions of years are likewise non-existent?

The Meteoritic Dust Clock

Looking up into the sky on almost any night, especially during the dark of the moon, we can observe streaks of light; they are meteors, or meteoroids, as the smaller ones are called. Sometimes we call them falling stars, which of course they are not. Meteors and meteoroids are pieces of rock-like material that hurtle through space. Their origin is not known, but they have occasioned much speculation.

They are composed of the familiar elements of iron, nickel, and silicate compounds, like those found in basalt from our earth's crust. On the average about 20 million meteors collide with the earth's atmosphere every 24 hours, like bugs on the windshield of a car. Naturally, all of these collisions, however small, slowly add to the layer of material on the earth's surface.

Hans Pettersson of the Swedish Oceanographic Institute calculated that about 14 million tons of meteoritic dust settle to the earth each year.[8] If this dust had been accumulating on the surface of the earth (and of the moon) for 5 billion years, the layer would by now be considerable. Assuming a density of 3 grams/cm^3 for the compacted dust, this layer should be 137 feet thick. Such a layer has nowhere been found, either on the earth, on the bottom of the oceans, or on the moon. More recent information suggests that the rate of meteorite dust fall may be even greater by a factor of three or more.[9]

Since the average meteor contains over 300 times the amount of nickel in earth rocks, the dust would have to be mixed throughout the upper three miles of crust to yield the present amount of nickel in the crust—assuming, of course, that the crust contained no nickel initially and that the rate of fallout has been constant for the past five billion years. Employing the same assumptions, Isaac Asimov concluded that the dust would account for all the iron in the upper one and a half miles of the earth's solid crust, which certainly also accounts for all the iron man has mined.[10] Again, since it is quite reasonable to suppose that the meteorite fallout rate has been higher in the past, as crater evidence indicates, and that the earth was created with a certain iron and nickel content, we may conclude that the earth is much younger than five billion years—as young in fact as a literal interpretation of the Bible would indicate.

The Population Growth Clock

The "explosion" of the world population has become a significant topic during the last few years. Scientists studying growth rates are especially concerned about the necessary requirements for life such as food, water, and space. Some scientists who specialize in these kinds of studies have made calculations that might help answer the question, How long would it take for the present world population to grow from just one family?

The rate of world population growth has varied radically during history as a result of many influences, including famines, pestilences, wars, and probably a number of catastrophic events. Estimates of the total human population at the time of Christ center at about 300 million. If the Flood occurred about 5000 B.C. and if the average length of a generation was forty years, Noah's family of eight people would multiply to 300 million by Christ's time if each family had an average of just 2.3 children. This corresponds to an average annual population increase of only 0.35 percent, whereas the present world population growth rate, considered by some to be catastrophic, is about two percent annually, almost six times as great as the hypothetical rate used in the above calculation.

If, on the other hand, the human race had been on earth for one million years with a growth rate of only 0.01 (1/100) percent annually, the resulting population would be 2×10^{43} people, i.e., the number 2 followed by forty-three zeros. This is enough people to fill completely more than a thousand solar systems solidly packed. Thus the theory that the human race had been multiplying for a million years or so seems absurd, even taking into account the fact that modern medicine and technology were not available. The consideration of reasonable population growth curves seems to support the biblical chronology of thousands of years, rather than the evolutionary chronology of several million years for man's history on earth.

The Age of the Mississippi River Delta

Additional striking evidence from sediments is to be found in the extensive studies of the delta of the Mississippi River during the past century. Charles Lyell, father of evolutionary geology, after a superficial examination, estimated the age of the delta to be only 60,000 years. This seems to be far short of what is required by current historical geology based on evolution.

But the detailed studies carried out over a period of many years by the U.S. Army Corps of Engineers with the cooperation of civilian geologists greatly reduced this figure. It now appears that the maximum age of the delta, that is, the time required for the Mississippi River to deposit the present accumulation of sediments making up the delta, is no more than 5,000 years. The total picture of sediments in the delta and underlying the delta fits the concept of Flood geology rather well.[11]

The Gas and Oil Seepage Clock

Trapped oil and gas deposits and the rates at which they leak through the layers of sediments to the surface of the earth again suggest a shorter time scale for the earth than evolutionists claim. Sometimes in oil well exploration a "gusher" results. The well goes wild and spews out oil and natural gas until measures are taken to bring the pressure under control. How can we explain this? It is believed that the oil was formed when organic materials were covered and trapped suddenly beneath heavy layers of earth and rock, usually under conditions of elevated temperature and pressure. The pressures in oil deposits result from three basic causes. Most of the pressures are due to the weight of all the layers of earth resting on top of the trapped oil and gas; the other causes of pressure are from the weight of oil pressing down upon itself and gases that may be present.

After rather detailed study of measurements of pressure in deep oil wells in various parts of the world, Dr. Melvin Cook concluded that the very high observed pressures require sudden deep burial.[12] Moreover, the containing rocks are porous so that to retain these pressures for periods greater than a few thousand years is apparently impossible under the observed permeabilities of the reservoir and trap formations. (Permeability determines the rate at which leakage may occur through the material.)

Geostatic Pressure

Geostatic pressure refers to the total force of the overlying layers of earth pressing down on any material beneath it. If an oil deposit is trapped beneath the thousands of tons of earth, the pressure may be evenly distributed throughout the liquid. The pressure of the earth's weight will push the oil up through the opening made by a drill.

The conclusion that oil and gas have remained trapped at such high pressures for millions of years does not seem to be valid. It would not be possible for the rocky sediments to maintain a sufficiently good seal for such a long time. Many non-creation scientists admit that the occurrence of fluids in reservoirs within the earth at excessive pressure is a mystery. They say, "These formations are millions of years old and the pressures are extremely high; we don't understand it, but there it is."

Creationists feel that they possess the answer to this mystery, for it fits within their basic assumption of global catastrophe. They believe that the excessively high-pressure oil and water reservoirs are not nearly as old as most geologists think. What may have happened about five thousand years ago was a tremendous catastrophe which caused a great deal of overthrusting, or the movement of large blocks of earth over one another. This type of violent action could have trapped rivers and lakes as well as animal life and all sorts of vegetable matter. The strata left overlying many of the trapped fluid formations would have produced high geostatic pressures. From that time on, the pressures have simply been decaying, sometimes very slowly but always fast enough that no excess pressures would remain at all if the formations were more than a few thousand years old.

As we conclude our consideration of non-radiometric methods for estimating the ages of the oceans, the atmosphere, and the rocks making up the earth's crust, it is now clear that there is a great deal of support for the short-term chronology of the earth which agrees with the Bible. Furthermore, many difficulties are occasioned by the non-radiometric long-term chronologies. It should be kept in mind, however, that each of these chronologies involves unverifiable assumptions. It is not possible to know for sure what the initial conditions were at time zero and whether or not the timers remained undisturbed and ran at a constant rate since time zero. We will see that radiometric methods suffer from similar shortcomings.

The Earth's Magnetic Moment

In 1835 the German physicist K. F. Gauss made the first measurements of the earth's magnetic dipole moment, that is, the strength of the earth's magnet. Additional evaluations have been carried out every decade or so since then to the present. The amazing fact about this global property of the earth is that it has decreased fourteen percent in 130 years!

In 1883 Sir Horace Lamb derived a rigorous mathematical-physical model for the magnetic moment of the globe, assuming that it is the result of a massive, circular electrical current flowing inside the earth. Today geophysicists agree that it is, indeed, an electromagnetic phenomenon, but they disagree on the form of the current producing it. However, in 1972 Dr. Thomas G. Barnes, professor of physics at the University of Texas in El Paso, published a revised and updated version of Lamb's mathematical theory based upon the latest understanding of the earth's metal core.[13] He showed that the magnetic moment should decrease exponentially according to a decay law similar to that for the decay of radioactive substances. (See graph on page 197.)

The magnetic moment of the earth appears to be decreasing with a half-life of only 1,400 years. The energy of the earth's magnetic field is decreasing with a half-life of just 700 years. Thus 7,000 years or ten half-lives in the past the magnetic energy extrapolates back up to a value $2^{10} = 1024$ times as great as its present value, and 28,000 years back it becomes 1.1×10^{12} times or roughly a trillion times as great as at present.

As the magnetic field energy decays, it is transformed into heat. The energy involved in this hypothetical extrapolation less than 30,000 years into the past would be sufficient to heat the entire earth to 5000°C and completely vaporize it by now. The earth obviously is not now either melted or vaporized. In the light of this analysis of the earth's decaying magnetism observed for 130 years, extrapolation of earth history 4.5 billion years into the past leads to an absurdity. The evidence supports an earth history of not much more than 10,000 years. And if it be objected that the argument based upon extrapolation of a presently observed process a mere 28,000 years into the past is questionable, our reply is that evolutionary theories of origins are based upon extrapolation billions of years into the past of processes which have never been observed.

It is significant that if the earth's magnetic dipole moment were increased by a factor of $2^5 = 32$ (corresponding to an extrapolation 7000 years in the past) a larger percentage of cosmic rays would be deflected before reaching the planet. Since the production of carbon-14 in the upper atmosphere is proportional to the cosmic ray influx, an important result would be a decrease in the amount of carbon-14 in the atmosphere and in living things 7000 years ago. Consequently, living things which died under such conditions would now yield apparent carbon-14 ages greater than their true ages.

The Cooling of the Earth

In the last century the British physicist Lord Kelvin, who happened to be a devout Christian, greatly upset the evolutionary theorists by demonstrating that the cooling of the earth from a molten state to its present temperature would only require some millions of years, rather than the hundreds of millions of years they had postulated at that time. Several decades later, radioactive elements were discovered in the earth's crust which continually produce heat beneath the surface. It was assumed that this new information completely invalidated Kelvin's conclusions.

However, more recent calculations show that even with the radioactive substances present in the crust, the problem for evolutionary geology remains.[14] Without radioactivity the time for cooling comes to 22 million years. With radioactivity the figure is 45 million years, still far too short to fit the evolutionary picture. The actual facts fit without difficulty into the biblical chronology of around ten thousand years for the age of the earth, because there is no need to assume that the earth was ever in a molten state in the first place.

Radiometric Clocks

In our study of different types of "earth clocks" used to measure the "ages" of various parts of the earth, we have found that they are unable to give exact values for the age of any given earth formation. Recall the age of the oceans calculated from the rate at which uranium salts flowed into them compared to the total amount of uranium in the ocean. This "clock" might have been running at a different rate long ago, or there may have been some uranium in the ocean when it was formed. We did conclude, however, that this clock tells us that the ocean may be as old as from 100,000 to 10,000,000 years. We know its age is greater than 3,000 years, because Greek historians wrote of sailing on the oceans.

Scientists long sought a more accurate means of dating the earth than those we have been studying, a method that would conform to all the requirements for an ideal or perfect timing device discussed earlier in this chapter. We will now consider how radioactive materials may be used to measure time. Radioactivity, a term introduced by Pierre and Marie Curie, refers to a remarkable physical process in which one element changes into one or more simple elements. A material like uranium, for instance, is continuously giving off radiation at a steady rate and gradually becoming lead.

When in 1907 Dr. B. B. Boltwood of Yale University suggested that the decay of radioactive elements could provide a method for dating rocks, it was thought that this was the absolute method that scientists had been looking for. Soon determinations of lead-uranium ratios in minerals were being made by chemical methods and age estimates calculated. However, the modern development of radiometric dating methods was made possible following the application by Aston in 1927 of the mass spectrograph to the study of the isotopic composition of lead. In 1936 Dr. A. O. C. Nier further improved this technique by developing the mass spectrometer. With this instrument it is possible to measure the ratios of the different isotopes of an element in a rock or mineral. Since these early developments, the radiometric dating methods have multiplied and become the principal basis for claims that the earth is, indeed, billions of years old.

The radioactive decay curve and half-life   The theory of radioactive decay depends upon the assumption that in a sample of atoms of any radioactive parent isotope each atom has an equal probability of decaying within a given period to produce an atom of the daughter isotope. If this is the case, the probably number of atoms decaying per unit of time will be proportional to the number of atoms remaining. If the initial number of atoms is very large (so that the random variations from the probable rate of decay become relatively very small) the number of remaining atoms decreases with what is termed an exponential decay curve which is shown in the accompanying graph.

In this illustration the initial number of radioactive atoms is taken to be 1,000,000. The probability of a particular atom's decaying in one second is taken as 10^{-4}, i.e., 1/10,000. This is called the specific decay rate. Therefore, at time zero with initial one million atoms present, the probable number of atoms decaying in the first second is $1,000,000/10,000 = 100$.

When 6,933 seconds have passed, half of the parent atoms will have decayed and the sample will consist of 500,000 parent atoms and 500,000 daughter atoms. Thus the time span of 6,933 seconds is called the half-life for this particular kind of radioactive atom. When one half-life has passed, the probable number of radioactive decompositions per second is 50, just half of the initial rate, since only half as many parent atoms are present. After the passage of another half-life period of 6,933 seconds there will be one-quarter of the initial number of parent atoms remaining, 250,000 and 750,000 daughter atoms. The expected rate of decay will be 25 atoms per second.

It is easy to see how, given certain assumptions, a radioactive parent-daughter couple can be used to date a rock or mineral specimen. If one knows the decay probability or half-life of the parent isotope, by analyzing the sample for the number of parent atoms and daughter atoms, the interval back to time zero can be calculated. It is assumed that the initial

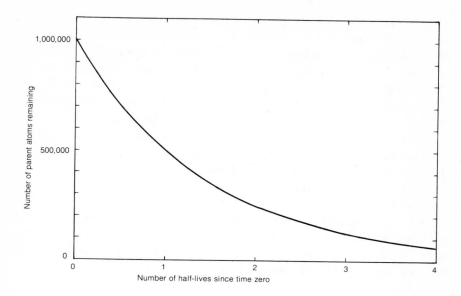

figure 8-3. Decay curve of a hypothetical sample of 1,000,000 radioactive atoms.

numbers of parent and daughter atoms are known, that the decay rate has not varied, and that neither parent or daughter atoms has entered or left the specimen.

For example, if it is assumed that only parent and no daughter atoms were present at time zero, then an analysis of 250,000 parent and 750,000 daughter atoms would be interpreted as meaning that an interval of two half-lives or 13,866 seconds has passed since time zero. Or if the rate of decomposition (i.e., counts per second) is measured and found to be 25 counts per second, assuming an initial 1,000,000 parent atoms, the same age of two half-lives is calculated.

There are many radioactive isotopes, each with its own decay rate or half-life, which could theoretically be used as radiometric clocks. Some have fast decay rates, others slow rates. Their different uses can be compared with those of a stop watch and an ordinary clock, one used to measure periods of seconds, the other of hours. As a concrete example let us consider the substance bismuth-210.

Bismuth-210 has a half-life of five days. During a period of five days a sample of bismuth will give off enough radiation to change one-half of the original bismuth atoms into thallium-206 atoms plus an equal number of atoms of helium-4. The block diagram depicts the course of radioactive decay of two differently sized samples of bismuth-210.

Sample "A" is all bismuth and has an original weight of 16 grams; Sample "B" is all bismuth and has an original weight of 40 grams. At the end of five days Sample "A" will still weight 16 grams, but its composition will have changed to 8 grams bismuth and 8 grams thallium. Sample "B" will still have a mass 40 grams, but its composition will have changed to 20 grams bismuth and 20 grams thallium. The diagram shows how this conversion will continue. Actually, the helium atoms which are emitted also have a definite mass. To be more precise, in the case of Sample "B," the mass of helium released in ten days is 0.57 grams, so the thallium produced is 29.43 grams. However, this does not alter the fact that three-quarters of the bismuth has decomposed in ten days, or two half-life periods.

It does not matter how much of a material one starts with, for during each half-life period one-half of the material will be converted to a new material. The values of radioactive half-lives do not seem to be greatly affected by any known chemical or physical conditions observed in nature. Because most half-lives are known to a fair degree of certainty and have not been observed to fluctuate substantially, we will assume they have been constant, and radioactive elements may serve well as clocking materials if they meet the other requirements of accurate timing.

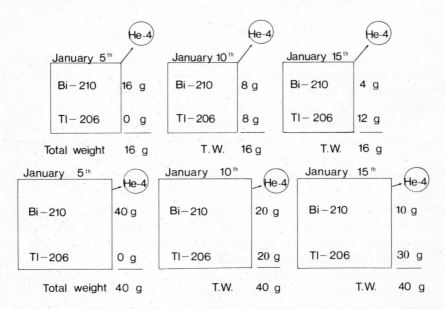

figure 8-4. A block of pure bismuth-210 is transformed to thallium-206 by radioactive decomposition. Half of the remaining bismuth changes every five days, so the half-life of bismuth-210 is said to be five days.

Another factor that must be considered is the setting of the radiometric "clock" at zero. The half-life data for a radioactive material gives the rate at which the clock runs, but how can we be sure of the amounts of material present at the start? If another 16-gram piece of material is found to have a composition of 8 grams of bismuth-210 and 8 grams of thallium-206, one really cannot be sure the material is only five days old unless there is some way of knowing its exact composition five days ago. Was it all bismuth-210? Or was there already some thallium-206 present? The two elements may have been combined just before the measurements were begun. And there are other factors that might lead one to incorrect conclusions about its age.

It is obvious that reasonable factors may have masked the real age of this material, now apparently five days old, before it was given to you. The same kinds of problems would be true for obtaining the age of any material containing radioactive elements. We cannot know the original composition of a material containing radioactive elements because they change. Their dating value can be based only on assumption of the original composition and the factors that may affect the composition throughout its existence.

Common Radiometric Methods

Now let us consider some of the radioactive elements commonly used in dating moon and earth rocks. A few of these elements are listed in the following table:

table 8. Parent/Daughter Isotope Pairs

radioactive parent isotope	non-radioactive daughter isotope	half-life
Uranium-238 (U-238)	Lead-206 (Pb-206)	4.5 billion years
Uranium-235 (U-235)	Lead-207 (Pb-207)	0.7 billion years
Thorium-232 (Th-232)	Lead-208 (Pb-208)	14.1 billion years
Rubidium-87 (Rb-87)	Strontium-87 (Sr-87)	47.0 billion years
Potassium-40 (K-40)	Argon-40 (Ar-40)	1.3 billion years

Scientists have determined the "ages" of meteorites, of moon rocks, and of earth rocks by measuring the ratio of one of the above parent/daughter isotope pairs and then calculating age by means of the half-life principle mentioned in our discussion above concerning Bi-210/Tl-206.

The generally accepted "age" of the earth, approximately 4.5 billion years, actually refers to the average of radiometric "ages" of selected meteorites which have fallen onto our earth, not of any earth rocks. Some meteorites show ages less than this, some greater. Earth rocks yield "ages" of about 3.6 billion years or younger. It is assumed by cosmologists that the earth and the moon and all the solar system were formed about 4.6 billion years ago. Supposedly 3.6 billion years marks the time of crystallization of the oldest earth rocks after a global, catastrophic event which, so to speak, reset earth's radiometric clocks.

Most biblical creationists hold that the earth and solar system are much younger, probably about 10,000 years old or less. In this view the ratios of daughter to parent isotopes basically reflect not radioactive decay over vast time spans, but conditions of the initial creation modified by subsequent events over a short time span.

It is true that a large structure of radiometric dating measurements has been built up in the past several decades which exhibits many concordant ages of earth rocks, moon rocks, and meteorites. On the other hand, there are numerous examples of discordances and inconsistencies which raise serious questions about the validity of the methods. The problems fall in three categories: 1. Anomalous ages, 2. discordant ages within one rock and between different methods, and 3. disequilibrium between members of radio decay series. Examples will be cited to illustrate each type of problem.

Anomalous ages
1. Volcanic rocks produced by lava flows which occurred in Hawaii in the years 1800-1801 were dated by the potassium-argon method. Excess argon produced apparent ages ranging from 160 million to 2.96 billion years.[15] In contrast with this, some moon rocks are considered to have lost up to 48 percent of their argon, and their K/Ar ages are judged to be too low. On the other hand, many lunar rocks contain such large quantities of what is considered to be excess argon that dating by K/Ar is not even reported.[16]

2. Some lunar rocks and soil from the Apollo 16 mission yielded "highly discordant" ages exceeding six billion years by lead methods. This is unacceptably high for current theories of lunar origins and disagrees with measurements made on other moon materials.[17]

3. Recent rocks from active volcanic sites studied in Russia, perhaps only thousands of years old, gave ages from 50 million to 14.6 billion years, depending upon which methods, samples, and corrections were used.[18]

4. A rock from Apollo 16 contains 85 percent excess lead which gives uncorrected ages ranging from seven to 18 billion years by three lead methods. Removal of lead by acid treatment makes possible a date of 3.8

billion years which is considered acceptable.[19]

Discordant ages within one rock and between different methods

1. Granite from the Black Hills in South Dakota yielded the following ages by the several methods: Sr/Rb, 1.16 billion; Pb^{206}/U^{238}, 1.68 billion; Pb^{207}/U^{235}, 2.1 billion; Pb^{207}/Pb^{206}, 2.55 billion; and Pb^{208}/Th^{232}, 1.56 billion.[20]

2. A series of volcanic rocks from Réunion Island in the Indian Ocean gives K/Ar ages ranging from 100,000 to 2 million years, whereas the Pb^{206}/U^{238} ages are from 3.2 to 4.4 billion years. The factor of discordance between "ages" ranges as high as 14,000 in some samples.[21]

The explanation offered by some uniformitarian geologists for these discrepancies is that these lavas brought with them the uranium and lead concentrations which had evolved during billions of years in former rocks which were then melted to form the magma source. When the lava solidified on the island the K/Ar clock took over to record the time since that most recent crystallization. But if in *these* rocks the Pb/U ratios were transported in with the original magma and tell nothing of the age of the present rock, how can one have confidence that *any* Pb/U "age" is a true age?

3. Certain rocks from Apollo 12, dated by Sr/Rb and several lead methods, yielded ages ranging from 2.3 to 4.9 billion years. The effort to explain the results involves hypothetical second and third events which reset some of the radiometric clocks at different times in the past.[22]

4. Lunar soil collected by Apollo 11 gave discordant ages by different methods: Pb^{207}/Pb^{206}, 4.67 billion; Pb^{206}/U^{238}, 5.41 billion; Pb^{207}/U^{235}, 4.89 billion; and Pb^{208}/Th^{232}, 8.2 billion years. Rocks from the same location yielded K/Ar ages of around 2.3 billion years.[23]

Disequilibrium between members of a radioactive decay series

In the radioactive decay series in which U^{238} is transformed into Pb^{206} there are fourteen successive decay steps and, therefore, thirteen intermediate radioactive nuclides. Once decay of uranium in a rock or mineral grain begins, the intermediates begin to build up in the rock, but they also begin to decay as soon as they are formed. After a certain time the members of the series reach concentrations which are in the proportions, approximately, of their half-lives. The radioactive decay series is then said to be in equilibrium. In the U^{238} series the equilibrium ratio of U^{234}/U^{238} is 5.5 x 10^{-5}.

1. The collection of volcanic rocks from Russia mentioned in item 3 of Anomalous Ages above presents only three examples of equilibrium be-

between these two nuclides, but eleven examples of disequilibrium. (See Footnote 18.) The deviations from the equilibrium value range from 55 percent deficiency to 36 percent excess in U^{234}. Ages obtained for these rocks by the lead methods range from 50 million to 500 million to 5 billion years, depending upon the correction techniques used. But equilibrium should be attained in only two million years. The volcanic rock is reportedly only thousands of years old, but the lead dating methods say tens of millions to billions. So the disequilibrium mixture of U^{238} and U^{234} must have come into the melt before the rock solidified.

But presumably there were billions of years for the two isotopes of uranium to come into equilibrium before that. How can disequilibrium of up to 55 percent be explained? The proposal that two chemically identical isotopes, U^{238} and U^{234}, could be in equilibrium in a melt but deposited in the crystalline rock in ratios up to 55 percent out of equilibrium cannot be supported by present knowledge of physics and chemistry. At present there is no explanation other than the view that the initial creation a few thousand years ago brought the uranium isotopes into being in various degrees of disequilibrium in different places in the earth.

2. Ten rock samples from Faial Azores, Tristan da Cunha, and Vesuvius display similar disequilibrium of the radioactive decay series.[24]

3. Certain moon rocks have been found with some radioactive isotopes out of equilibrium by up to 10 percent.[25]

A Last Look at the Moon

On May 8, 1975, the California State Board of Education held a public hearing at which about three dozen citizens expressed their reasons for believing that textbooks should be adopted which present some of the scientific evidence in support of the creation model of origins. One of the presentations included a summary of the radiometric dating results on twelve Apollo moon rock samples.[26] The inconsistencies and anomalies were striking. The uranium/lead and thorium/lead methods gave results varying from 3.36 to 28.1 billion years, and the potassium/argon method results spread from 2.2 to over seven billion years. Of course, any age over 4 to 5 billion years is considered "unacceptable" because the moon is supposed to have evolved at about the same time as the earth, which is supposed to have evolved about 4.5 billion years ago.

The spread between values by different methods applied to single rock samples was also striking. For example, one sample gave ages of 4.31 to 8.20 billion by lead methods and over seven billion years by the potassium/argon method. Another sample gave lead ages ranging from 5.4 to 28.1

billion years. The spreads of values from single samples of rock were from 1.9 to 22.8 billion years.

As one reads the research reports and the lunar conference reports concerning moon rocks, the impression is gained that the collection of a great mass of facts has resulted in the raising of more questions than have been answered. It would seem that one unanswered question is the age of the moon.

The examples given above indicate some of the problems that are found with radiometric dating methods. They suggest that it is not uncommon for radioactive parent and/or daughter nuclides to be added to or lost from rocks and mineral crystals. They show that as yet unexplained disequilibrium exists between nuclides in decay series. These examples also reveal the magnitude of the discordances which occur between different methods and between different minerals within a single rock specimen.

Radioactive Halos and Instantaneous Creation

Another radiometric evidence which is difficult to reconcile with a great age for the earth comes from the studies by Robert V. Gentry of radioactive halos.[27] These are spherically shaped zones of radiation damage in rock crystals surrounding microscopic inclusions of certain radioactive elements such as uranium, thorium, and polonium, which emit alpha particles. Each radioactive isotope emits radiations with characteristic energies. The energy of an alpha particle as it is ejected from a radioactive atom determines how far it can smash through the surrounding crystal before it stops. The crystal structure along its path is damaged and becomes discolored. The distance the alpha particle travels before it is stopped is roughly proportional to its energy. Thus each inclusion in the crystal is surrounded by spherical shells of discoloration, the outer radii of which provide a measure of the energies of the alpha particles. The energies are characteristic of the atoms which emitted the alphas, so it is possible to identify the radioactive isotopes which the inclusions originally contained.

Dr. Gentry has apparently established the wide occurrence in igneous rocks of radioactive halos formed by three isotopes of the element polonium, ^{210}Po, ^{214}Po, and ^{218}Po. Supposedly these rocks crystallized over periods of hundreds or thousands of years from magmas deep in the earth, probably hundreds of millions of years after the initial formation of the earth. But the half-lives of the three polonium isotopes are only 138 days, 164 microseconds, and 3 minutes, respectively. On the traditional theory of rock formation over vast time spans, how could there be any of these very rapidly decaying polonium isotopes left to form inclusions in the rock crystals by the time the magma had finally cooled sufficiently for crystals to form?

This evidence seems to point to the instantaneous creation of rocks which contain polonium radiohalos. Since these rocks are widely distributed, it would follow that the earth itself was created instantaneously. Dr. Gentry considers that his findings bring into question the entire structure of radiometric chronologies.

Some Conclusions

The above examples of problems and difficulties in the various systems of radiometric age analysis bring into question the validity of the fundamental assumptions upon which the systems are all built. Assuredly much radiometric dating information has been assembled which appears to show extensive agreement between measurements and methods. On the other hand, if in many cases the assumptions lead to contradictory or absurd results, how can we be sure that the assumptions are valid in any case? Furthermore, the assumptions have to do with supposed events in the distant past for which there were no human observers, and the basic time scale for these alleged events has already been agreed upon on the basis of evolutionary, materialistic philosophical principles. Therefore, is not the evidence adduced in support of imagined scenarios of geologic activity and radioactive decomposition actually circumstantial? And do not the complex corrections, rearrangements, and reinterpretations of data devised to explain or remove discordant results take on a strong *ad hoc* character?

Surely, in the light of the scriptural evidence and the many physical evidences for a young earth, biblical creationists are justified in rejecting such great-age chronologies built on evolutionary presuppositions.

On the other hand, there is still a great deal of work remaining for creationists involved in developing a creation-flood model for the interpretation of the data of the geological sciences. One important problem is the correct interpretation of the so-called isochrons, a special type of graphical correlation of isotope ratios in different rocks or in different minerals of a given rock. Isochrons are used particularly with the strontium-rubidium method.

Sometimes these isochrons are poor, but sometimes they are quite good, fitting well with the interpretation which assigns very great ages to the rocks. Careful study and reevaluation of the geological field methods, petrology, analytical procedures, and other aspects connected with the use of isochrons is needed. The challenge is for dedicated Christian men and women of science who, as the Lord calls them, will pursue research in this and other fields of science with the object of discovering truth, glorifying God, and defending His Word, the Holy Scriptures.

Carbon-14 Dating

The discussion thus far has dealt with radiometric clocks which have long half-lives and should be appropriate for obtaining dates of objects having ages from, say, one-tenth to several times their half-lives. However, what radio "clock" can be used to date objects from King Tut's tomb or from an ancient Inca temple? Dr. Willard Libby of U.C.L.A. first suggested that carbon-14, which is formed in and distributed throughout our atmosphere and thus exists in all plants and animals, could be used to date objects of any age from recent times to about 40,000 years ago.

The discovery of this method was an important contribution to the study of ancient civilization (archaeology) and also to the study of ancient plant and animal fossils (paleontology). Events in earth history of interest to geologists have been dated by this method. One example would be the dating of trees buried in a recent glacier.

As in the case of all other radiometric dating methods, the carbon-14 method is based upon a combination of reproducible scientific data and certain assumptions about events and processes in the ancient past. Here are the basic elements of the method:

1. Ordinary carbon atoms have nuclei composed of six positively charged protons and six neutrons having no electrical charge. The mass of a proton is about equal to that of a neutron, about one atomic mass unit (1 AMU). Thus an ordinary carbon atom can be represented by the symbol, $^{12}C_6$, where the subscript tells the number of protons in the nucleus, and the superscript tells the mass of the atom in AMU. We will sometimes write this kind of carbon as carbon-12, or C-12. All carbon atoms have six protons, but some have different numbers of neutrons in their nuclei. These are different isotopes of the element carbon.

One isotope of carbon is carbon-14, which has six protons and eight neutrons. Its symbol is $^{14}C_6$. Carbon-14 atoms are continually being produced in the upper atmosphere as a result of cosmic radiation from outer space. The high-energy atomic nuclei which compose cosmic radiation smash into atoms in the atmosphere at high velocity. In the debris of these collisions are many neutrons. When one of these neutrons collides with the nucleus of an ordinary nitrogen-14 atom, a nuclear reaction sometimes takes place.

Nitrogen-14 atoms contain seven protons and seven neutrons in their nuclei, and the corresponding symbol is $^{14}N_7$. When a neutron reacts with a nitrogen-14 nucleus, it knocks a proton out of the nucleus and replaces it. The result is an atomic nucleus containing six protons and eight neutrons. Thus the atom has been transmuted from nitrogen-14 to carbon-14. This nuclear reaction can be represented as follows:

$$^{1}n_0 + {}^{14}N_7 \rightarrow {}^{14}C_6 + {}^{1}p_1$$

The symbol for the neutron $^{1}n_0$ means that its mass is 1 AMU and its charge zero. The symbol for the proton, $^{1}p_1$, means that its mass is 1 AMU and its charge is $+1$. About 10,000 grams (22 lbs.) of carbon-14 are being produced annually by this reaction.

Ordinary carbon, carbon-12, is stable, but carbon-14 is unstable, decomposing radioactively with a half-life of about 5,730 years. The radioactive decay reaction is

$$^{14}C_6 \rightarrow {}^{14}N_7 + \beta^-$$ (The symbol, β^-, represents a beta particle, a negatively charged electron which is emitted from a nucleus.)

2. This carbon-14 combines with oxygen to form carbon dioxide gas which diffuses down to mix with all the atmosphere.

3. Plants use carbon dioxide in their life cycles and become radioactive. Animals and people eat plants and become radioactive. Ordinarily C-12 from living things contains nearly one part of C-14 to every trillion parts of C-12. Actually, this means that if we placed one gram of ordinary carbon from a living thing under a Geiger counter, we would observe about 900 counts (or beta particles from C-14 disintegrations) per hour. After the living thing dies, this count would decrease according to the curve on page 197. The C-14 is changing back to N-14 with a half-life of 5,730 years.

4. When an organism dies it stops taking on more radioactive carbon-14, so the amount in the dead object begins from the moment of death to decrease at a rate which reduces the amount by a factor of one-half each 5,730 years, the half-life of carbon-14.

5. Thus, if we obtained some charcoal from an ancient Cro-Magnon campfire in France and found that one gram of purified carbon yielded a count of 225 counts per hour, we would conclude that the date of the campfire was about 11,460 years before the present, if the assumptions underlying the method are valid.

Most of the radio-carbon dates determined for objects of known historical age back to about 250 B.C. agree with their historical age reasonably well. For instance, the Dead Sea Scrolls were found to yield a C-14 date of about 2,000 years before the present. However, this is not true of objects of interest to geologists and paleontologists. The following table lists some of the discrepancies.[28]

table 9. Samples of Carbon-14 Dating

Description of Sample	C-14 Date (Yrs. before present)	Geological Date (Yrs. before present) —approximate—
W-169. Keilor Skull, Victoria	8,500	Pleistocene (300,000—1,000,000)
L-137. Peat and wood buried under Pleistocene fossil remains	8,000 to 10,200	1,000,000—2,000,000
Gr N-2022. Neanderthal Mandible from Libya	40,700	35,000—100,000
UCLA-1292. Sabertooth Tiger LaBrea tar pits	28,000	100,000—1,000,000
Gin-93. Mammoth scapula in Cro-magnon burial site, Siberia	11,000	20,000—35,000
TA-121. Mammoth bones, Komi, USSR	10,455	35,000
I-1149-1150. Natural Gas Alabama & Miss. in Cretaceous and Eocene formation	34,000 30,000	50,000,000— 100,000,000
MO-334. Coal, Kirgizia	1,680	100,000,000

The above is just a sampling of many similar dates in the literature. One can understand such statements as the following: "As a result of radio-carbon dates, all the previous interpretations of Pleistocene lake history, depth and position in geologic time must be reassessed."

Is the C-14 reservoir in balance? It is obvious that the radio-carbon method is valid only over that period for which the C-14 content of the atmosphere has been constant. This can only be the case if the production rate has equalled the decay rate throughout the ages in which the specimens dated lived.

As new studies have been made it has become increasingly evident that the total decay rate of C-14 on the earth may be about 30 percent less than the total production rate of C-14 in the upper atmosphere. Dr. Suess comments, "It seems probable that the present-day inventory of natural C-14 does not correspond to the equilibrium value, but is increasing."[29] If the C-14 content of the atmosphere is out of balance now, as we go back in time it becomes more and more out of balance.

Reinterpreting Carbon-14 data It is possible to correct C-14 dates for such a non-equilibrium condition. Dr. Melvin Cook has recalculated some of the dates given in the literature. A sampling of these is given in the following table.[30]

table 10. Comparison of Carbon-14 Dating

Sample No.	Historical or Geological age	Amt. at equilibrium C-14 age uncorrected	Amt. not in equilibrium C-14 age corrected
C-1	4650 ± 75 yrs.	3979 ± 350 yrs.	3320 ± 350 yrs.
C-752	3925 - 4325 yrs.	3945 ± 106 yrs.	3300 ± 106 yrs.
C-576	2050 ± 100 yrs.	1917 ± 200 yrs.	1720 ± 200 yrs.
C-744	6707 ± 300 yrs.	5266 ± 450 yrs.	4300 ± 450 yrs.
C-818	——	25,000 yrs.	15,000 yrs.
C-438	8000 yrs.	8631 ± 540 yrs.	6530 ± 540 yrs.
C-630	Glacial wood (Wisconsin)	10,676 ± 750 yrs.	7900 ± 750 yrs.
C-558	Folsom bone	9883 ± 350 yrs.	7400 ± 350 yrs.

The reason for non-equilibrium of C-14 in the biosphere is a subject for speculation. Perhaps the rate of C-14 production in the past was smaller than at present. If the earth's magnetic dipole moment is decreasing with a half-life of only 1,400 years as we reported above, the influx of cosmic rays only a few thousand years in the past must have been less, with resultant lower rate of C-14 production.

Atmospheric conditions, particularly the amount of moisture in the upper atmosphere were probably much different before the Flood, and could have affected the rates of C-14 production. The greater abundance of vegetation and animal life prior to the Flood (which is indicated in the fossil record) may have brought about dilution of C-14 because of a larger amount of ordinary carbon in the biosphere compared with the present. It follows that specimens which died in the Flood would have such low content of C-14 at death that they would now appear to be very old, perhaps 50,000 years or more, even beyond the limits of the C-14 method. With production of C-14 rapidly increasing from a low pre-Flood value, fossils produced for some centuries after the Flood would have very low C-14 content and thus would now yield very large, erroneous radiometric ages.

Professor Robert L. Whitelaw of Virginia Polytechnic Institute and State University applied a correction somewhat similar to Dr. Cook's to over 15,000 carbon-14 dates published in the journal, *Radiocarbon*.[31] When the results were arranged in three groups and according to the corrected carbon-14 ages, significant patterns in the data became evident.

Most striking was the evidence that roughly 5,000 years before the present, large numbers of men, animals, and trees died. Following this, the rate of deaths dropped to a very low value and then began to increase again. This is what would be expected as a result of the Flood which occurred a little over 5,000 years ago according to the best biblical chronology.

These compressed chronologies have been based upon the assumption that the deep ocean carbonates are continually mixing with the surface layers. Recent data indicate that such is not the case.[32] It has been determined that plankton, the microscopic plants in the surface layer, deplete this layer of carbon dioxide, more of which is then absorbed from the atmosphere. Thus the plankton is in equilibrium with the C-14 of the atmosphere, as is likewise the entire food chain of sea animals which derive their sustenance ultimately from plankton.

This information provides the basis for a different C-14 chronology which has been proposed by Read and Stokes. They assume that the C-14 production mechanism was turned on at the time of the Flood and that the C-14 balance between the atmosphere and oceanic plankton was established within about 500 years. During this period the C-14 content of living things would increase approximately linearly and finally approach a value slightly less than the present value. Following this initial rapid build-up period, the C-14 content of the atmosphere and the plankton and other living things would very slowly increase from around 1,500 B.C. to the present.[33]

The effect upon radio-carbon dating would be even more dramatic than in the case of Cook's system. The corresponding corrections on radio-carbon ages would compress all such ages within the past 5,200 years to correspond to biblical chronology. The radio-carbon ages for the period from 1500 B.C. to the present would remain substantially unchanged, and the rest would be compressed within the preceding 500 years. Fossils produced at the time of the Flood, since they contained little or no C-14, would yield zero assay of radio-carbon and would be undatable by this method.

More recent data obtained by carbon-14 dating of sequences of three rings has indicated, however, that for the period before 250 B.C., carbon-14 dates are low, the errors increasing to about 700 years, 4,600 before the present.[34] There is also evidence of a discontinuity in the data at around 5,000 years before the present. Sidney P. Clementson has interpreted this data in terms of a different model which agrees with the biblical chronology.[35]

In this model, lack of complete mixing of the upper and lower atmospheres greatly reduces the rate of introduction of carbon-14 into the biosphere. Thus the carbon-14 concentration in living things before the Flood was quite low. At the time of the Flood large-scale mixing in the atmosphere brought down accumulated carbon-14 into the lower atmosphere and thus into the biosphere, and the low mixing rate was subsequently reestablished. Thus the excess carbon-14 has been slowly decaying and thereby causing the concentration in living things gradually to decrease toward an equilibrium value which is lower than that adopted by Dr. Libby on the assumption of complete atmospheric mixing.

Another recent effort to develop an interpretation of radio-carbon data which fits biblical chronology is reported by Harold Camping in *Adam When?*[36] This analysis succeeds in achieving some good correlations between radio-carbon data and the interpretation of biblical chronology which places the creation at 11013 B.C. However, a considerable number of assumptions are involved, the most radical one being the assumption that deep space water dumped on the earth at the time of the Flood contained a large quantity of radio-carbon. Camping's complex and carefully thought-out hypothesis should receive careful critical evaluation.

Even without new analysis and corrections, carbon-14 data has shaken up many previously held evolutionary interpretations. The method definitely requires corrections, because lack of equivalence of the total decay and production rates indicates that carbon-14 must be increasing on the long term, whereas the tree-ring data show that it must have been decreasing for some thousands of years previous to the Christian era.

Thus the most basic assumption of the radio-carbon method, that the specific carbon-14 content of the biosphere carbon has been constant for many thousands of years, is in error. The best model on which to base corrections will hopefully become clear with the accumulation of more information concerning the atmosphere, the earth's magnetic field, the effects of the Flood upon the oceans and atmosphere, and other factors. We believe that increasingly strong support for biblical chronology will develop as these matters are better understood.

A New Chemical Method for Dating Bones

In 1972 a new method for determining the age of bones was announced by Dr. Jeffry Bada of the Scripps Institution of Oceanography.[37] This technique is based upon the rate of a purely chemical reaction in the bone and involves no radioactive element. Bones incorporate as part of their structure a protein called collagen, which contains L-isoleucine among its constituent amino acids. The amino acids in living systems are generally of the L form, which is the mirror image of the D form. When a creature dies, the amino acids all begin to shift slowly to the D form until an equilibrium mixture containing equal amounts of the two forms is produced. Dr. Bada measured the rate in bones of this change for L-isoleucine and then analyzed the amino acids of some ancient bones to find the ratio of the L to the D form of isoleucine. Then from his value of 110,000 years for the half-life of the L form he calculated values for the ages of the bones. It is reported that these values agreed well with the ages based on carbon-14.

Any such agreement between methods, of course, provides support for the validity of both methods. However, there are some problems with this dating as with the others. In order to apply the method it is necessary to know the temperature history of the bone, because the rate of change of the amino acid depends upon the temperature. The chemical conditions surrounding the bone also affect this rate. As a consequence of these problems, the method is generally being used in cases in which it is possible to calibrate it against the carbon-14 method in the particular location and stratum containing the bone to be dated. This method is still quite new, but apparently it has not added much that is really new to the long-term chronologies required by all evolutionary theories. On the other hand, recent critical evaluation of the uncertainties inherent in the method raises some serious questions as to its validity.[38]

Conclusions

Generally speaking, the evidence as it has been presented indicates that the radiometric and non-radiometric clocks being used by scientists to time earth events fall short in one or more of the requirements for the ideal clock which we studied earlier in this chapter. In particular, the last four of the requirements listed on page 183 are normally not met by the usual methods for measuring.

There is no way to determine whether or not the "timer" was set at zero when it was started. As a matter of fact, if the world was created, we would expect it to display an appearance of age from the very beginning. Attempts to date it, then, would generally be expected to make it appear older than it really is.

Similarly, the requirements that the "timer" run at a uniform rate and that it not be disturbed in any way are not subject to experimental verification. We cannot prove that these requirements have been met over the years since the earth came into existence. We know, however, of several kinds of events which could have disturbed the timer or the rate at which it has run. The development of the industrial age, great storms on the sun, and variations in cosmic radiation are examples of such disturbances. There is also good evidence for a worldwide cataclysmic Flood which could have disturbed timers. For these reasons, present methods of dating the earth are open to question.

Thus we see that neither of the two major theories of origins—the theory of special creation or the theory of evolution—can be *proved* by today's methods for dating the earth. However, what evidence we can gain through these methods tends to support the creationist's view of a recently-created earth rather than one which evolved into its present condition over a long period of time.

Jesus Christ, Lord of Time and the World

Time is a created thing. This is clear from the definition of time offered in the opening section of this chapter and from the first verse of the Bible, "In the beginning God created the heaven and the earth." Heaven and earth include the entire physical universe composed of space, matter, energy, and time. Without space, matter, and energy, there can be no possibility of a succession of events in a real world. Thus time also was created in the beginning, the beginning of all things including time—the beginning, that is, of all things except God the Creator.

While the Scriptures show that creation was the work of all three Persons of the triune Godhead, in a unique way the Son is said to be the Creator. In John 1:3 we read, "All things were made by him; and without him was not any thing made that was made." And in Colossians 1:16, "For by him were all things created . . . all things were created by him, and for him." But in the opening verses of the Epistle to the Hebrews an especially significant aspect of creation is attributed to Jesus Christ: "God . . . hath in these last days spoken unto us by his Son, whom he hath appointed heir of all things, by whom also he made the *worlds*." The word *worlds* is the Greek word *aion* from which comes the English word "aeons" or "eons." The meaning relates to the vast ages of unending time.

Jesus Christ is the Lord of everything not only because the Father has made Him heir of all things, but also because Jesus Christ is the Creator of the ages. That is to say, the entire plan of the ages, the outworking of every purpose of the triune Godhead, has been created by the Son of God, whose sacrificial death, bodily resurrection, and providential upholding of all things guarantee perfect fulfillment to the glory of God the Father. The consummation of all things in Jesus Christ is pictured for the believing heart in the pages of the Revelation or Apocalypse (Unveiling), the final book of the Bible. There will be no part of God's creation—no creature, no angel, no man or woman or child—who will not in that day bow the knee to Christ the Lord.

It is the right of Jesus Christ not only to receive glory, honor, and praise in that day of consummation, but to be honored and acknowledged as Creator even today in this present age. Thus *The Creation Explanation* has been written to demonstrate how the facts of the sciences support what the Bible says about creation and the providential rule over the world by Jesus Christ. To believe that the world and its creatures are the result of a series of fortuitous accidents is to deny Jesus Christ the honor due Him as the Creator. Truly to honor Christ as Creator is also to receive Him as Savior and Lord, to know Him and through Him the Father, which is life eternal (John 17:3).

9
The Ultimate Design

Our chief concern in *The Creation Explanation* has been to discover in the natural world evidences for intelligent, purposeful design. Such evidence, we have seen, is to be found at every level of the universe, from the nucleus of the atom to the most distant galaxy. This evidence accords with the biblical revelation of the creation of all things by a Creator. The Bible affirms the origin of all things—the source and ground of all being, all reality—to be the infinite-personal Spirit, God the Creator. And the Bible claims some three thousand times to be the Word of God to man.

We wish to draw *The Creation Explanation* to a close with a consideration of three vital questions: First, is there conclusive evidence outside of the Bible which supports the scriptural revelation that the Creator is a personal Being, not merely a force that moves or a substance that composes all things? Second, is it reasonable to believe that the Creator has something to say to man whom He has created? Third, is it reasonable to believe that the Bible is, indeed, the Word of God to man?

Ultimate Evidence of the Designer

The design which we have discovered in the universe points to an intelligent Designer who must be a personal Being. But there is even more powerful evidence for the existence of a personal Creator. Let us analyze the essential attributes of man, those things which make him man, profoundly different from all other creatures. These essential attributes are: 1. intellect—the capacity to know, reason, remember, and use symbols, as for example, in spoken and written language; 2. affectional nature—the capacity to have feelings such as love, fear, compassion, anger, and hate which are of a higher quality than the instinctive passions of animals; 3. moral nature—the sense of personal responsibility to exercise moral judgment and to do that which is right; and 4. will—the power to decide and to act in accord with personal decisions.

The intellect, the affections, and the moral nature of man influence his will as he decides and acts. This is the personal being, man, the highest being in the natural world. Is not this human nature marvelous in its complexity and capacities? How meaningful life is because man is able to enter into personal relationships with other humans and with God. David the Psalmist marvelled at the handiwork of God in the creation of man: "I will praise thee; for I am fearfully and wonderfully made: marvellous are thy works; and that my soul knoweth right well" (Psalm 139:14).

Is it possible, then—is it reasonable to believe—that this essential human nature could have its origin in impersonal atoms and physical law? Can all that man is, his personality and character, his attainments in literature, art, science, and technology, his aspirations, religious awareness, and faith—all this—be nothing more than the natural effects of material atoms in motion, chemical reactions, and electrical currents? Is there any intellectual capacity in atoms? Are there any feelings? Is there any sense of moral responsibility? Can atoms make decisions or choices and proceed to act according to personal will? Obviously not! At least we have no evidence of personal nature in atoms.

Therefore, is it not basically an act of irrational faith to believe that random interactions of atoms produced man, the personal being? Is there any experimental evidence that life, consciousness, personality, intelligence, purpose, and will developed spontaneously in a primeval ocean or slime pit? There is none.

Then the origin of personal human nature must be found in a higher personal source, an infinite-personal source, a spiritual Being who created the universe and made man in His own personal-spiritual image. Surely this is the only rational conclusion that can be drawn from observation of the essential attributes of man. Our conclusion, then, is that the existence of human nature with its essential attributes affords conclusive evidence for the real existence of the infinite-personal Creator-God of the biblical revelation. And this evidence is entirely independent of the

Bible. Thus we see that the Bible is reasonable and in agreement with the observed facts when it reveals the Creator-God of the universe to be a personal Being, the infinite Spirit who is the source and ground of all being. The ultimate design, the ultimate evidence of design in the universe, is the personal-spiritual nature of man, for the pattern is the image of the Creator Himself.

He Has Spoken to Man

The answer to our second question—does the Creator have anything to say to man?—flows naturally from our first conclusion. One of the principal characteristics of man the personal being is his continual communication with his friends and neighbors. This is one of the factors which makes human culture and society so infinitely more meaningful than anything the animals do. And our communication is carried on primarily with the use of symbols called words, the only medium by which propositional truth can be communicated to man.

Well, then, if God created man in His own image, a personal being who continually desires to communicate with other men, is it not reasonable to believe that the Creator, the infinite-personal Spirit, should desire to communicate His truth and love to man? Is the Creator dumb? Does not puny, ignorant, limited man need to receive the wisdom and knowledge of God? And would the Creator withhold from man the truth that he needs for his life, happiness, and fellowship with the Creator? The only reasonable response to these questions is to affirm that the Creator must have something to say to man.

He Has Spoken in the Bible

Our third question may be rephrased as follows: Is it reasonable to believe that God has spoken to man by means of prophecies and revelations written down by chosen men and collected in a book? The typical complaint against the Bible's being the Word of God holds that because the Bible was written by fallible men, it is therefore full of human errors and cannot be the Word of God. Our response to this and the typical exchange that might ensue between this author (A) and an unbeliever (U) runs thus:

A. Did you ever write a letter?
U. Sure.
A. What did you write it with?
U. With a pen or a pencil.

A. Then you didn't write it. The pencil did.

U. Oh, no. I made the pencil write.

A. Then *you* are able to make the pencil put your thoughts, your words on paper?

U. Yes.

A. Is not the God who created the prophets and the apostles even more able to use *them* as His divinely controlled writers to put His truth for man in words collected in a book? After all, He not only created the prophets, but He also arranged their family history and their life experiences so that they were prepared to be living pens, through whom the divine revelation flowed, so that the Bible is at once a divine and a human book, yet infallibly preserved from error, for God is absolutely sovereign in the control of all His creatures. In 2 Peter 1:21 the Bible says, "For the prophecy came not in old time by the will of man: but holy men of God spake as they were moved by the Holy Ghost."

So it is entirely reasonable to believe that the Creator God has a personal message for man whom He created a personal being in His own image, and that He has communicated this message in words. It is reasonable that the infinite-personal God should have used chosen personal men to speak and write His message to man. It is reasonable that this message should be preserved in permanent form in a book for men of all times and conditions who are seeking to know God and His will for their own lives. Finally, it is reasonable to believe that the Bible is the Word of God, for it reveals the real existence of the infinite-personal God Whom we are led to believe exists because of the fact that personal human nature could only have its source in a Creator who is Himself a personal Being.

Here *The Creation Explanation* case rests. You, the reader, must come to your own conclusions based upon the evidence from the creation. The persuasive evidence for intelligent, purposeful design is all around us and within us—in inanimate nature, in living creatures, and in the nature of man himself. May these evidences lead you to faith in the God of creation, the God of the Bible, the God and Father of our Lord Jesus Christ—to stronger faith if you are already a believer, and to a new-found faith if you have not before trusted in Jesus Christ. This faith does not come as a result of studying science, but hopefully the examination of scientific evidence which we have just concluded can remove some of the roadblocks to faith. The faith itself comes through the message of the gospel contained in the Bible, the message that "Christ died for our sins according to the scriptures; and that he was buried, and that he rose again the third day according to the scriptures" (I Corinthians 15:3, 4).

We believe that biblical faith produces full confidence in the entire

Bible as the Word of God, including the Genesis record of creation. This faith alone can redeem an individual or a nation from the destructive effects of the evolutionary faith. It can do far more. It can give value and meaning to an otherwise meaningless universe and blessed fulfillment to an otherwise empty life. With this faith one can go forth into life and into the world with the purpose of glorifying God in all things, confident that every created thing bears witness to the truth of the Scriptures which are our only divine rule for faith and life.

Jesus said,
"The Scripture
cannot be broken."
John 10:35

A Creation Model

As every reader of this book surely knows, materialistic, evolutionary scientists have a theoretical model for the origin and development of the universe, the world, life, and man. But is there a rational creation model into which the data of the sciences can be fitted? Yes, there is a creation model, and we wish to offer here a tentative or provisional development of it which may serve as a basis for further study by other students of creation-science. Limited aspects of this model were suggested in Chapter 3.

In science, systems of theories, called models, serve as frameworks for the observational data of the sciences. They provide tentative explanations for the observed facts and they also serve as guides to scientific research. The evolutionary model has for more than a century influenced a major part of research, particularly in such fields as geology, paleontology, biological sciences, and anthropology. Remember, however, that scientific models have an essential philosophical character, especially models relating to origins, for as we pointed out in Chapter 5, the scientific method cannot be applied to questions of origins in the same way that is possible with, say, a question about the mechanism of genetic inheritance. The philosophy of materialism inspires the evolutionary model, whereas the philosophy of biblical theism informs the creation model.

The outline for the creation model is found in the first eleven chapters of Genesis, the opening book of the Bible. We will now give a summary of a creation model which we believe to be true to the biblical record and also in better accord with the data of science than is the evolutionary model. We make no claim to finality except for those general principles and specific details which are expressly stated in the Scriptures. We hope that this provisional creation model will encourage Christians to study and research in creation-science, biblical chronology, and general scientific research for the glory of God.

Gen. 1:1 **Ex. 3:14, 20:11** **John 1:1-3** **Col. 1:16, 17** **Heb. 1:1-3, 11:3**	The infinite-personal Spirit, God, created the physical universe and the spiritual creation by His power and word. Space, matter, energy, and time all had a beginning. Before or outside of time exists only God who alone is infinite, eternal, and unchangeable. He is the ground and source of all being.
Gen. 1:2	Initially the earth was dark, formless, disorganized except that it was surrounded by waters, perhaps in violent motion. Thus the earliest sedimentary rocks would be laid down without fossil content because life had not yet been created.
Gen. 1:1-25 **Ex. 20:9-11** **Ps. 115:16** **Gen. 1:3-5**	In six normal days the entire work of creation was accomplished and the surface of the earth transformed into a proper environment, complete with the entire complex biosphere, for man's abode. In the first day the earth was provided with light and a day-night cycle, and the first day closed.
Gen. 1:6-8	On the second day the watery envelope around the earth was separated into liquid waters which entirely covered the globe, and a surrounding canopy of water in vapor and cloud form, with the open atmosphere (firmament) or the first heaven between.
Gen. 1:9-13 **Gen. 2:15**	In the third day one huge continental mass was lifted up out of the waters to provide dry land for plant life. Plant life was created, for the most part probably as seeds which then rapidly grew at a miraculous rate, filling the soil with their root networks, establishing the plant foundation for the biosphere. The plant kinds,

though relatively more plastic than the animal kinds and therefore suitable for man's intelligent selective breeding and control, were nevertheless created to vary only within the limits of their respective kinds.

Gen. 1:14-19   On the fourth day the sun, moon, and stars were either created or brought into a condition which made them suitable as a basis for telling time, seasons, years and days.

Gen. 1:20-23   On the fifth day God created sea life and flying creatures such as birds and perhaps insects.

Gen. 1:24-31   On the first part of the sixth day God created land animal life of all sorts. The higher animal kinds, though generally much less plastic than some plant kinds, were created with considerable potential for variation. But the genetic boundaries of the kinds are absolute. God may have created original specimens of a kind with great genetic potential so that in the course of time through the genetic process of segregation, numerous species could have arisen within the boundaries of that kind. Or He may have created a number of potentially interbreeding types of species within a kind. Then,

Gen. 1:26-28   after the beautiful earth environment was completed in its primeval perfection, God created man in His image,

Gen. 2:7-14   gave him dominion over all the world and its creatures, and made him a steward, particularly in the Garden of

Gen. 2:15-17   Eden. Adam, using the language originally given to him

Gen. 2:19-20   by God, first demonstrated his dominion and stewardship, as well as the intellectual capacity of primal, unfallen man, by classifying and naming all of the land animals and birds. Although made from the dust of the

Gen. 2:18-25   earth as were the plants and animals, Adam's race was founded in an entirely different manner. One man was first created holding within himself all the potential of the race, and from his side Eve was created, so that the entire race generated from them would be one in Adam. Therefore, Adam could represent the race in the test of obedience in Eden. At the close of the sixth

Gen. 1:31-2:1   day the work of creation was completed, and God saw that it was very good, containing no trace of imperfection or evil.

Gen. 2:2-3 On the seventh day the Creator rested from His work of creation, bringing to a close the creation week.

Gen. 1:7, 2:6 The level of the land surface originally was probably generally lower and more even than at present, with rather low mountains. Also the sea level was probably much lower than the modern level, so that the total dry land area was considerably greater than at present. The large amount of water vapor enveloping the globe probably produced a "greenhouse effect," causing a semi-tropical climate over most of the world, so that lush vegetation and forests extended over a much greater proportion of the globe than at present. The water vapor canopy also would screen out more of the cosmic radiation from space, as would also a much stronger earth magnetic field which probably existed at that time. As a consequence, mutations and other deleterious effects of cosmic rays on living organisms were largely or completely shielded out of the environment.

Gen. 1:29-30 In Eden before the fall, man was not subject to death. Nevertheless, the biblical data suggest a natural biochemical order, because man and animals lived by eating plants as food. Therefore, the laws of physics and chemistry, including the Second Law of Thermodynamics, were apparently in effect. But God had no doubt provided protective arrangements to maintain the original perfection of His created beings. For example, the tree of life was supplied to enable man to live forever. Even today our bodies have repair systems which continually function to correct damage to the DNA molecules of our genes.

Gen. 2:9, 3:22-24

Gen. 2:17 With the fall of man by his disobedience into the estate of sin and misery, death by sin came upon all men, just as God had promised. The divine curse placed upon man was for his sake also placed upon the world, in fact, upon the entire creation. Thus a perfect creation began to decay. The perfect natural order which the Creator would, no doubt, have supplied

Rom. 5:12
Gen. 3:16-19

Rom. 8:19-23

with sustaining organizing power, had not sin entered the scene, was allowed to suffer the progressively degenerating effects of the curse. The presently observed Second Law of Thermodynamics fits this picture. Man became immediately spiritually dead, losing his original righteousness, and became subject to the morally and spiritually degrading effect of sin, as well as the physically degenerating influences of a decaying physical order. The entire plant and animal creation was dragged into a parallel downward course, a path not of evolution, but of devolution. Nevertheless, for man a spiritual path upward through the work of a Redeemer was promised and made available to man.

Gen. 3:15, 21

Gen. 4-5

The conditions of life on the earth from Eden to the Flood were probably basically as described earlier, yet with local disruptions and increasing dislocations of the perfectly balanced order of the initial creation. Man's mental and physical capabilities were still very great. Culture, technology, and cities were rapidly developed. The ungodly line of Cain multiplied as did the godly line of Seth, and a civilization dominated by the materialistic thinking and desires of unregenerate human hearts filled much of the earth. Even the children of believers were drawn into the ungodly relationships and the whole earth was corrupted.

Gen. 6

Finally, God had to judge and cleanse the world. One godly family was chosen by God to preserve the race. By the time the ark was completed and the Flood came, only eight believed strongly enough to break with the world system and go God's way. The remainder of the race perished, along with the air-breathing animals, in a global flood catastrophe so physically stupendous and so ominous in its portent of judgment for sinful men, that very few people today want to believe that it ever happened.

Gen. 7-8

II Pet. 3:3-7

Gen. 7:11

The waters which inundated the entire surface of the earth probably came from three, perhaps four sources. First, the excess water in the antediluvian vapor canopy condensed and fell as rain. Second, juvenile water from the crust of the earth poured through fissures into the ocean. Third, the relative levels of the land surface and ocean bottom changed, the land sinking and the ocean floor rising, until every mountain top was covered. Fourth, God may have brought additional water from space by miraculous means. The Flood was accompanied by violent movements of the earth's crust, and by volcanic activity of momentous proportions. Tremendous tidal waves and rushing currents scoured and deeply eroded the continental surface. Entire forests were ripped up and transported large distances to be dumped where the currents slowed. The sediments formed from the eroded materials were dropped in vast sheets, deeply burying the plant remains, much of which was converted to coal, and animals were fossilized by the billions, giving plain evidence of their sudden death. The currents shifted, reversed, and laid down layer after layer of sediments, fossils, and plant remains.

On the bottom of some of the sequences of strata, some of the original sedimentary layers from the creation week were preserved, or sometimes they were eroded away and redeposited elsewhere. In general, bottom-dwelling sea creatures tended to be buried first, whole communities composed of many different species being buried together. Amphibious creatures and other animals living near the continental margins were often trapped next, and the more mobile dry land animals often were able to escape the rising flood waters for longer periods and thus were entombed in strata above the other types of animals. Humans were usually able to protect themselves longer, fleeing to higher and higher ground before they were finally swept away to their death. Thus, their bodies were subjected to the most violent effects of the flood waters, and many were left strewn on the surface after the Flood, subjected to rapid decay, and therefore left few fossils.

Although the preceding scenario describes the formation of the most common fossil sequences in the strata, the violence and erratic character of the currents and tidal waves associated with the global flood resulted in many anomalous sequences. This explains the numerous areas where so-called reversed strata occur, such as in the famous Lewis Overthrust in Glacier Park. There actually was no "overthrust," but the erratic action of water laid down non-fossiliferous sediments on top of shallow sea sediments containing many marine fossils.

When the flood waters subsided, seeds soon began to sprout and twigs and branches of many kinds of plants were able to take root quickly. The ark, a 30,000-ton vessel some 450 feet long, disgorged its precious cargo of animals and humans which overspread the ruined earth's surface, taking directions determined by the providence of a sovereign Creator. The land mass was still, for the most part at least, connected in one great supercontinent. This explains how certain animal types are found only on particular continents, for example, most of the marsupials such as kangaroos in or near Australia.

Following the Flood, the family of Noah began the slow and difficult process of reestablishing the human race on the earth. They brought through the Flood much of the culture and technology of the pre-Flood civilization. Thus civilization could develop relatively rapidly. No doubt the living conditions were rigorous in those first centuries after the Flood. The earth's crust was shuddering from its recent ordeal. Tremendous torrents of lava poured over large areas of the world, and high mountain chains were pushed up to dominate many landscapes.

The global climatic pattern was completely upset and changed by the Flood. The thick water vapor canopy was now gone, so average earth temperatures dropped suddenly, perhaps as much as fifteen degrees. Great ice caps spread from centers near the poles and subjected large areas of the land surface to glacial action. If the Flood was, indeed, at around 5000 B.C., perhaps there were a number of glacial advances and retreats in the next 2000 years. The center of human population expansion in the Middle East would not be directly affected by the glaciers, but the pioneer elements of mankind which pushed out rapidly to the far reaches of the globe after the Flood would be greatly affected. Probably there were a number of post-Flood catastrophes which swamped large segments of the animal and plant populations which rapidly occupied the land after the Flood. Perhaps one or more of these events accounted for the tremendous destruction of life now evidenced by the frozen mammoths and other creatures as well as the vast bone deposits found in some of the Arctic islands.

It should be pointed out that the pioneer groups of humans who extended the frontiers of the race were mostly living and traveling as small, isolated breeding populations. They tended to undergo much more rapid degenerative changes and genetic alterations, especially since they would also be under the pressure of difficult living conditions on the outer reaches of human exploration. Their fossil remains would be expected to show some differences from those of the average human types, the peoples which remained closer to the cradle of civilization. Animal populations may also have tended to change rather rapidly within the limits of their created kinds as they overspread the earth.

Another effect which may have contributed to more rapid genetic changes and to shortening of human and animal life-spans is related to the post-Flood world climate. The removal of the water canopy allowed more cosmic radiation to reach the earth's surface. This and other conditions differing from those before the Flood may have increased the rate of deleterious mutations, thus accelerating the rate of degeneration of all **Gen. 5 & 11** creatures. Genesis 11 records a rather rapid decrease in human longevity.

Gen. 10:8-12 By a thousand years after the Flood another materialistic civilization had been built in the Middle East, with large cities and increasingly centralized control of religion, government, and culture. Mankind was uniting in a cooperative system that was man-centered and anti-God. God broke this up by confusing their **Gen. 10:25** languages, scattering the peoples as different nations.

Perhaps at this time in the days of Peleg, God also divided the major dry land mass physically, producing the pattern of separate continents we know today. At this time when plates of the earth's crust were moved rapidly by forces known only to God, further upthrusting of the major mountain chains occurred, and this continued for perhaps another thousand years as the continents moved into their modern relationships on the globe.

In the meantime the great ancient civilizations, the Sumerian and the Egyptian, had developed and left their remains which so puzzle the cultural anthropologists who wonder where they came from, fully developed in art, technology, government, and religion. The

Gen. 11:31-12:5

stage of history was now set for God to choose Abraham and separate him from the polytheistic culture of the Chaldeans, to bring him into a very small land, Palestine, to serve the God of Creation. This land would for some two thousand years be the scene of God's direct dealings with Adam's race. Even now this land is again becoming the center of events which promise to shake the world and drive the course of human history until the end of the age.

This creation model is in many respects tentative, not final or complete. It is offered as a framework for understanding the data of science in a manner which recognizes the authority of the Bible as the verbally inspired and infallible Word of God. It may also serve as a guide to Christians who desire to pursue scientific research in channels which will be blessed by God because His truth has been accepted as the foundation for expanding human knowledge of His creation.

Biblical Chronology

Some Christians including a number of scholars of the past and present have held that the language of the Bible permits the possibility that the earth may be millions or billions of years old. While we realize that those who espouse this view may be sincere in their faith, we nevertheless cannot accept it as a reasonable interpretation of the Scriptures. This question is a complex one which really requires more space than is available in a brief appendix, but we will offer an outline of biblical reasons for believing the earth is young.

What the Scriptures Seem to Say

Ayone who simply picks up the Bible and reads the opening chapters without preconceptions will never get the idea that a vast span of time was required for the creation. Neither does the subsequent history leading to the appearance of Abraham give the impression of millions of years rather than a few thousands.

The Meaning of the Word "Day"

Many have assumed that the days of creation are actually enormous periods of time, or "revelational days" which refer to lengthy time spans, or the initial days of long time periods. There are, however, many reasons for understanding them to be six successive, normal solar days.

1. In Genesis 1:5 and 14-18 the words *day* and *night* are used nine times in such a way that they could only refer to either a normal day or the light or dark period of a normal day.

2. The expressions *morning* and *evening* are each used more than one hundred times in the Old Testament, and they always refer to normal days.

3. The word *day* occurs over two hundred times elsewhere in the Old Testament with ordinals, i.e., first, second, third, etc. In all of these cases outside of the first chapter of Genesis, the reference is to a normal day.

4. The Hebrew word for *day* and its plural, *yom* and *yamim*, are translated to mean normal days in some 1900 cases, but only in 65 cases are they translated "time" in the King James Version. Thus the usage is literal in about 95 percent of the cases. In the other cases, either the context or an associated adjective indicate that a meaning other than a normal day is intended.

5. In Exodus 20:8-11 a reason for the Fourth Commandment is given. Men shall work six days and rest the seventh because the Creator made all things in six days and rested the seventh. It is difficult to see how the Author of the inspired Scriptures can mean anything other than a creation week of six successive normal days.

A "Gap" Between Genesis 1:1 and 1:2?

Many Christians hold this view, probably for the most part because it has been promoted for many decades in the footnotes of the Scofield Reference Edition of the Bible. Once again we feel we must disagree with many of our brethren whom we love and respect in the Lord, for we believe there are too many weighty reasons for rejecting this interpretation. Space permits listing only a few of these reasons.

1. There is no hint of such a gap in the text of Genesis 1:1, 2. Surely if there were a vast period of time with momentous events on the primeval earth leading to a judgment and cataclysmic destruction, there would be some clue in the text, but there is none. A strange kind of exegesis is required to read a great time gap between these two verses.

2. Some propose that the word *hayetha* should be translated "became" rather than "was" in verse 2. While this is a possibility, another word is normally used for "was." *Hayetha* is translated "was" about 4900 times in the Old Testament and "became" only 64 times.

3. If this gap is used to explain the geological strata and the greater

part of the fossil record, death was in the world on a massive scale before Adam. This appears to contradict Romans 5:12.

4. Finally, it is difficult to see how God could, during the creation week, repeatedly pronounce His handiwork "good" and His finished creation "very good" if the rocks carried a burden of fossilized evidence from sin, rebellion, and judgment of a previously created order, and if a fallen angel, Satan, the author of that rebellion, were lurking somewhere in the shadows.

Interpretation of the Biblical Genealogies

The construction of a biblical chronology depends upon the interpretation of the genealogies of Genesis 5 and 11. If these genealogies are assumed to be reporting direct father-son relationships, the resulting chronology places the creation at about 4000 B.C., as in the traditional chronology of Bishop Ussher first published in 1654. There is, however, evidence that the Hebrew expression translated "begat" does not always refer to a direct father-son relationship, but that it can also signify a more distant connection. This led some to propose that the listed patriarchs were heads of dynasties perhaps hundreds of thousands of years long. This, however, makes the genealogies like rubber and reduces biblical chronology to absurdity.

A recent contribution (Chapter 8, footnote 1) adopts as the interpretive principle the idea that each successive named patriarch was born the same year as his predecessor and was of his blood line. The application of this assumption leads to a chronology which places the creation at about 11,000 B.C., the Flood at about 5000 B.C.

Another approach makes use of the Septuagint version of the Old Testament. This is a translation from the ancient Hebrew into Greek dating to about two centuries before Christ, and it has somewhat different numerical data for the ages of the patriarchs. A chronology built primarily on the Septuagint information places creation at about 5650 B.C. and the Flood at 4000 B.C. It is the present authors' opinion that further progress in biblical studies may well occur which will confirm one or the other of these lines of interpretation.

In any event, it is clear that the Bible teaches that the age of the earth is to be measured in thousands of years, not in millions. Probably the majority of informed students of the problems of creation-science would consider that a date for creation of around 10,000 B.C. is not out of line with the scriptural account, and that this would correlate satisfactorily with the essential data of the sciences interpreted in terms of biblical catastrophism.

Theistic Evolution

Theistic evolution is the view that God, indeed, created all things, but that He used evolutionary processes to accomplish His work of creation. Some believers in Christianity hold this view, considering that it is consistent with the teachings of the Bible.

Upon careful examination, however, theistic evolution is found to conflict seriously with both the Bible and the scientific evidence, as well as with the theory of evolution held by the majority of the materialistically oriented members of the scientific community. In the authors' estimation, theistic evolution may be held as an explanation of origins only at the expense of such radical compromise of the Bible as to imperil the whole structure of Christian doctrine. An outline of the major objections to this view follows.

Conflicts with the Teachings of the Bible

1. The expression, "after their kind," occurs ten times in Genesis 1, strongly implying the kind of tight boundaries between the kinds which have been discovered by the science of genetics.
2. The creation of man from the dust followed by the creation of one

woman from his side cannot be reconciled with any evolutionary origin of man without destroying the integrity of the language of the Bible. Problems such as these would raise serious questions concerning the vital doctrines of the verbal inspiration and infallibility of the Scriptures.

3. Any evolutionary theory requires vast periods of time, but no such time span is indicated in the Bible (See Appendix B).

4. Such a view raises serious questions concerning the attributes of God, particularly His sovereignty. According to Psalm 33:9, " . . . he spake, and it was done; he commanded, and it stood fast." But according to theistic evolution, God spoke and then had to wait a billion years or more.

5. The biblical doctrine of man and of redemption is grounded in the unity of the entire race in Adam (Romans 5:12-21, I Corinthians 15:21-23, 45-50).

6. Any effort to correlate the creation days of Genesis with the eras and periods of historical geology fails abysmally. For example, in Genesis land plants were created first, but historical geology has simple marine animals evolving first.

Conflicts with Scientific Evidences

1. Theistic evolution must face the same scientific difficulties which materialistic evolution does, as presented in *The Creation Explanation*.

2. There is no scientific evidence for a slow evolutionary process guided by divine intelligence.

Conflicts with Evolutionary Theory

1. Evolutionary theory by definition leaves no place whatsoever for teleology (purpose) or for any divine influence in nature. The standard view of evolutionary scientists is pure materialism.

2. Evolutionary theory provides for no distinctions between animal and human evolution. Man is supposedly only the most advanced of the animals. Evolutionary theory will not allow for a divine creation of man's soul after the materialistic evolution of his body. The soul, too, must be explainable by physics and chemistry.

It appears that those who would embrace some scheme of theistic evolution must soon find themselves in an intellectual "no man's land," where they will be called upon to defend themselves against formidable logical arguments directed from both the creationist and the evolutionist camps. It is our position that the most secure and reasonable position, both biblically and scientifically, is the one promoted in this book which is based upon a straightforward, essentially literal understanding of the opening chapters of Genesis. Recognizing that some Christians may continue to disagree, we would not impugn their faith, but we sincerely urge them to consider afresh the plain teaching of the Scriptures in dependence upon their Author, the Holy Spirit.

Basic Probability Theory

If there are several different possible outcomes of any kind of operation, the sum of the probabilities of the various outcomes is equal to unity, i.e., the number 1. In this case, in N random constructions of a protein molecule the possible outcomes are either 1. all failures to produce an active enzyme, i.e., zero successes, or 2. at least one success. Thus,

$$P_{\substack{\text{all} \\ \text{failures} \\ \text{in N trials}}} + P_{\substack{\text{at least} \\ \text{one success} \\ \text{in N trials}}} = 1.$$

Also note that if the probability of failure in one trial is $(P_f)^N$, the probability of failure for two trials is $(P_f)^2$, and for failure all N times in N trials is $(P_f)^N$. Thus, in rolling a six-sided die once, the probability of getting any particular result, say the number 3, is 1/6. The probability of failing to get a 3 in one trial rolling of the die is 1 - 1/6 = 5/6. Then in four trials, for example, the probability of never rolling a 3, i.e., of failing to get a 3 in at least one of the trials is $(1 - 1/6)^4 = (5/6)^4$. So we conclude that in four trials the probability of succeeding in rolling a 3 at least one is

$$P_{\substack{\text{at least} \\ \text{one success} \\ \text{in 4 trials}}} = 1 - P_{\substack{\text{all} \\ \text{failures} \\ \text{in 4 trials}}}$$
$$= 1 - (1 - 1/6)^4$$
$$= 1 - (5/6)^4 = 1 - 625/1296$$
$$= 0.4825$$

Footnotes

Chapter 1

[1]Schildknecht and Holoubek, *Angew. Chem., 73* (1961), p. 1.

[2]Aneshansley, Daniel J., *Science, 165,* July 4, 1969, pp. 61-63; Farb, Peter, *The Insects,* Life Nature Library, Time, Inc. (1962), pp. 120-121.

[3]Gennaro, J. F., *Natural History, 78,* August, 1969, pp. 36-43.

[4]Carr, Archie, *Land and Wildlife of Africa,* Time, Inc. (1964), pp. 62-63; Warren, James V., *Scientific American, 231,* No. 5, Nov., 1974, pp. 96-105.

[5]Griffin, Donald R., *Echoes of Bats and Men,* Garden City, N.Y.: Doubleday Anchor (1959).

[6]Farb, Peter, *op.cit.,* pp. 125-132.

[7]Shute, Evan, *Flaws in the Theory of Evolution,* Craig Press, Nutley, New Jersey (1961), p. 136.

[8]Sauer, E. G. F., *Scientific American, 199,* No. 2, Aug., 1958, p. 42; Emlen, Stephen T., *ibid.,* 233, Aug., 1975, pp. 102-111.

[9]Palmer, J. D., *Natural History, 76,* Nov., 1967, pp. 54-57; Keeton, William T., *Scientific American, 231,* Dec. 1974, pp. 96-107.

[10]Sisson, R. F., *National Geographic, 141,* May, 1972, pp. 694-701.

[11]Roessler and Post, *Natural History,* May, 1972, pp. 30-37.

[12]Odum, Eugene P., *Fundamentals of Ecology,* 3rd Edition, W. B. Saunders Co., Philadelphia (1971), pp. 273-274.

[13]Zeiller, Warren, *Natural History,* Dec., 1971, pp. 36-41.

[14]Eisner and Eisner, *Natural History, 74,* Mar., 1965, pp. 30-37.

[15]Pramer, David, *Science, 144,* No. 3617, April 24, 1964, pp. 382-388.

[16]Osborn, Fairfield, *The Web of Life,* New York: Devin-Adair (1953).

[17]Pauling, Linus, *Nature of the Chemical Bond,* 3rd Edition, Ithaca, N.Y.: Cornell Univ. Press (1960).

[18]Meldau, Fred John, *Why We Believe in Creation, Not in Evolution,* Denver, Colo.: Christian Victory Pub. Co. (1959), pp. 23-51.

Chapter 2

[1]Gal-Or, Benjamin, *Science, 176,* 7 April 1972, p. 15.

[2]Tribus and McIrvine, *Scientific American, 224,* Sept. 1971, pp. 179-188.

[3]Morowitz, Harold J., *Energy Flow in Biology,* New York: Academic Press (1968), pp. 58-75.

Chapter 3

[1]The approach and much of the data of this section are adapted from *The Fossils Say NO,* by Duane Gish, Creation-Life Publishers, San Diego, Calif (1973).

[2]Romer, Alfred, *Vertebrate Paleontology,* p. 23, Univ. of Chicago Press (1966).

[3]*Ibid.,* pp. 13, 166-167.

[4]The greater part of the data of this section are found in *The Genesis Flood,* by Whitcomb and Morris, Presbyterian and Reformed Pub. Co., Philadelphia (1961); and Morris, Henry M., *Scientific Creationism,* pp. 101-110, Creation-Life Publishers, San Diego (1974).

[5]Velikovsky, Immanuel, *Earth in Upheaval,* Dell Pub. Co. (1955), pp. 81-87, 151.

[6]Twenhofel, W. H., *Principles of Sedimentation,* 2nd edition, p. 144, New York: McGraw-Hill (1950); Stair, Ralph, *Scientific Monthly, 83,* July 1956, p. 11.

[7]Read, John G., *Mountains of Ararat,* filmstrip-tape album by Creation-Science Research Center, San Diego, Calif. (1973).

[8]Segraves, Kelly L., *Search for Noah's Ark,* filmstrip-tape album by Creation-Science Research Center, San Diego, Calif. (1974); Cummings, Violet M., *Noah's Ark: Fable or Fact?,* Creation-Science Research Center, San Diego, Calif (1973).

[9]Northrup, Bernard E., *Creation Research Society Quarterly, 6,* Dec. 1969, p. 129.

[10]Burdick, Clifford, *Creation Research Society Quarterly, 9,* June, 1972, p. 25.

[11]Axelrod, D., *Evolution, 13,* pp. 264-275 (1959).

[12]Leclerque, S., *Evolution, 10,* pp. 109-113 (1956).

[13]"Footprints in Stone," produced by Films for Christ, Peoria, Illinois.

[14]*Why Not Creation?,* Walter E. Lammerts, editor, article by William J. Meister, Sr., pp. 186-193, Presbyterian and Reformed Pub. Co. (1970).

[15]Romer, Alfred, *op.cit.,* pp. 328, 362.

[16]Birch and Ehrlich, *Nature, 214,* 22 April 1967, p. 352.

Chapter 4

[1]Curtis, Helena, *Invitation to Biology,* New York: Worth Publishers, Inc. (1972), pp. 18-21.

[2]Moore, John N., and Slusher, Harold S., Editors, *Biology: A Search for Order in Complexity,* Grand Rapids, Mich: Zondervan Pub. House (1971), pp. 14-15, 61-66.

[3]Curtis, Helena, *op.cit.,* pp. 27-47, 82a-82k.

[4]*Ibid.,* pp. 49-81.

[5]*Ibid.,* pp. 205-254; Moore and Slusher, *op.cit.,* pp. 141-149.

[6]Odum, Eugene P., *Fundamentals of Ecology,* 3rd edition, Philadelphia: W. B. Saunders, Co. (1971), pp. 37-105.

[7]Curtis, Helena, *op.cit.,* pp. 438-456.

[8]*Ibid.,* pp. 117-166; Moore and Slusher, *op.cit.,* pp. 83-104.

[9]*Ibid.,* pp. 167-202; Moore and Slusher, *op.cit.,* pp. 105-118; Watson, James D., *Molecular Biology of the Gene,* 2nd ed., W. A. Benjamin, Inc., New York (1970).

[10]Watson, James D., *op.cit.,* p. 508.

[11]*Ibid.,* pp. 299-329; Curtis, Helena, *op.cit.,* pp. 146-166; Moore and Slusher, *op.cit.,* pp. 441-461.

[12]Campbell, Lengyel, and Langridge, *The Proc. Nat. Acad. Sci. U.S., 70,* (1973), pp. 1841-1845.

[13]Betz, Brown, Smyth, and Clarke, *Nature, 247,* Feb. 1, 1974, pp. 261-264.

[14]Hickman, C. P., *Integrated Principles of Zoology,* C. V. Mosby Co. (1961), pp. 671-672; Moore and Slusher, *op.cit.,* pp. 74-81.

[15]Miller, S. L., *Science, 117,* p. 528 (1953).

[16]Oparin, A. I., *The Origin of Life,* New York: Dover Pub. Co. (1953).

[17]Medvedev, Zohres A., *The Rise and Fall of T.D. Lysenko,* New York: Columbia Univ. Press (1969), pp. 128, 135, 181-182.

[18]Miller and Orgel, *The Origins of Life on the Earth,* Englewood Cliffs, New Jersey: Prentice-Hall (1974), pp. 83-128, 135-151.

[19]Paecht-Horowitz, Berger, and Katchalsky, *Nature, 228,* p. 636 (1970).

[20]Calvin, Melvin, *Chemical Evolution,* New York: Oxford Univ. Press (1969), p. 178.

[21]Miller and Orgel, *op.cit.,* p. 164.

[22]Morowitz, Harold J., *Energy Flow in Biology,* New York: Academic Press (1968), p. 99.

[23]Trincher, Karl S., *Biology and Information,* Plenum Publishing Corp. (1965), pp. 71-76.

[24]Kornberg, A., *Scientific American,* Oct., 1968; *Science, 163,* p. 1410 (1969).

[25]Polanyi, Michael, *Chemical and Engineering News,* August 21, 1967, pp. 54-66; *Personal Knowledge: Towards a Post-Critical Philosophy,* Univ. of Chicago Press (1958), pp. 328-335.

Chapter 5

[1]The material on culture is adapted from R. Clyde McCone and Everett W. Purcell, *Man and His World,* Science and Creation Series, Book 5, Creation-Science Research Center, San Diego, Calif.

[2]Popper, Karl R., *The Logic of Scientific Discovery,* New York: Basic Books, Inc., (1959), pp. 40-42, 78-92.

[3]The material on the origin of civilization is adapted from R. Clyde McCone, in *Symposium on Creation IV,* Donald W. Patten, editor, Baker Book House, Grand Rapids, Mich., pp. 123-133 (1972).

[4]White, Leslie, "The Development of Culture," *The Development of Civilization to the Fall of Tome* (1959), p. 284.

[5]Frankfort, Henri, *The Birth of Civilization in the Near East,* p. 1.

[6]Adams, Robert M., "The Origin of Cities," *Scientific American,* CCM, (Vol. 203 1960), p. 154 ff.

[7]*Ibid.,* pp. 165, 166.

[8]Frankfort, Henri, et.al., *Before Philosophy* (1949), p. 140.

[9]Wooley, C. Leonard, *The Sumerians* (1965), p. 9.

[10]Leakey, Richard E., "Skull 1470," *National Geographic Magazine,* Vol. 143, No. 6, June, 1973, p. 819.

[11]Taieb, Maurice, and Johanson, Karl, as quoted in *Scientific American, 231,* Dec. 1974, p. 64.

[12]O'Connell, Patrick, *Science of Today and the Problems of Genesis,* Christian Book Club of Amer., Hawthorne, Calif. (1969), pp. 139-142; Cousins, Frank W., *Fossil Man,* Evolution Protest Movement, Hants, England (1971), pp. 40-45.

[13]O'Connell, Patrick, *ibid.,* pp. 105-138.

[14]Custance, Arthur C., "Fossil Man in the Light of the Record in Genesis," *Why Not Creation?,* Walter Lammerts, ed., Presbyterian and Reformed (1970), pp. 194-229; *Creation Research Society Quarterly, 11,* December, 1974, pp. 157-159.

Chapter 6

[1]Glasstone, Samuel, *Sourcebook On Atomic Energy,* 3rd edition, Van Nostrand Reinhold Co., pp. 96-134 (1967).

[2]Quoted by Glasstone, *op.cit.,* p. 82.

[3]*Ibid.,* pp. 432-472.

[4]Read, John G., *The Origin of the Solar System,* filmstrip and printed text, Creation-Science Research Center, San Diego, Calif. (1973); Hoyle, Fred, *Astronomy,* Crescent Books, Inc., pp. 269-281 (1962).

[5]Kaula, W., M., *An Introduction to Planetary Physics,* John Wiley and Sons, Inc., N.Y., p. 429 (1968).

[6]Reeves, H., *Icarus, 19,* pp. 604-616 (1973).

[7]Spitzer, L., *Origin of the Solar System,* Jastrow and Cameron, editors, p. 45 (1963).

[8]*Nature, 247,* Feb. 15, 1974, p. 427; *Scientific American, 233,* Aug., 1975. Dr. Fred Hoyle is reported to have developed a complex mathematical model based upon numerous assumptions which reportedly predicts the rate of solar neutrino production which has actually been observed.

[9]Rasool, Ichtiaque, *Science, 183,* Feb. 8, 1974, p. 504.

[10]Lyttleton, R. A., *Mysteries of the Solar System,* Oxford Clarendon Press, p. 110 (1968).

[11]Joss, P. C., *Astronomy and Astrophysics, 25,* No. 2, pp. 271-273, reported in *Creation Research Society Quarterly,* H. L. Armstrong, editor, *11,* Dec. 1974, pp. 161-162.

[12]Lyttleton, R. A., *op.cit.,* p. 134.

[13]Read, John G., *The Search for Extraterrestrial Life,* filmstrip and printed text, Creation-Science Research Center, San Diego, Calif. (1973).

[14]*Science, 176,* p. 975 (1972); Nakamura *et.al., Ibid., 181,* p. 49 (1973).

[15]Slusher, Harold, *Science and Scripture,* Sept.-Oct., 1971, p. 26.

[16]Mulfinger, George, *Creation Research Society Quarterly, 7,* June, 1970, pp. 7-24; Slusher, Harold, *Bible-Science Newsletter,* Jan., 1975, pp. 1-3.

[17]Hoyle, Fred, *op.cit.,* pp. 252-270.

[18]Abell, George, *Exploration of the Universe,* Holt, Rinehart, Winston, p. 566.

[19]Abell, George, *ibid.,* pp. 576-589.

[20]Burbidge, G. R., *Nature Physical Science, 246,* Nov. 12, 1973, pp. 17-24.

[21]Dingle, Herbert, *Science at the Crossroads,* Martin Brian and O'Keefe, London (1972).

[22]Moon and Spencer, *Journal of the Optical Soc. of America,* Aug., 1953, pp. 635-641.

[22]Boardman, Koontz, and Morris, *Science and Creation,* Creation-Science Research Center, San Diego, Calif., pp. 187-191 (1973).

[24]St. Peter, Roger L., *Creation Research Society Quarterly, 11,* December, 1974, pp. 143-155.

Chapter 7

[1]MacRae, Allan A., in *Modern Science and Christian Faith,* Wheaton, Ill: Van Kampen Press (1954), pp. 231-232.

[2]Unger, Merrill F., *Archaeology and the Old Testament,* Grand Rapids, Mich: Zondervan Publishing House (1954), pp. 27ff.

[3]Mayr, Ernst, *Population, Species, and Evolution,* Cambridge, Mass: Harvard Univ. Press (1970), p. 12.

[4]Dickerson, Richard E., *Scientific American, 226,* April, 1972, p. 58.

[5]Estimated from various data in Alfred Romer's *Vertebrate Paleontology,* 3rd ed., University of Chicago Press (1966).

[6]*Evolution–Science Falsely So-called,* 19th ed., International Christian Crusade (1974), pp. 20-25.

[7]Lammerts, Walter E., in *Why Not Creation?,* Nutley, N.J.: Presbyterian and Reformed Pub. Co., (1970), p. 301.

[8]Crow, James F., *Bulletin of Atomic Scientists, 14,* Jan., 1958, pp. 19-20, quoted in *The Genesis Flood,* by Morris and Whitcomb, p. 401.

[9]Moore, John N., and Slusher, Harold S., editors, *Biology: A Search for Order in Complexity,* Grand Rapids, Mich: Zondervan Publishing House (1971), p. 420.

[10]Kaufmann, David A., *A Challenge to Education II-A,* Walter Lang, Editor, Bible-Science Association, Inc., Caldwell, Idaho, pp. 119-130 (1974).

[11]Merton, P. A., *Scientific American, 226,* May, 1972, pp. 30-37.

[12]*Ibid.,* p. 32.

[13]Kaufmann, David A., *op.cit.,* pp. 124-125, quoted by permission.

Chapter 8

[1]Camping, Harold, *Adam When?,* Frontiers for Christ, Alameda, Calif., pp. 52-90 (1974); Teachout, Richard A., *Bible-Science Newsletter,* 15 Jan. 1971, pp. 1-7.

[2]Cook, Melvin, *Prehistory and Earth Models,* Max Parrish, London, pp. 14-15 (1966).

[3]*Chemical Oceanography,* Riley, J. B., and Skirrow, G., eds., Vol. 1, pp. 164-165, London: Academic Press (1965).

[4]Martin, Dean F., *Marine Chemistry,* Vol. 2, pp. 228-229, Marcel Dekker, Inc., New York (1970).

[5]*Ibid.,* pp. 233-263.

[6]Cook, Melvin, *op.cit.,* pp. 10-14.

[7]Nevins, S. E., *Creation–Acts, Facts, Impacts,* p. 164, Institute for Creation Research Publishing Co., San Diego (1974).

[8]Pettersson, Hans, *Scientific American, 202,* Feb. 1960, p. 132.

[9]Hawkins, G. S., *Annual Review Astronomy and Astroophysics, 2,* pp. 140-164 (1964), cited by W. M. Kaula in *An Introduction to Planetary Physics,* p. 249, John Wiley & Sons, Inc., New York (1968).

[10]Asimov, Isaac, *Science Digest, 45,* Jan. 1959, p. 35.

[11]Allen, Benjamin F., *Creation Research Society Quarterly,* Vol. 9, Sept. 1972, pp. 96-114.

[12]Cook, Melvin, *op.cit.,* p. 260; *Chemical and Engineering News,* 29 May 1972; *Science, 160,* 614 (1968).

[13]Barnes, T. G., *Creation Research Society Quarterly,* Vol. 9, No. 4, March 1973, p. 222.

[14]Ingersoll, Zobel, and Ingersoll, *Heat Conduction With Engineering, Geological and Other Applications,* pp. 99-107, Univ. of Wisconsin Press (1954).

[15]Funkhouser and Naughton, *Journal of Geophysical Research, 73,* No. 14, July 15, 1968, p. 4601.

[16]Turner, Grenville, *Science, 167,* CO Jan. 1970, p. 466.

[17]Tera and Wasserburg, *Earth and Planetary Science Letters, 17,* (1972), p. 36.

[18]Cherdyntsev, *et.al., Geological Institute, Academy of Sciences,* USSR, Earth Science Section, 172:178. The data is reproduced by Sidney P. Clemmentson in *Creation Research Society Quarterly, 7,* No. 3, Dec. 1970, p. 140.

[19]Nunes and Tatsumoto, *Science, 182,* 30 Nov. 1973, p. 916.

[20]Zartman, *et.al., Science, 145,* 31 July 1964, p. 479.

[21]Oversby, V. M., *Geochimica et Cosmochimica Acta, 36,* Oct. 1972, p. 1167.

[22]Tera and Wasserburg, *Earth and Planetary Science Letters, 14* (1972), p. 281.

[23]Wang, *et.al., Science, 167,* 30 Jan. 1970, p. 479.

[24]Oversby and Gast, *Earth and Planetary Science Letters, 5* (1968), p. 199.

[25]Tatsumoto and Rosholt, *Science, 167,* 30 Jan. 1970, p. 461.

[26]Read, John G., *What Is the Scientific Certainty of Evolution?,* Scientific-Technical Presentations, P.O. Box 2384, Culver City, Calif.

[27]Gentry, Robert V., *Science, 184,* 5 April 1974, pp. 62-66; Gentry, Robert V., *et.al, Nature, 252,* Dec. 13, 1974, pp. 564-566.

[28]These samples are selected as representative from the more than 15,000 radiocarbon dates that have been published in *Radiocarbon* and *Science.*

[29]Suess, A. E., *Journal of Geophysical Research, 70,* No. 23, pp. 5937 and 5947 (1965).

[30]Cook, Melvin, *Prehistory and Earth Models,* pp. 1-10, London: Max Parrish (1966).

[31]Whitelaw, R. L., *Creation Research Society Quarterly, 7,* No. 1, June 1970, p. 56.

[32]Keeling and Waterman, *Journal of Geophysical Research, 73,* No. 14, (1968), p. 4529.

[33]Read, John G., unpublished paper.

[34]Renfrew, Colin, *Scientific American, 225,* Oct., 1971, pp. 63-72.

[35]Clementson, Sidney P., *Creation Research Society Quarterly, 10,* March, 1974, pp. 229-236.

[36]Camping, Harold, *op.cit.,* pp. 178-229.

[37]Bada, Jeffrey L., *Earth and Planetary Science Letters, 15,* (1972), pp. 223-231.

[38]Gish, Duane, *ICR Impact Series, No. 23,* Institute for Creation Research, San Diego (1975).

Bibliography

Chapter 1
Davidheiser, Bolton, *Evolution and Christian Faith,* Nutley, N. J.: Presbyterian and Reformed Pub. Co. (1969).
Meldau, Fred John, *Why We Believe in Creation, Not in Evolution,* Denver, Colo.: Christian Victory Pub. Co. (1959). (This publication contains some inaccuracies but also much useful information.)
Odum, Eugene P., *Fundamentals of Ecology,* 3rd edition, Philadelphia: W. B. Saunders Co. (1971).
Shute, Evan, *Flaws in the Theory of Evolution,* Nutley, New Jersey: Craig Press (1961).
Scientific Studies in Special Creation, Walter E. Lammerts, Editor, Nutley, N.J.: Presbyterian and Reformed Pub. Co. (1971), pp. 243-268.
Symposium on Creation IV, Donald W. Patten, Editor, Grand Rapids, Mich.: Baker Book House (1972), pp. 57-107.

Chapter 2
Clark, Robert E. D., *The Universe–Plan or Accident?,* Philadelphia: Muhlenberg Press (1971), pp. 15-42.
Fabun, Don, Energy: *Transactions in Time,* Beverly Hills, Calif.: Glencoe Press (1971).
Morowitz, Harold J., *Entropy for Biologists: An Introduction to Thermodynamics,* New York: Academic Press Inc. (1970).

Wilson, Mitchell, *Energy* (Life Science Library), Time-Life Publishers (1967).
Scientific Studies in Special Creation, Walter E. Lammerts, Editor, Presbyterian and Reformed Pub. Co., Nutley, New Jersey (1971), pp. 60-71.
Why Not Creation?, Walter E. Lammerts, Editor, Presbyterian and Reformed Pub. Co., Nutley, New Jersey (1970), pp. 67-79.

Chapter 3
Clark, Robert E. D., *The Universe–Plan or Accident?,* Philadelphia: Muhlenberg Press (1961), pp. 117-140.
Daly, Reginald, *Earth's Most Challenging Mysteries,* Nutley, New Jersey: Craig Press (1972).
Gish, Duane, *The Fossils Say NO,* Creation-Life Publishers, San Diego, Calif. (1973).
Morris, Henry M., *Scientific Creationism,* Creation-Life Publishers, San Diego (1974).
Segraves, Kelly L., *Jesus Christ, Creator,* Creation-Science Research Center, San Diego, Calif. (1973).
Velikovsky, Immanuel, *Earth in Upheaval,* New York: Dell Pub. Co. Inc. (1955).
Whitcomb, John C., and Morris, Henry M., *The Genesis Flood,* Philadelphia, Pa.: Presbyterian and Reformed Pub. Co. (1961).
Scientific Studies in Special Creation, Walter E. Lammerts, Editor, Presbyterian and Reformed Pub. Co., Nutley, New Jersey (1971), pp. 125-135, 156-168, 184-197, 234-242, 285-298.
Symposium on Creation III, Donald W. Patten, Editor, Baker Book House, Grand Rapids, Mich. (1971), pp. 33-102.
Symposium on Creation IV, Donald W. Patten, Editor, Baker Book House, Grand Rapids, Mich. (1972), pp. 9-44.
The Fossil Record, The Geological Society of London, London, England (1967).
Why Not Creation?, Walter E. Lammerts, Editor, Presbyterian and Reformed Pub. Co., Nutley, New Jersey (1971), pp. 114-242.

Chapter 4
Boardman, Koontz, and Morris, *Science and Creation,* Creation-Science Research Center, San Diego, Calif. (1973), pp. 113-140.
Coppedge, James F., *Evolution; Possible or Impossible?,* Grand Rapids, Mich.: Zondervan Pub. House (1973).
Gish, Duane T., *Speculations and Experiments Related to Theories on the Origin of Life: a Critique,* Creation-Life Publishers, San Diego, Calif. (1972).
Curtis, Helena, *Invitation to Biology,* New York: Worth Publishers, Inc. (1972).
Miller, Stanley L., and Orgel, Leslie E., *The Origins of Life on the Earth,* Englewood Cliff, N.J.: Prentice-Hall (1974).
Watson, James D., *Molecular Biology of the Gene,* 2nd edition, New York: W. A. Benjamin, Inc. (1970).
Biology: A Search for Order in Complexity, John N. Moore and Harold S. Slusher, Editors, Grand Rapids, Mich.: Zondervan Pub. House (1971).
Scientific Studies in Special Creation, Walter E. Lammerts, Editor, Presbyterian and Reformed Pub. Co., Nutley, New Jersey (1971), pp. 136-155, 169-183, 269-284, 308-329.

Symposium on Creation I, Baker Book House, Grand Rapids, Mich., (1968), pp. 11-32.
Symposium on Creation III, Donald W. Patten, Editor, Baker Book House, Grand Rapids, Mich. (1971), pp. 145-150.
Symposium on Creation IV, Donald W. Patten, Editor, Baker Book House, Grand Rapids, Mich. (1972), pp. 45-56.

Chapter 5
Cousins, Frank W., *Fossil Man,* Revised Edition, Hants, England: Evolution Protest Movement (1971).
Macbeth, Norman, *Darwin Retried,* Boston: Gambit Inc. (1971).
O'Connell, Patrick, *Science of Today and Problems of Genesis,* 2nd edition, Hawthorne, Calif.: Book Club of America (1969). (Note: While this book is written by a Roman Catholic priest, directed primarily to a Catholic audience, it nevertheless contains a most useful compilation of factual data, especially on human fossils and the Flood.)
Popper, Karl R., *The Logic of Scientific Discovery,* New York: Basic Books, Inc. (1959).
Smith, A. E. Wilder, *Man's Origin, Man's Destiny,* Wheaton, Ill.: Harold Shaw Pub. (1968).
Symposium on Creation I, Grand Rapids, Mich.: Baker Book House (1968), pp. 81-89.
Symposium on Creation III, Donald W. Patten, Editor, Baker Book House, Grand Rapids, Mich. (1971), pp. 121-144.
Symposium on Creation IV, Donald W. Patten, Editor, Baker Book House, Grand Rapids, Mich. (1972), pp. 9-44, 123-133.
Why Not Creation?, Walter Lammerts, Editor, Presbyterian and Reformed Pub. Co., Nutley, New Jersey (1970), pp. 185-229.

Chapter 6
Boardman, Koontz, and Morris, *Science and Creation,* Creation-Science Research Center, San Diego, Calif. (1973).
Chesnut, D. Lee, *The Atom Speaks,* Creation-Science Research Center, San Diego, Calif. (1973).
Hawkins, Gerald, *Splendor in the Sky,* Revised Edition, Harper-Row Pub. (1969).
Whitcomb, John C., Jr., *The Early Earth,* Grand Rapids: Baker Book House (1972).
Scientific Studies in Special Creation, Walter E. Lammerts, Editor, Presbyterian and Reformed Pub. Co., Nutley, New Jersey (1971), pp. 22-31.
Why Not Creation?, Walter E. Lammerts, Editor, Presbyterian and Reformed Pub. Co., Nutley, New Jersey (1970), pp. 24-66.

Chapter 7
Davidheiser, Bolton, *Evolution and Christian Faith,* Nutley, N.J.: Presbyterian and Reformed Pub. Co. (1969), pp. 231-281.
Klotz, John W., *Genes, Genesis, and Evolution,* Second Edition, Saint Louis: Concordia Pub. House (1970), pp. 120-321.

Shute, Evan, *Flaws in the Theory of Evolution,* Nutley, New Jersey: Craig Press (1961), pp. 49-61, 78-83, 147-162.
Evolution–Science Falsely So-called, 18th ed., Toronto, Canada: International Christian Crusade.
Scientific Studies in Special Creation, Walter E. Lammerts, Editor, Presbyterian and Reformed Pub. Co., Nutley, New Jersey (1971), pp. 136-155.

Chapter 8
Boardman, Koontz, and Morris, *Science and Creation,* Creation-Science Research Center, San Diego, Calif. (1973), pp. 141-182.
Dalrymple, G. B. and Lanphere, M. A., *Potassium-Argon Dating,* San Francisco, Calif.: W. H. Freeman and Co. (1969).
Hamilton, E. I., *Applied Geochronology,* New York: Academic Press (1965).
Slusher, Harold S., *Critique of Radiometric Dating,* Creation-Life Publishers, San Diego, Calif. (1973).
Scientific Studies in Special Creation, Walter E. Lammerts, Editor, Presbyterian and Reformed Pub. Co., Nutley, New Jersey (1971), pp. 72-102, 198-205.
Why Not Creation?, Walter E. Lammerts, Editor, Presbyterian and Reformed Pub. Co., Nutley, New Jersey (1972), pp. 80-113.

Index

Abell, George   152
Abiogenesis, theoretical difficulties   97
Adam, creation of   223
   unity of race in   236
Adams, Robert   117
Adenine   80
Adenosine-5'-phosphate   85
Affectional nature, human   216
Amber, Baltic, fossils   51
Amino acid racemization dating method   210
Amino acids   67, 165
Amniotic egg, reptilian   42
Anatomy, comparative   162-165
Andes Mountains, recent   47
Andromeda Galaxy   151
Anemones, sea   10
Animalia, Kingdom of   69
Anthropology
   cultural   105-119
   physical   119-131
Ants, symbiosis with plants   9
Apheloria corrugata, millipede   10
Ararat   50
Archaeopteryx, fossil bird   43
Argyroneta, spider aquanaut   8
Ark of Noah   227
Asimov, Isaac   190
Asteroids   140
Atavistic structures   171
Atomic structure   133-137
Atomic theory   133
ATP (adenosine triphosphate)   89
Australopithecus   120, 124, 126, 129, 130

Bada, Jeffry   210
Balance of nature   73
Baluchaterium   59
Barnes, Thomas G.   194
Bats, echo location   6

Bee, integrated design   6
Beetle, Bombardier   2
"Big Bang" theory   155
Biosphere   70, 71
Birch, L. C.   60
Biston betularia, peppered moth   174
Bohr, Niels   135
Bombardier beetle   2
Bone Cave, Cumberland   51
Boule, Marcellin   127
Brachinus tschernikhi, Bombardier beetle   2
Brahe, Tycho   107
Breuil, Abbé   127
Bull's horn acacia   10
Burdick, Clifford   48, 50, 53

Cain   225
Calaveras fossil skull   120, 125
Calvin, Melvin   100
Cambrian rocks, fossils   41, 57
Camping, Harold   210
Canopy, water vapor   224
Carbohydrates   67, 68
Carbon dioxide   16, 23, 68
Carbon-14 data reinterpreted   208-210
Carbon-14 dating   126, 128, 205-210
Carbon-14, increasing inventory   207
Carboniferous rocks, fossils   57
Carnivores   72
Castenedolo fossil   120, 125
Catastrophism, biblical   40
Cells   65ff.
   complexity   66
   size   65
Cellulose   67
Cenozoic rocks, fossils   59
Centrioles   67
Cepheid variable stars   150
Cetacea, no fossil ancestors   44

Chadwick, James   *134*
Change, processes of   *21*
Check valves, giraffe carotid artery   *5*
Chemical energy   *30, 31*
Chloroplasts   *67, 68*
Christ Jesus, Creator   *19, 140, 212*
   faith (trust) in   *213, 218*
   Lord of time   *212*
   Savior   *213*
Chromosomes   *67*
   human   *78*
Chronology, biblical   *181, 231-233*
Civilization
   evolution of, theory   *116*
   origin   *115-119*
Class (zoological classification)   *69*
Classification (taxonomy)   *68-70, 162-165*
Cleaner relationships, symbiotic   *9*
Clementson, Sidney P.   *209*
Coal   *49, 57*
Code, genetic   *86*
Codons, of genetic code   *86*
Coelacanth, "living fossil"   *55*
Comets   *140, 144*
Community, biological   *71*
Coney   *176*
Conservation of energy   *32*
Conservation of matter-energy   *32*
Cook, Melvin   *208*
Cooling of earth   *194*
Cordaites, fossil conifer   *57*
Cosmic radiation   *205, 224*
Creation Model   *55, 220-229*
Cretaceous rocks   *47*
Cro-Magnon man, fossils   *206*
Cultural evolution   *117-119*
Custance, Arthur C.   *130*
Cyanide   *10*
Cyclic change   *24*
Cytidine-5'-phosphate   *85*
Cytochrome *c,* evolution, theory   *165-169*
Cytoplasm   *65*
Cytosine   *80*

Dakota Indians
   language   *105, 116*
   world view   *111*
Dalton, John   *133*
Daly, Reginald   *50*
Darwin, Charles   *93, 114*
David, Psalmist, taught of God   *21*
Days of creation   *222-224, 231-233*
Dead Sea Scrolls, age   *207*
De Broglie, Louis   *137*
de Chardin, Teilhard   *44, 128*
Degeneration of cultures   *115*
Degeneration, natural law of   *32ff.*
Deoxyadenosine-5'-phosphate   *79*
Deoxycytidine-5'-phosphate   *79*
Deoxyguanosine-5'-phosphate   *79*
Deozyribose   *81, 82*
Deoxythymidine-5'-phosphate   *79*
Design   *1-19*
   in atomic nucleus   *139*
   in atoms   *133-137*
   in solar system   *140-143*

Designer, ultimate evidence   *215-219*
Diatomaceous earth deposit   *51*
Dickerson, Robert   *165*
Dinosaurs   *58*
   ornithischian   *58*
   saurischian   *58*
Diplodocus dinosaur   *58*
Disorder, entropy measure of   *35*
Distribution, animal and plant   *172*
DNA (deoxyribose nucleic acid)   *64, 67, 224*
DNA, replication in cell   *78-85, 87*
   accuracy   *82*
   rate   *82*
Dobzhansky, Theodosius   *91*
Dolphin, sonar   *6*
Dominant traits   *75*
Doppler effect   *152, 153*
Drosophila (fruit fly)   *90*
Dubois, Eugene   *44, 127*

Earth-sun system, design   *16-18, 143*
Echo location   *6*
Ecology   *12, 70-73*
Ecosystem   *71*
Eden, Garden of   *224*
Ehrlich, P. R.   *60*
Electromagnetic force   *28*
Electron   *134, 136, 137, 139*
Elements, chemical, in oceans   *185*
Elements, essential to life   *18*
Embryo, development of   *169-171*
Endoplasmic reticulum   *66*
Energy   *24ff.*
   conservation of   *32*
   pyramid   *72*
Entropy   *33-35*
   probability and   *34, 35*
Enuma Elish, Babylonian creation myth   *160*
Enzymes   *67, 165*
   altered by mutations   *92-94*
Eohippus (Hyracotherium)   *176, 177*
Eolidoidea, sea slug   *10*
Ephemeral markings   *52*
Equilibrium   *34*
Equus Scotti, fossil horse   *176*
Errors, in science, causes   *113*
Escherischia coli   *66, 89, 92*
Eukaryotic cell   *69*
Eve, creation of   *223*
Extinction, of species   *59-61*

Faith   *19, 38, 40, 61, 90, 98, 102, 104,*
   156, 159, 178, 180, 213, 218, 219
Falsifiability, criterion of science   *108*
Family (zoological classification)   *69*
Fats (lipids)   *67*
Fault breccia   *47*
Feather, bird   *162*
First law of thermodynamics   *32*
Fish, French angel   *9*
   yellow-tailed goat   *9*
Fisher   *73*
Flight, no evidence of origin   *43*
Flood, Genesis   *40, 225-227*
Food chains   *72, 73*
Force   *24*
   in atomic nucleus   *140*

Fossils   *41ff.*
  horse   *175*
  humanoid, analysis   *124*
  humanoid, classification   *119-128*
  humanoid, interpretation   *124*
  polystrate   *49*
  produced by Flood   *226*
Frankfort, Henri   *117*
Free energy   *31*
Friction   *27, 29*
Fungi, Kingdom of   *69*
Fungus, cowboy   *11*

Galactose   *92*
β-Galactosidase   *92, 93*
Galaxies   *149-152*
  distances to   *151*
  evolution, theory   *151*
Gametes (sex cells)   *75*
Gauss, K. F.   *193*
Gecko, lizard   *3*
Genes   *78*
  size   *85*
Genetic code, origin unknown   *100*
Genetic load   *60, 94*
Genetics   *77ff.*
Gentry, Robert V.   *203*
Genus (zoological classification)   *69*
Geologic column   *42*
Geostatic pressure   *192*
Gingko tree   *173*
Giraffe   *5*
Glaciation   *227*
Glucose   *92*
God, the Creator   *1, 12, 16, 18, 19, 21, 73,*
  77, 88, 90, 104, 112, 133, 139, 149, 156, 159
  161, 164, 180, 212, 213, 215-219
  the Father   *212, 213, 215, 216, 217, 218*
Golgi bodies   *67*
Grand Canyon   *188*
Gravitational force   *28*
Greeks, natural philosophy of   *107*
"Greenhouse effect," of atmosphere   *17, 224*
Guanine   *80*
Guanosine-5'-phosphate   *85*
Gunn, James   *155*

Haeckel, Ernst   *169*
Haldane, J. B. S.   *96*
Half-life, radioactive   *196*
Halos, radioactive   *203*
"Heat death" of universe   *35*
Heat, energy   *29*
  capacity of water   *16*
  of fusion, water   *15*
  of vaporization, water   *15*
Helium, atmospheric   *185*
Helix, double, DNA   *79, 82, 83, 84*
Herbivores   *72*
Heredity   *73ff.*
Himalaya Mountains, recent   *47*
Hippopotamus graves   *51*
Holy Ghost (Holy Spirit)   *218*
Homeostasis   *63, 64*
Homo erectus (Pithecanthropus)   *127, 129, 130*
Homo habilis   *120, 126, 129*
Homo sapiens   *127*

Howell, B. F.   *188*
Humanities, contrasted with science and
  history   *112*
Hutton, James   *186*
Huxley, Julian   *91*
Hydrogen bond   *15, 79, 80, 81, 82, 85*
Hydrogen cyanide   *10*
Hydrogen peroxide   *2*
Hydroquinone   *2*
Hypothalamus, and bodily temperature
  control   *178, 179*
Hyracotherium (Eohippus)   *176, 177*

Ice, crystal structure   *15*
Incas, of Peru, degeneration   *115*
Indus Valley, civilization   *118*
Information, coded, genetic   *37, 63, 64, 89, 90*
Information theory, genetic code and   *37*
Intellect, human   *1, 18, 19, 38, 105, 216*
Intelligence, origins and   *38*
Isochrons, strontium-rubidium   *204*

Jacobsen, Thorkild   *117*
Java Man (*Homo erectus*)   *44, 127, 129, 130*
Jesus Christ, Creator   *19, 140, 212*
  faith (trust) in   *213, 218*
  Lord of time   *212*
  Savior   *213*
Josephus, Jewish historian   *106*

Kaufmann, David A.   *177*
Keith, Sir Arthur   *125*
Kelvin, Lord (William Thompson)   *194*
Kepler, Johannes   *107*
Kerkut, C. A.   *176*
Kinds
  biblical   *40*
  created   *164. 223*
Kinetic energy   *25, 34*
Kingdom (zoological classification)   *69*
Kornberg, Arthur   *101*
Khorana, H. G.   *101*
Krakatao Island   *172*

Lactose, metabolism   *92*
Lamb, Horace   *194*
Lammerts, Walter   *48, 174*
Languages, and "primitive" cultures   *115*
  all complex   *116*
Leakey, Louis   *44, 124, 126*
Leakey, Richard   *44*
Leeuwenhoek, A. van   *95*
Lewis Overthrust   *47, 227*
Libby, Willard   *205*
Library in a molecule   *89*
Life   *63ff.*
  and energy laws   *35*
Light transit time problem   *154*
Linnaeus, Carolus   *68, 69*
Lipids (fats)   *67*
"Living fossils"   *54*
Lizard, gecko   *3*
Lyell, Charles   *182, 186*
Lysenko, T. D.   *96*
Lysosomes   *67*
Lyttleton, R. A.   *144*

Magellanic Clouds   *151*
Magnetic field, of earth   *18, 193-194, 224*
Mammoths, frozen   *51, 228*
Man   *105ff.*
   place in world   *18*
   study of, creationist approach   *111*
Man, person nature   *18, 216ff.*
Mars, planet   *145*
Materialist's dilemma   *90*
Mayas, of Yucatan, degeneration   *115*
Mayr, Ernst   *94*
Meanders, incised   *47*
Mechanism, evidence of design   *102-104*
Meiosis   *79*
Meister, William J., Sr.   *54*
Membrane, of cell   *65, 66*
Mendel, Gregor   *74, 75*
Mendel's Laws   *74-76*
Mendelyeev, D. I.   *137*
Merton, P. A.   *177*
Mesopotamian River Valley, civilization   *118*
Mesozoic rocks, fossils   *58*
Metabolism   *30, 36, 63, 64*
Meteor showers   *140*
Meteorites, in sediments   *49*
Meteoritic dust   *190*
Milky Way Galaxy   *150, 151*
Miller, Stanley   *96, 100*
Millipede, *Apheloria corrugata*   *10*
Missing links, evolutionary   *44*
Mississippi River delta, age   *191*
Mitochondria   *67*
Mitosis   *79*
Mold, predatory soil   *11*
Molecular genetics   *78*
Monera, Kingdom of   *69*
Monkey Puzzle tree   *173*
Moon, Parry   *154*
Moon
   radioactivity of   *145*
   rock, discordant ages   *202*
Moral nature, human   *216*
Morowitz, Harold   *101*
Morris, Henry M.   *46, 50*
Muller, H. J.   *173*
Mutations   *75, 90-95, 173-175*
Myrmecophytes (ant plants)   *10*
Myth, modern, evolution   *110*

Navigation, bird   *8*
Neanderthal   *44, 121, 124, 126, 130*
Nebular Hypothesis   *141, 148*
Nematodes   *11*
Neutrinos, solar   *142*
Neutron   *134, 139, 205*
Nevins, Stuart E.   *189*
Nile River Valley, civilization   *118*
Nitrates, in oceans   *185*
Noah   *227*
Norfolk Pine   *173*
Nuclear force   *28*
Nucleolus   *67*
Nucleotides   *79, 82*
Nucleus of atom   *137, 139*
Nucleus, of cell   *65, 67*
Nudibranch (sea slug)   *10*

Oceans, age   *184*
Ochoa, Severo   *101*
Olenelus fauna   *57*
Olmo fossil   *120, 125*
Oort, Jan   *144*
Oparin, A. I.   *96*
Orb web   *7, 8*
Order (zoological classification)   *69*
Organelles   *65-67*
Orgel, Leslie   *100*
Orohippus   *176*
Overthrusts, geologic   *47, 227*
Ozone, atmospheric   *17*

Palestine, stage of history   *229*
Paluxy River fossil footprints   *54*
Parallax of stars   *147, 150*
Pasteur, Louis   *96*
Peking Man (Sinanthropus)   *44, 121, 127, 128*
Pennsylvanian strata   *57*
Periodic Table of Elements   *137, 138*
Petroleum seepage clock   *192*
Pettersson, Hans   *190*
Pheromones   *7*
Philosophy and beginnings   *159ff.*
Phosphoric acid   *81*
Photographic process   *30*
Photosynthesis   *12, 23, 36, 68*
Phylum (zoological classification)   *69*
Physiology, philosophy, assumptions and   *177*
Phytoplankton   *72*
Pigeon, navigation   *8*
Piltdown fossil fraud   *128*
Pithecanthropus erectus (*Homo erectus*)   *44, 121, 124, 126, 127, 129, 130*
Planets, rotations   *142*
Plantae, Kingdom of   *69*
Pliohippus, fossil horse   *176*
Polanyi, Michael   *103*
Polar, water molecules   *14, 15*
Pollen, fossil   *53*
Polonium, radioactive halos   *203*
Population, biological   *71*
Population, growth   *191*
Porcupine, predator control   *73*
Porpoise, sonar   *6*
Potassium-argon dating   *126*
Potential energy   *25, 34*
Poynting-Robertson effect   *145*
Pramer, David   *11*
Precambrian rocks   *47, 53*
Predation and defense   *10*
Prehistory, contrasted with history and science   *112*
Probability theory, of protein formation   *98-102, 239*
Prokaryotic cell   *69*
Pronuba moth, yucca and   *13*
Proper motions, of stars   *150*
Proteins   *67*
   comparative structure, evolution   *165-169*
   synthesis by chance, probability   *98-102*
   synthesis in cell   *88*
   synthesis in cell, rate   *89*
   synthesis on Montmorillonite clay   *100*
Protista, Kingdom of   *69*
Proton   *134, 136, 205, 206*

Protoplasm   *65, 67*
Pyramid of biomass   *72*
    of producers and consumers   *71*

Quasars, energy and red shift anomalies   *153*

Radioactive decay curve   *196, 197*
Radioactive disequilibrium   *201*
Radiometric ages
    anomalous   *200*
    discordant   *201*
Radiometric clocks   *195*
Radiometric dating of fossils   *128*
Radiometric dating methods   *199*
Read, John   *209*
Recessive traits   *75*
Red shift, galactic   *151, 152, 153*
Redi, Francisco   *95*
Reeves, H.   *143*
Reproduction   *63, 64, 73, 74*
Response   *63, 64*
Revelation, source of absolute truth   *109*
Rho-factor, in protein synthesis   *85*
Ribosomes   *67, 88*
RNA (ribose nucleic acid)   *67*
    messenger RNA   *85*
    polymerase   *85*
    transfer RNA   *88*
Romer, Alfred   *41, 44*
Rudimentary structures, organs   *171*
Rutherford, Ernest   *134*

Sandal prints, with trilobites   *54*
Satellite, artificial   *27*
Satellites, of planets   *140*
Schildknecht, H.   *2*
Schwann, Theodor   *65*
Science, contrasted with history and
    humanities   *112*
Science, self-correcting   *114*
Science and technology, pre- and
    post-Flood   *106*
Scientific method   *107-110*
Second law of thermodynamics   *33ff., 71,
    156, 224, 225*
Sediments, marine   *189*
Seth   *225*
Shrimp, cleaner   *9*
Sigma-factor, in protein synthesis   *85*
Sin, effect on creation   *224*
Sinanthropus (Peking Man)   *44, 128*
Sirenia, no fossil ancestors   *44*
Slug, sea   *10*
Solar system, age   *144-146*
Solar system, origin, symposium   *141, 143*
Solomon, biblical author   *24*
Species   *69, 163*
    extinction of   *60*
Spectroscope   *135*
Spectrum   *136*
Spencer, D. E.   *154*
Spiders   *7, 8*
Spinnarets, spider   *7*
Spontaneous generation   *95*
    on early earth, theory   *96-98*
Star Pine   *173*
Starch   *67*

Stars, classification   *149*
    distances to   *147*
    evolution of, theory   *146-149*
    types   *147-148*
Stegosaurus dinosaur   *59*
Stinging cells   *10*
Stomata, on plant leaves   *66*
Strontium-rubidium dating   *204*
Suction cups   *4*
Suess, Hans E.   *207*
Sugars   *68*
Sumerian civilization   *118*
Surtsey Island   *172*
Swanscombe fossil skull   *121, 126*
Symbiosis   *9, 10*

Taxonomy   *68-70, 162-165*
Theism, biblical   *90*
Theistic evolution   *235-237*
Thompson, J. J.   *134*
Thompson, W. R.   *115*
Thymine   *80*
Tigris-Euphrates River Valley, civilization   *116*
Time, and evolution   *182*
Time, defined and measured   *182-184*
Transcription of RNA   *85*
Translation of mRNA   *86-88*
Triceratops dinosaur   *59*
Tribolites, in sandal print   *54*
Trincher, Karl   *101*
Tyrannosaurus (Rex) dinosaur   *59*

Ultraviolet light dilemma   *97*
Unger, Merrill, F.   *160*
Uniformitarianism   *40*
Uranium, in oceans   *184*
Uridine   *85*
Uridine-5'-phosphate   *85*

Variation
    limited genetic   *77*
    within biblical kinds   *40*
Velikovsky, Emmanuel   *145*
Venus, planet   *145*
Vestigial structures   *171*
Virchow, Rudolf   *65*

Wadjak skull   *127*
Wald, George   *182*
Warbler, navigation   *8*
Wasp, fig gall   *13*
Water   *14ff.*
Water cycle   *24*
Water vapor canopy   *224*
Whales (sonar)   *6*
Whitcomb, John C.   *50*
White, Leslie   *117*
Whitelaw, Robert L.   *208*
Will, human   *216*
Wonder net   *5*
Wooley, C. Leonard   *118*
Work   *24ff.*

Yir Yoront people, world view   *106*
Yucca, and pronuba moth   *13*

Zagros Mountains, civilization   *116*
Zinjanthropus   *120, 126, 129*
Zooplankton   *72*